TEACHING SURGEONS' HANDS TO HEAL

A Urological Surgical Chairman's Chronicle:
The History of the Department of Urologic Surgery,
University of Minnesota
1969 – 1993

Elwin E. Fraley, MD

authorHOUSE®

AuthorHouse™
1663 Liberty Drive
Bloomington, IN 47403
www.authorhouse.com
Phone: 1-800-839-8640

Published by AuthorHouse 06/23/2014

ISBN: 978-1-4969-1950-2 (sc)
ISBN: 978-1-4969-1949-6 (e)

Library of Congress Control Number: 2014910780

"Rise and follow me,
I'll make you worthy.
Rise and follow me,
I'll make you fishers of men."[1]

—Jesus Christ

My philosophy, in essence, is the concept of man as a
noble heroic being with his own happiness as the moral
purpose of his life, with productive achievement as
his noblest activity, and reason as his only absolute.[2]

—Ayn Rand

[1] Vincent, Rhonda. "Fishers of Men." http://www.lyricsmania.com/
fishers_of_men_lyrics_rhonda_vincent.html. Retrieved on July 2, 2011.
[2] Rand, Ayn. (1957) Appendix to: *Atlas Shrugged*. Random House. New York.

To my wife, Jeanne, and my children: George, William, Elwin, Karen, Christopher, and Andrew, and their families.

Much of what I have achieved, I owe to my wife, Jeanne, the love of my life. In good times and bad, her humanity and equanimity were, and continue to be, anchors for the entire family. She steadied the ladder of my career as I climbed it. As Shakespeare noted in Othello, *"The General's wife is the General's General."*

She helped make our lives the special, unique rose garden of which T. S. Elliott wrote:

> No peevish winter wind shall chill
> No sullen tropic sun shall wither
> The roses in the rose-garden which
> is ours and ours only.[3]

In all of our married life, I have never heard anyone speak an unkind word about her, which is a lot more than I can say about myself. I have always argued that you have a good marriage when you look forward to going home at night, and I always did.

I also dedicate this book to all the residents, fellows, and faculty who made it all possible. We were and are a family.

---

[3] no_peevish_winter_wind_shall_chill_no_sullen. (n.d.). *Columbia World of Quotations*. Retrieved July 02, 2011, from Dictionary.com website: http://quotes.dictionary.com/no_peevish_winter_wind_shall_chill_no_sullen.

Contents

ABOUT THIS MANUSCRIPT

One of the major helpers in the preparation of this book, especially in terms of getting it finished, final editing, and getting it to the publisher has been Keith W. Kaye, MD, former Professor of Urology at the University of Western Australia in Perth, Australia. He is now retired from active practice, but he was of great help in this book and probably it would never have been without his help.

I wrote this story, but enlisted Dave Racer, President of DGR Communications, Inc., and CEO of Alethos Press, to assist in editing. Mr. Racer is an author, publisher, and public speaker, with a background in health-care reform; he teaches American government, with an emphasis on the founding documents, and the US Constitution. Information about Dave Racer can be found at www.daveracer.com.

Donald L. Morton, MD, 1934–2014
During the preparation of this book, I learned of the death of my mentor, colleague, and very close friend Don Morton. Don's death will leave a void in all our lives. I am sure when they enter his name in the book of life, one word will suffice: Excelsior.

Cover: Robert C. Hinckley painting "First Operation under Anesthesia." Used with Permission:
The Boston Medical Library in the Francis A. Countway Library of Medicine.

Introduction

"There is no shortcut to excellence."
—Anonymous

"Gladly Lerne, Gladly Teche."
—Chaucer, *Canterbury Tales*

Before launching into this book, I will deal with some housekeeping items.

This history is primarily about how to structure a residency program to train young urologic surgeons. The chronicle also details what the training program we built at the University of Minnesota contributed to our specialty over twenty-five years. But the story is also about much more. Our department changed the paradigm of a surgical discipline of urology by inventing the field of endourology. The science historian Thomas Kuhn gave *paradigm* its contemporary meaning when he adopted the word to refer to the set of practices that define a scientific discipline at any particular period of time. The invention of the field of endourology also gave impetus to evolving less-invasive approaches to, or treatments of, surgical disease in fields other than urology. More details on this technical and conceptual contribution are detailed later in this book.

This story is set in an academic research and training hospital. It is important for readers to understand the importance of such institutions to the future of American and world medicine, as well as mankind in general. Furthermore, during the past several decades, the changing political environment and declining financial resources in the state of Minnesota and the nation as well have impacted the professional lives of physicians, as well as the viability of our academic medical centers. This change occurred in part because we went from a free-market model in physicians that encouraged or incentivized entrepreneurs and their creativity to a different model that will, in my opinion, have the opposite effect on medical progress and the advanced training of young physicians. Creativity and progress are most often linked to freedom in any country.

The reader, among other things, will gain an understanding of the field of surgery: how surgical leaders are chosen, how surgeons are trained, and how to evaluate a surgeon if the reader, or an associate or loved one, should ever need one. The latter is important information to have because most Americans will have surgery of one type or another at least once and sometimes multiple times in their lives.

WHY HISTORY IS IMPORTANT

As I approached the writing of this book, I thought about the nature of the task, and I eventually concluded that recording history is analogous to an academic mortality and complications conference. In such conference cases in which there was an error or death reviewed, mistakes are analyzed and strategies for doing a surgery better are developed.

History is especially important to our country because there is no American "race," so our country is defined *entirely by its history*. We were founded as a nation that values freedom, individual responsibility, and limited government above all else. These ideas and beliefs are expressed in the founding documents that define the concept of America.

Our ancestors and founders came to America when there was absolutely nothing here except opportunity, and they created a "land of opportunity" that still attracts people from all across the world. At last count, more than a million people immigrate to this country legally each year. The country was founded on a capitalist economic model; another definition of capitalism is economic and personal freedom. It is a model in which, according to John Locke and others, private property is the foundation of liberty or freedom. Whether or not the reader is religious or not, it seems to the author that it was providential that less than 2 million people clinging to life on the east coast could produce two of the most important governing documents in human history, defeat a colonial power with the most powerful navy and army in history at that time, and produce the pantheon of giant men it did. America would be well served if we, in a population of 300 million, could find a single individual leader equivalent to George Washington, Thomas Jefferson, John Adams, James Madison, Benjamin Franklin, or many others, like the fifty-three additional signers of the Declaration of Independence.

Throughout history, only a small percentage of human beings have experienced true political and economic freedom. By some estimates, less than 5 percent of the 100-plus billion people who have lived on earth have ever been completely free, and even today only a small number of nations have citizens who know freedom. I define *freedom* today as having a minimum of force directed against any citizen— that is, government force backed by guns. Within the broad sweep of history, a monarch, despotic ruler, or ruling oligarchy has almost always kept other humans as subjects under some form of control by forces detrimental, especially economically, to such individuals and their families. In contrast, America's founders created a nation where individuals were to be free from such controls by others, and with inalienable rights not ceded to them by the state. The United States remains one of the few places on earth where people remain truly free *sui generis*, although to a lesser extent than during the founding. Right now our country is undergoing a massive expansion of a government that will result in greater and greater state control over its citizens and force them to do things not consistent with their being free, using powers not enumerated in our constitution. We may be creating exactly the same type of government from which our ancestors fled. What is even more disturbing is that Americans are so willingly relinquishing their freedoms, the freedoms that our heroes died for and the freedom that sustained or has been the protective rib cage for the greatness and exceptional nature of America for so many years.

American history—our history—also includes a clear exposition of our founding ideals, such as that our citizens were entitled only to the unalienable rights, sometime referred to as natural rights, to life, liberty, and the pursuit of happiness, as well as equal treatment under the law, as stated so clearly in the first two paragraphs of the Declaration of Independence. Mankind of course recognizes the Declaration of Independence as one of the most important documents in history and thus on a par with *The Magna Carta* in terms of being charters of freedom. In addition, the other pillar of our founding, the United States Constitution, is the most enduring document of its kind in the history of civilization. Our constitution is exceptional in that it enumerates the powers of government and sets limits on that enumerated power. The constitution is what gave us an enumerated republic. It is therefore one of the most brilliant governing documents ever created because it was designed to limit the power of government to control the lives of Americans, or in other words, to use force against them.

One of the best comments ever made regarding the Declaration of Independence was the Independence Day speech given by President Coolidge. What follows is an example of Coolidge's sentiments:

> About the Declaration there is a finality that is exceedingly
> restful. It is often asserted that the world has made a great

deal of progress since 1776, that we have had new thoughts and new experiences which have given us a great advance over the people of that day, and that we may therefore very well discard their conclusions for something more modern. But that reasoning cannot be applied to this great charter. If all men are created equal, that is final. If they are endowed with inalienable rights, that is final. If governments derive their just powers from the consent of the governed, that is final. No advance, no progress can be made beyond these propositions. If anyone wishes to deny their truth or their soundness, the only direction in which he can proceed historically is not forward, but backward toward the time when there was no equality, no rights of the individual, no rule of the people. Those who wish to proceed in that direction cannot lay claim to progress. They are reactionary. Their ideas are not more modern, but more ancient, than those of the Revolutionary fathers.
—President Calvin Coolidge, July 4 address, 1926

Thomas Paine's *Common Sense* was the third of the four most seminal documents of the founding (the fourth being *The Causes and Necessities for Taking Up Arms,* attributed to Thomas Jefferson in 1775). As a whole, all these documents were written by America's founders, and they create a framework of enduring freedom that is the envy of the world.

By contrast, the constitution of the European Union (EU) enumerates what the governance mechanism of Europe may do, not how its power is restricted. It is possible that this is why the European Union is so shaky and may not last much longer in its present form. By the way, that constitution was founded on a false premise—that the Europeans could create a structure that would allow a collection of countries that are well down the road to serfdom to compete with America the exceptional. The assumption behind the European Union was that Greeks, Italians, and Spaniards would be as industrious as, say, the Germans. This document, conceived and written by the coercive collectivists otherwise known as progressives, has been in trouble from the outset. Although the document was signed by twenty-five countries in Europe, it was not ratified by either the French or Dutch voters. There is serious trouble ahead for Europe, especially as the financial viabilities of the various nation-states begin to stratify them economically one from the other.

History also makes our leaders in all fields more responsible because they know future historians will hold them accountable, and many have acted as if they were conscious of history's judgment—the "legacy thing," so to speak. Lincoln argued that our leaders would not escape history's judgment even after "the silent artillery of time"[4] has had its effect.

Many United States presidents had an abiding interest in history. Clifton Truman Daniel, Harry Truman's oldest grandson, tells the story in Prologue Magazine (Spring 2009, vol. 41, no. 1) about a visit President Truman made to their home in New York City. Clifton and his brother, young children at the time, tried to sneak past their grandfather one morning to get to the TV to watch cartoons. Truman, whose head was buried in the morning newspapers, hailed them and made the two- and four-year-olds get up on the couch beside him. Truman retrieved a book from the library and began reading to the boys. When Clifton's parents awakened and came down for breakfast, President Truman was reading Thucydides's *The History of the Peloponnesian Wars* to his young grandsons. Truman had a lifelong interest in history and was very well read in the field.

---

[4] Lincoln, Abraham. (1838), "The Perpetuation of Our Political Institutions: Address Before the Young Men's Lyceum of Springfield, IL." January 27, 1838. http://www.abrahamlincolnonline.org/lincoln/speeches/lyceum.htm Retrieved on June 4, 2014.

However, no US president has summarized the importance of our history more cogently than President Ronald Wilson Reagan, or as some like me refer to him: *Ronaldus maximus*:

> So we've got to teach history based not on what's in fashion but what's important: why the Pilgrims came here, who Jimmy Doolittle was, and what those thirty seconds over Tokyo meant. You know, four years ago, on the fortieth anniversary of D-Day, I read a letter from a young woman writing of her late father, who'd fought on Omaha Beach. Her name was Lisa Zanatta Henn and she said, "We will always remember, we will never forget what the boys of Normandy did." Well, let's help her keep her word. If we forget what we did, we won't know who we are. I'm warning of an eradication of the American memory that could result, ultimately, in an erosion of the American spirit. Let's start with some basics: more attention to American history and a greater emphasis on civic ritual. And let me offer lesson number one about America: All great change in America begins at the dinner table. So tomorrow night in the kitchen I hope the talking begins. And children, if your parents haven't been teaching you what it means to be an American, let 'em know and nail 'em on it. That would be a very American thing to do.[5]

History is a narrative, a story of events and people. One purpose of history is to provide a record from which future generations can benefit if they study and reflect intelligently on what went before them. For anyone who has been through surgical training, written history is almost like reading the proceedings of a mortality and complications conference.

---

[5] Reagan, Ronald. (1989) Farewell Address of President Ronald Reagan. January 11, 1989. Washington, DC.

This book's story is mostly about young men and their teachers and mentors who stood for high principles and were more often than not the embodiment of *American exceptionalism*. This is the story of a surgical training program, the people it guided toward excellence, and the free market, entrepreneurial setting in which they worked. Military historians like to describe the West Point Class of 1915 as the class "the stars fell on" because it produced Eisenhower, Bradley, Van Fleet, and many other military luminaries. I believe it would be appropriate to argue the same could be said to a lesser extent of our training program at Minnesota because of the quality of the outstanding men it produced—when the stars fell on it.

Some of our trainees became famous in their field after they completed their training with us as they helped transform their surgical specialty. It is not hyperbole to say that the Minnesota trainees in urologic surgery have cast the broad, bright light of progress and excellence across urologic surgery, an imprint that should last for several generations. Even though some of the resident colleagues of the academic stars did not become as famous, they nonetheless have lived productive lives as practicing surgeons, and they made a positive impact on their patients and their communities. All evidence suggests that our residents have produced an enviable record of community service and superb patient care: they all have the admiration and respect of everyone who trained them.

This history also limns how Minnesota's cultural and political environments affected the ability of committed academicians and their trainees to maintain a standard of excellence, financial stability, and some measure of tranquility in their professional and personal lives.

Although this narrative describes happy and exhilarating moments associated with advancing our specialty, there were also some times that were sad and depressing, especially as time wore on in a changing society and practice environment in the university system. It could be argued, therefore, that a more apt theme for this history might be borrowed from Dickens's *The Tale of Two Cities*: "It was the best of times; it was the worst of times." But even if I had used that quote for that purpose, I would have ended up by arguing that, on balance, it was the best of times during my run.

The history also sets forth my concerns about the future of medicine in general and academic medicine and America's academic training centers in particular and gives the reasons for my pessimism. I wish I were more optimistic about the future of both of my former professions—professor and surgeon. Unfortunately, my perception of the future of medicine and today's academic centers has introduced a dimension of personal sadness that I never thought I would experience outside of harm or death coming to a loved one. I certainly hope I have become a Cassandra in error.

Most Americans do not grasp that what happens in academic medicine will be a predictor for what happens in medicine as a whole. As some would argue, "A fish rots from the head back." Today's academic medical centers are in the process of producing tomorrow's physicians, and bear serious study if we are to see what lies ahead in the practice of medicine.

Finally, the medical profession often promotes a sense of history, especially for a surgeon. Every time a surgeon requests an instrument in the operating room, he or she asks for it by its appellation, more often than not another surgeon's name: the DeBakey clamp, the Richardson retractor, the Cooley vascular clamp, the Mayo or Metzenbaum scissors, and so on. Thus almost always as the surgeon performs an operation, he or she is reminded of the surgical legacy and the giants who went before them and how much is owed to them.

In the last analysis, the reader should recall that George Orwell argued in his classic book *1984* that the way to destroy a nation (or an institution) is to first destroy its history. Remember Winston Smith, the protagonist in *1984*: Smith's job in the Ministry of Truth was to keep rewriting history so that the government would always be right. This is why it is important that what happened in our department while I was its chairman—indeed, at all times—should be recorded accurately and completely, because the facts may be valuable as a guide to the future and should not be subject to revision, which would render them nonhistory.

Writing this particular history has given me the privilege of reliving our department's halcyon days. Ralph Clayman, a resident alumnus and former chairman of urology and now dean at the School of Medicine in Irvine, California, called his experience in our department "a magic time." It is understandable then that this project has provided for me one last "Indian summer" in the evening of my life.

THE IMPORTANCE OF THE ACADEMIC TRAINING AND RESEARCH CENTERS

The training of most surgeons today occurs in one of the nation's leading university-affiliated academic medical centers, such as the University of Minnesota Hospitals and Clinics, which is the venue for this story. All of our major American academic medical centers (AMCs) are important: they are not only national treasures, but also examples of "American exceptionalism" writ large, and a resource for all nations. Although many Americans may take these great institutions for granted since they have just "been there" all their lives, they should realize that similar centers do not exist to the same extent in any other country.

America's public and private sectors have made a costly investment to create and sustain these AMCs over the last century, and they will be very expensive to maintain. So the question is, will the resources and public policy commitment be there to sustain them in the future? This book advocates that these American academic research and training centers need to be preserved if at all possible, as they are the source for much of the progress in medicine. It is reasonable to predict that they will provide the innovative advances in the medicine of tomorrow just as they have done in the past. They are, in a word, *American "national treasures,"* which Americans and the world cannot afford to see fall into decline.

Men of great vision began establishing these AMCs at the turn of the twentieth century, or what later also became known as *the Century of American Medicine.* The impetus for this effort was, like many other grand efforts, supported by one of America's robber barons, Andrew Carnegie. Of course, there are many other institutions, such as the University of Chicago and the Rockefeller Institute, that were founded by Rockefeller and the other titans of America's great wealth. The effort in establishing our free-market medical-care system led to seventy-two Nobel Prizes in medicine, while the Soviets received just one and that was in 1904 for Pavlov's work on conditioned reflexes.

The University of Minnesota Hospitals and Medical School have a sterling history of innovation and clinical achievements. It has produced outstanding trainees, leaders, and innovators, especially in the fields of cardiovascular surgery, transplantation, pediatrics, neurosurgery, otolaryngology, and urologic surgery—among others. Thus it was, at one time, a superb training and research environment. But many of these Minnesota-initiated advances were achieved at a time when university physicians had great personal and economic freedom, and this allowed them to express their entrepreneurial and creative or "animal" spirits. Michel Paparella, MD, the chief of otolaryngology at the University of Minnesota, who was recruited two years before I was, said the physicians were described as "entrepreneurs" by the people who recruited him. During that time, the school encouraged and rewarded innovation. That is not only the Minnesota formula for success, but also the economic model for our country. Milton Friedman said, "No one has succeeded in organizing society in a better way than the free-market capitalism model in terms of producing a high standard of living and happiness." Today the entrepreneur is as rare in university medicine as the wooly mammoth is in the state parks. The university and other physicians have lost much of their economic freedom. They now operate in a system that is anything but entrepreneurial, which may produce drastic negative impact on physicians and medicine.

PROLOGUE

Before beginning the story about the Department of Urologic Surgery at Minnesota, I have set forth a brief distillation of some experiences and influences that shaped my philosophy about leadership and the care and feeding of young people that I brought to my chairmanship in Minnesota.

My educational and clinical background was not atypical for individuals who were chosen to direct a surgical training program in America in the mid-last century. If there was one thing about my career that was unusual, it was that a major university appointed me to a leadership position in a surgical specialty when I was thirty-three years old. That was not unique, but it was unusual.

I was born in the hamlet of Sayre, population 10,000, in northeast Pennsylvania. Democratic political consultant James Carville once said, "In Pennsylvania there is Philadelphia and Pittsburgh, with Alabama in between." Sayre was definitely more Alabama, where, to paraphrase President Obama, "We clung bitterly to our guns, Bibles, and religion." To paraphrase the musical *Annie*, many people in that area experience "A Hard-Luck Life."

Our varsity football field was only ninety-five yards long and had not a stick of grass. We called the field either the "dirt" or "mud bowl," depending on the weather. At one end of the field, if you ran much behind the goalposts, you smacked into the brick wall of the high school building. At the other end of the field, the back of the end zone was bounded by a fence demarcating private backyards. We only kicked field goals and extra points at the high school end of the field so we did not lose the football since the homeowners could not be relied upon to return the footballs. The high school was so poor we used our practice footballs during the games. Our uniforms were ill-fitting, having been worn many times by others in past seasons to the point where the numbers were indistinct. It was a big deal when we received new jerseys our senior year.

One thing that characterized that geographic area in those days was frugality. Remember, the generation before ours had been through the Great Depression, and many individuals like my father were forced to quit school early in order to work to help support their families. He became very successful in business, but he and his friend always carried a large roll of one-, five-, ten, twenty-, and larger dollar bills held together by a couple of rubber bands; my dad called the roll his "wad." Men of the depression, like Banker Bob in Garrison Keillor's radio show in Minnesota, always wanted to be close to their money. No one in our family ever trusted banks. My dad and my grandfathers had secret hiding places for their money, not even known by their children or grandchildren.

But to illustrate what the money we have poured into education has actually produced, my old high school now has a new athletic complex and the football field is artificial turf—that is correct, artificial turf. I want readers to realize our world-class level of spending on education, second only to Switzerland, has gone for good purposes—like artificial turf!

Those early years were, for the most part, happy ones, since I was blessed with a large family of aunts, uncles, and doting grandparents, especially my paternal grandparents. My parents were supportive of my going to college, something they could not even dream of during the depression, and they helped in countless ways, even after Jeanne and I married when I was still at Princeton. Because we lived in close proximity in a small town, I had known my wife for many years before we married.

Figure 1. My paternal grandparents, Harry and Anna Fraley

The main activities available to a young boy in those days in that area were reading, bird-watching, scouting, and sports or the high school band. I spent at least part of some summers working on my grandfather Fraley's farm. We had no "couch potatoes," since television in the home did not come along until I was ready to graduate from high school. Some of the townspeople would sit before their small TV sets and watch the test pattern for an hour before the programming started at seven o'clock in the evening. The first program, which started at seven, was "Kukla, Fran, and Olive"— really exciting.

Scouting was truly a worthwhile experience: I made Eagle Scout, with more than fifty merit badges before I moved on. I was a scout camp counselor at an early age, and assumed assistant scoutmaster positions on several occasions. I had the privilege of leading one troop in an expedition to the 1951 International Boy Scout Jamboree

Figure 2.
My merit badge sash

in Bad Ischl, Austria, which gave me leadership experience early in life (which was always one of the goals of the Boy Scouts). The scouts in that troop were from all across the country and included two child prodigies, one of whom entered the University of Chicago at age fourteen. I learned the War Between the States was not really over, because our troop was camped next to a troop from southern states in Austria. It was a contest for the time we were encamped to see whether "Battle Hymn of the Republic" or "Dixie" could be sung the loudest. We saw the extensive ruins of war throughout Germany, and while we were at the jamboree, we lived on black bread and cheese, our main rations in Austria. That foreign experience only reinforced my appreciation for our wonderful country.

Because I was good-sized for my age, I talked my way into the boy scouts at the age of age ten, when the usual starting age was twelve. By twelve I had already received my Eagle Scout award, when I was delighted to receive a letter from President Eisenhower.

There were important lessons I learned about racial prejudice growing up. There were only two black families in my hometown or even in the surrounding area. One of the families had a boy my age, the late Dick Jackson, who became one of my best childhood friends. Dick was well liked, but life was not easy for him. In fact, it was probably tougher than most of his peers realized at the time. For example, there were two barbers in town, one of whom refused to cut Dick's hair. The other one would cut his hair if he came at five o'clock and only if I came with him. That barber pulled his shades down so no one in town would see him actually cutting Dick's hair. Haircuts were thirty-five cents in those days. When Dick needed a barber, he would call me and we would get it done just as if it were a normal part of life.

Dick and I were close friends all during high school. Dick was a marvelous athlete, who went on to Cornell, where he was the second black football captain in Ivy League history. (The first was Levi Jackson at Yale.) The fact that in our senior year we had an undefeated, and until the last game, un-scored upon, season attracted a lot of interest by college scouts. Looking back, we were on the edge of a new era for black athletes in our country, especially at the professional level. The people in our town, including my parents, ended up helping pay Dick's Cornell tuition during his last two years in college after Cornell claimed their scholarship well had run dry. One of the Cornell coaches went around town with a tin cup collecting enough money to keep Dick in college his last two years. Even in those days liberals were famous for starting something they would not or could not finish if it involved spending their own money.

Many people in that small town, some of whom were declared bigots, were so proud of Dick's achievements they willingly contributed to paying part of his tuition. I learned about my father's generosity from one of his employees. He never brought the subject up to me. It was against the ethos of that time to brag about anything, including boasting by heroes returning from war about their heroics. That is why veterans came home from World War II, folded their uniforms and put them in mothballs, and then went back to their work and their families. For example, John Bradley, one of the Iwo Jima flag raisers on Mount Suribachi, won the Navy Cross, second in rank only to the Medal of Honor, but his family only found that out by going through his belongings after he died. Jimmy Doolittle responded to a written inquiry about the Tokyo raid by stating in a letter I own, "The Tokyo raid was a job to be done and we did it as best we could." I wonder what a great nation's sailors, like those in nineteenth-century England, were thinking when Admiral Nelson, after he was killed in the battle of Trafalgar, was returned back to his country in a barrel of brine so he could be buried in loving English soil; I speculate that those sailors were determined not to leave any man behind. That English toughness or manliness ebbed away with time, as did their empire, which is what I fear is our fate.

> History is strewn with the wrecks of nations which have gained a little progressiveness at the cost of a great deal of hard manliness, and have thus prepared themselves for destruction as soon as the movements of the world gave a chance for it.[6]

Other points about societal attitudes in those times: A black bride could not get her photo published in the very liberal *Washington Post* until 1957, the year I graduated from Princeton. I guess the Post ascended to its position of moral superiority much later in time. During the West Point graduation ceremonies, the faces of Jewish cadets were printed on perforated pages so they could easily be torn out if a visitor were offended to look at them. In Florida there were many private yacht clubs, one of which had employees in white duck pants and blue blazers who stood on the dock and shouted through a big white megaphone at incoming vessels thus: "Are there any Jews

---

[6] Bagehot, Walter. (1904) *Physics and Politics: Or, Thoughts on the Application of the Principles of "Natural Selection" and "Inheritance" to Political Society.* D. Appleton and Company. New York. P. 61.

on board? Jews are not welcome here." One such club in the Florida Keys had several US presidents as members or past members, and their photos were displayed throughout the club. Just let today's media loose on that story!

Like most of the young men in high school, I had a passion for sports. As such, I played all major sports at the varsity level; I was captain in football and basketball during my senior year. Everyone learned a lot of life's lessons from participating in sports, including that you had to drive yourself without mercy to perform and remain focused even when fatigued. Sports are often the experience of conquering failure. That determination translated to the operating room later in my life.

THE PHYSICIAN WHO CHANGED MY LIFE

An experience with a local physician bent the arc of my life in a new direction. Donald Guthrie, MD, established what eventually became a large clinic and hospital in our town long before I was born. Dr. Guthrie received his surgical training, such as it was back then, at Penn and Mayo. He started his practice in Sayre in the early twentieth century in what was then a fifteen-bed nursing home that had served before Guthrie arrived as the home of a railroad baron. Incidentally, at

Figure 3. Donald L. Guthrie, MD

one time, the railroad repair facilities in Sayre served as a Lehigh Valley Railroad hub, where engines and railroad cars were repaired;

that enterprise was one of the two largest such repair facilities in the world. The railroad repair shops attracted a lot of Italians and Ukrainians and Polish immigrants as workers, and their children were one of the toughest bunches of hard-nosed football players in Pennsylvania.

Guthrie was an entrepreneur in every sense and a dynamo of a human being. During his long career, he achieved international fame and was a founder of the American Board of Surgery. He and my father were good friends. In addition, my father-in-law, at age forty, after he had been a successful professional athlete and civil engineer, interned at the hospital started by Dr. Guthrie—the Robert Packer Hospital. My father-in-law ended up in family practice and was close with my father. In fact, the two of them promoted my dating my wife initially and then became worried we would run off and get married, which is exactly what we did between my junior and sophomore years at Princeton.

The Guthrie family had a distinguished history in medicine and surgery. His father, George Washington Guthrie, served as one of the founders of the American College of Surgeons. And his son, Donald L. Guthrie, was also a founder of the American Board of Surgery.

Over the years, Guthrie built the hospital and clinic from literally nothing into what today is a three-hundred-plus-bed hospital and clinic. His hospital dominates medicine in northeastern Pennsylvania and southern New York State. The Robert Packer Hospital and Guthrie Clinic even have a research arm, with laboratories and residency training programs in affiliation with several Philadelphia-based medical schools.

Notice that there is a clinic in Guthrie's name, and it is associated with a hospital of another name, the Robert Packer Hospital. Guthrie learned his lessons well at Mayo. In Rochester, Minnesota, there is the Mayo Clinic, and the main hospital is St. Mary's Hospital. That way, no one ever is reported as having died at the Mayo Clinic, but rather the demise is reported from St. Mary's. The Mayos thought out all the angles, and I mean all of them. When it came to advancing the Mayo Clinic, the famous brothers were about as nuanced as a couple of *Vlad the Impalers*.

Guthrie took me under his charge at a tender age as a summer intern after I told him my life's goal was to become a surgical chief like him. As far back as I can remember, I thought I wanted to be a surgeon, probably based on my awareness of Guthrie's accomplishments. I became Guthrie's "professional son," not unlike what Robert Caro described in his LBJ biography *The Years of Lyndon Johnson: The Path to Power*. Caro, who lived next to me my first year at Princeton, documented how LBJ became Sam Rayburn's "professional son" shortly after arriving in Washington, DC, and the rest is history. The Guthries did not have children.

During the times Dr. Guthrie and I were together in his office or on the ward, I learned much about the art of medicine. He also taught me how to calculate the amount of starch required to prepare the bedding that was changed each day, and how to estimate the amount of coal it would take to run the hospital's power plant all winter. Guthrie was probably my first interaction with a polymath.

Shortly after arriving in Sayre, Dr. Guthrie developed a long-range plan for building his little hospital into a major medical center. He told me that his concept was to establish a circle of affiliated referring family physician clinics at a distance of sixty to one hundred miles in all directions from his hospital, and to arrange for those clinics to direct all their referral patients to him. In fact, he bought some of those outlying practices, so some of the primary care physicians were his employees. This he referred to as the Guthrie Circle concept. Guthrie was far ahead of his time in that type of thinking. (This

Guthrie strategy became the model of our outreach program at Minnesota years later.) In a sense, he had his own little Guthrie HMO; as Harry Truman said, "The only thing that is new is the history you do not know."

Guthrie also wrote a brilliant paper on how to organize a hospital so that the best people were the first to welcome patients into the hospital. Guthrie believed it was important to "disarm" a patient's fears as he or she entered the hospital for treatment. Entering a hospital, especially for major surgery, carried significant risk in those days when open-drop ether was one of the main techniques for anesthesia. My tonsillectomy was done under open-drop ether, and I still remember that awful, unpleasant "burned-rubber" odor. Little did I imagine that one day I would be standing or sitting in the Ether Dome, where ether anesthesia was first used in surgery at the Massachusetts General Hospital in Boston. Physicians and hospital administrators get so caught up in their work, they often forget how much little considerations mean to patients who are shouldering the terrible burden of sickness. Guthrie developed the bedside manner into an art form. I share some recollections about his approach to sick patients from that period when I made rounds with Dr. Guthrie as a student observer. Guthrie would take the hands of a female patient in his own and look her straight in the eye, saying, "My dear, you are such a brave soldier: such a braaaaave soldier." Needless to say, this was not viewed as corny in any sense in those days, and it seemed therapeutic in many cases. Maybe physicians should regress to the bedside manners of those days.

Before MRIs and CAT scans, the practice of medicine was as much an art as a science. Physicians relied on shaping a patient's mind while bending it toward the drive to get well. Giving reassurance and emotional support to anxious and sick patients was one of the main therapeutic tools of the physician of that time, and Dr. Guthrie was a master of those techniques.

Dr. Guthrie also introduced me to the concept of the "lipstick sign": the first tangible sign that a female patient had turned the corner toward recovery from surgery was when she had applied lipstick for the first time postoperatively. The male counterpart to the lipstick sign was shaving.

Another phenomenon I observed was patients who would take Dr. Guthrie's hands and kiss them and bless them preoperatively so as, I suppose, to bless his work. Better to have the Almighty guiding a surgeon's hands than not. We had a large Catholic population in our area, and whether or not this act was derived in some way from the Catholic traditions or rituals was never clear to me. (I speculate as to the Catholic origin of such a gesture because the only patients who did that to me were Catholic patients from Italy with aniline dye-induced bladder cancer.)

Dr. Guthrie or his nurse saw every one of his patients once or sometimes twice per day—something else important I learned from him and which I incorporated into my practice at Minnesota. During my residency training, the standard held by my chief Wyland Leadbetter at the MGH was that all patients had to be seen at least twice per day—often once by staff and twice by a resident.

Guthrie and Pete Hopkins, the local Ingersoll-Rand plant manager, directed me toward Phillips Exeter Academy in preparation for college, but I passed on that suggestion until later. They knew our small-town schools were not the best preparation for entering an Ivy League school. The advice concerning Exeter was some of the best advice and mentoring I ever received.

Before leaving Sayre, I had no idea of Guthrie's national reach or standing in American surgery. However, as is explained later, a Princeton encounter with a volunteer mentor in medicine clarified that issue.

Most Americans probably realize that small towns are, to apply a well-worn cliché, the backbone of this country. Every time the claxon horn of war sounds, small-town Americans come forth in droves to defend freedom. I cannot recall a single draft dodger in our area during World War II. Believe me, in that small town, everyone knew everything about their neighbors; whether that was good or bad is still unresolved in my mind, but it had a decidedly dampening effect on draft dodging.

I was about seven when the war started. A total of a dozen or so of my family and close friends went off to the war in 1941 and 1942. After a close friend's father was killed, I was so mad I decided it was time for me to enlist, so after hitchhiking twenty miles north to Elmira, New York, I thought I had convinced the sergeant at the recruiting station I was eighteen, although in fact, I was about ten years old. The recruiter played along, and after some paperwork was completed, they had me in the back room, where a medical examination was done and my physical abilities were tested by having me do some strenuous calisthenics. About halfway through the charade, my mother appeared at the front door with a look on her face that would have turned wine into vinegar. When we arrived home, I could have sued her for cruel and unusual punishment under the Fourteenth Amendment, as I might have done in today's world. To borrow a line from the movie *The Shining*, my mother and father "corrected" me—almost. Needless to say, I never even entertained pulling such a trick again.

One day I noticed the face of the school principal, Irving Hazard, peering into our classroom through a small glass window in the classroom door. He pointed at me and motioned for me to come with him. Mr. Hazard had suffered paralysis in one side of the face from polio, so his visage pressed up against the window glass was a bit intimidating—scary one might say—so I went with him immediately. It was Charlie Caldwell, the Princeton head football coach, on the phone for me. Caldwell had been Coach of the Year, and he had an undefeated team recently featuring Dick Kazmaier,

1951 winner of the Heisman Trophy, so Princeton was riding high at the time. He told me they wanted me at Princeton to play football and asked if I could come for an interview. I had no idea where Princeton was, but I agreed to go to see him. As it turned out, I had to hitchhike to Princeton to meet with the coaches. In those days, I did not know that such a beautiful place and campus existed. Cornell was picturesque, with the Cayuga Lake, one of the Finger Lakes, and they had offered me a full scholarship, but I concluded it was not Princeton. I was particularly taken by the old football stadium—Palmer Stadium—and the rest of the athletic facilities, which were in sharp contrast to our ninety-five-yard dirt bowl. The Gothic architecture was breathtaking. I had the same awe for Princeton's history and grandeur as F. Scott Fitzgerald expressed in his novel *This Side of Paradise*. I went through the admission process and was rejected, despite Coach Caldwell's support.

I had plenty of other opportunities for college, but I was fixed on Princeton after I visited the campus. So I revisited the Exeter idea after talking with Coach Caldwell and others. Exeter was always looking for one-year postgraduate "ringers," so they encouraged me to apply and eventually I was accepted for a single postgraduate year. It helped that I wrote my own letter of recommendation to Exeter. A friend's wife was Hazard's secretary, so she gave me some school stationery. When Hazard received a thank you from Exeter for the letter he knew he did not write, he called me out of class and asked me what I knew about the matter. I knew I was busted and so I confessed I wrote my own letter under his name, but I reassured him I did not say anything he would not have said. That did not cut it, of course, but he did not pursue the matter further.

if you applied yourself growing up in a small town and were successful in student government, sports, and other activities, you developed a positive self-image and a self-confidence that would serve you well the rest of your life, especially in tough times. You also learned the values that bound Americans together, like integrity, caring for your neighbors, and pride in your work and your country. You were taught very conservative financial principles by the depression survivors and that you should never waste anything. For the most part, these were happy times, and I often recall what Cecil Rhodes (Rhodesia, Rhodes Scholarships) said: "To be born an Englishman in the nineteenth century was like winning the first prize in the lottery of life." Being an American at the time I was growing up was like winning the Powerball jackpot of life. It was a time of American exceptionalism and world hegemony writ large.

You do not realize until you leave a small town how competitive the outside world really is and how good you had it growing up, comforted and Bubble-Wrapped at every turn by friends, parents, and relatives. You were treated almost like a God if you were a good athlete, and all in all, you were inclined to think you were something special. I was in fact prone to the Churchillian "I am a glowworm" concept. Winston Churchill said that he knew all men were worms, but he fashioned himself a glowworm.

PHILLIPS EXETER ACADEMY

Life started to get really hard the day I stepped on the playing fields at Exeter, which was my particular introduction to prime time. Football players had to report two weeks before classes began for twice-a-day fall practices. The athletes were smarter and in many cases also bigger and faster than in high school. It was a short time thereafter when classes started and I really learned I was far from the big shot I thought I was in high school. No one asked, not even once, for my high school press clippings.

Phillips Exeter Academy (PEA), for those readers who may not be familiar with the school, is one of the finest college preparatory schools in the nation. The school has college-level facilities, and most of the faculty could have taught at the university level if they had chosen to do so. The school is situated in a typical small New England town in rural New Hampshire. It is an ideal environment for concentrated study, but little else. Again, I had never even heard of Exeter until Donald Guthrie and Pete Hopkins suggested I consider it. In 1953 most high schools, especially in small towns, were a stark contrast to Exeter both in terms of faculty and also the facilities. Since then, the massive spending on education has made more local schools somewhat more competitive with Exeter and its brother schools.

I spent a single post-high school or PG year at Exeter, where I learned what the word *excellence* really meant—at least in academic affairs. I had to become an indefatigable worker just to keep up with the other students, many of whom were already functioning at a college level in advanced placement courses. So it was a year spent playing catch-up. It is no mystery why PEA students qualified for advanced placement in the best schools, or how many of them even skipped their freshman year and entered Ivy League or other colleges as sophomores after they graduated from Exeter.

There were 208 students in our graduating class, 108 of whom were accepted at Harvard, thereby constituting more than 10 percent of the 1953 Harvard freshman class. Phillips Andover Academy, the other bookend of the Phillips Academies, located in Andover, Massachusetts, was a Yale feeder, as reflected in the careers of both presidents George H. W. and George W. Bush. Exeter was populated in part by some of America's first families: names like Rockefeller, Heinz, Trippe (Pan Am Juan Trippe, the father) and so on were commonplace. One day while returning to my room from across campus, there was a long gray limo parked in front of an underclassman dorm. Two men in gray chauffer uniforms, including tight-fitting tailored gray gloves and spats, were busy loading multiple pieces of baggage into the limousine. The car belonged to the Heinz family of 57 Varieties fame, and a young Heinz, who had been excused from school for two weeks, was getting ready to go to London for the coronation of Queen Elizabeth. I think this lower classman was the Heinz who grew up to become a United States Senator.

Life at Exeter was rigorous, but in retrospect, it was worth every bit of the sacrifice of time and effort. In the end, I was much better prepared for college and a career, thanks to Exeter. I learned to write during that year, and I learned how to take a one-question blue-book exam as given in college, which I never saw in high school. Even the sports were far more demanding than high school in that many of our games were against college freshman teams.

Although all the teachers were superb, my English teacher, Darcy Curwen, was one of the most unforgettable characters I have ever met. On the first day he warned us: "If you write as well as the average Exeter student, you will get a D; if you write as well as the best Exeter student, you will get a C-; if you write as well as Shakespeare, you will get a B; and if you write as well as I do, which of course has never happened, you might get an A-." I worked literally all night on my first theme paper and was devastated when it was returned with a big red shovel on the title page; inside the shovel blade was written: "This is the worst theme paper I have ever read, F-." An F- was referred to by the students as a "flag-neg," translated meaning Flagrant Neglect. That was the lowest grade possible and suggested you were not even trying and possibly did not belong at Exeter. I was told two of those grades in one reporting period was a ticket home. To top it all off, I flipped up the title page, and he had only corrected the first four lines. I was in a rage and went storming into his office and asked him how he could give me that grade having read only four lines. Curwen's answer? "You do not need to eat a whole apple to know it is rotten." What could I say? And so it went, but his one-on-one tutoring, a feature of Exeter, helped to improve my writing, so I am forever grateful to him and the other Exeter teachers. I learned later that many Exeter students had had a similar experience with Curwen. Sometime after college acceptance letters arrived, I was notified by the College Boards that I had received the second-highest grade in the English Composition Achievement Test in the country. I thought at the time, thank you again, Darcy.

When I interviewed with the director of admissions at Princeton, who came to Exeter for the interview process, as did all the major Ivy League schools, he noted my low grade in English and asked who my master (teacher) was. I told him Curwen, and he just smiled and quickly moved on. I thought a salesman of ice to the Eskimos had a better prospect than I did of getting into Princeton after that interview. The Princeton representative, a Mr. Edwards, did note at the end of the interview that coach Charlie Caldwell had some interest in me, but it was just a passing remark and did not appear important to the interviewer. One thing I knew was that my house master, Robert Kessler, who was a Princeton graduate at age nineteen and an all-American lacrosse player, had written a strong recommendation for me, and it certainly was not based on my grades at the time he wrote that letter. If I had to guess, it was that letter that got me into Princeton. The only thing I can think of that might have helped me with Bob Kessler was that I started a Boy Scout troop in my "spare" time and his son Andy was in the group. The troop met in Kessler's living room much of the time. This was before, even at Exeter, students became more interested in smoking pot than tying knots.

When the thick envelope indicating I had been accepted at Princeton came on April 15, I was more than relieved. In those days all the acceptance or rejection letters arrived at Exeter precisely on April 15. The rejection letters were in very thin envelopes, but mine was thick so I knew what it said before it was opened. If I had been turned down again, I would have been forced to go to Cornell, Brown, or Lafayette, where I was accepted in high school; I considered, at the time, that any of them would have been a fate worse than death. I wanted to go to Princeton; it was, in fact, an obsession. I feel to this day that, at least in part, I "willed myself" into Princeton—with Exeter's help.

I owe Exeter more than I can ever repay for even more reasons than I have already enumerated. A year there was the only way I was ever going to be accepted at Princeton. At Exeter I met an outstanding group of dedicated teachers and gifted students, who lived and worked in a cloistered *Catcher in the Rye*-like world unknown to most Americans. These schools were modeled after the British "public schools" (actually the English public schools, as most people know, are private schools similar to Exeter)—like Eaton and Harrow. The prep school network, located mainly in New England, is famous for producing students who later become part of America's elite, including several presidents and other leaders of the United States.

PRINCETON UNIVERSITY

For most of us, undergraduate years in an all-male university were the near final preparation for adult life. I was particularly blessed, having had time at Exeter and Princeton; these institutions taught me the concept of American exceptionalism, and thus, what the word *excellence* really meant. The professors and the administrators, as well as the students, made Princeton an extraordinary experience. Alumni of my generation had great appreciation for what Princeton gave us.

Princeton's founders built the institution on Judeo-Christian values during "the great (religious) awakening" that occurred in pre-War for Independence of America. Thus, one value the institution tried to impart back then was, "To whom much is given, much is expected" (Luke 12:48). Many of us made that admonition from Luke one of the animating forces in our lives, even including our choice of a profession. Again, there are those who argue that the only thing we (Princetonians) owed society was ourselves and our best efforts, but I emphatically disagree. The attitude that someone who was given the exposure to Exeter and Princeton owed our society nothing back is perverse, cynical, and unjustified.

Princeton and its surrounding area are rich in American history. The school is located a short distance from where General George Washington crossed the Delaware. It also is near to the site of the Battles of Trenton and Princeton, the turning points in our Revolutionary War, during which troops rolled back and forth in the outskirts of what is now the town, before Washington's army eventually defeated the British. My wife, Jeanne, and I married between my junior and sophomore years and lived in a carriage house on an estate near Pennington, New Jersey, a few miles from Princeton, where there was a historic monument in a nearby field marking it as a site of a General George Washington encampment during the war.

Princeton's central administration building, Nassau Hall, served as the seat of the colonial government for a time, and the Continental Congress met there. Nassau Hall is the iconic Princeton landmark, which explains why "Going Back to Old Nassau" is the school's alma mater.

I did have a very interesting experience that took me back in time to Sayre. Princeton University had many famous alumni who retired in the town of Princeton. Some of these individuals acted as volunteer mentors to students who had either defined their career goals or were leaning in one direction or the other. I made an appointment with one of the mentors in medicine, Professor Allen Oldfather Whipple, the former chief of general surgery at Columbia University School of Medicine in New York City. This was the individual who designed the Whipple Operation for pancreatic cancer that is still done today.

When we first met, he asked where I was from, and when I said Sayre, Pennsylvania, which I thought would mean little to him, his eyes brightened and he launched into a long exposition about Donald Guthrie and spontaneously told me Guthrie was one of the most respected surgeons in the country and that he had an international reputation. He also mentioned with a wry smile that the Guthries threw legendary parties in their home. I just smiled and thanked him while thinking *maybe Sayre is not such a backwater after all.*

Figure 4. Allen Oldfather Whipple, MD
With Permission: Archives & Special Collections,
Columbia University Health Sciences Library

HARVARD MEDICAL SCHOOL (HMS)

I went from Princeton directly to Harvard Medical School (HMS). The education at HMS was beyond superb. The strength of the school came from the broad exposure it provided to the many teaching hospitals in the Harvard system, and the thousands of patients who were treated in them. The students, of course, were self-driven and intelligent, and at the time, among the best students of medicine in the world. In the course of my four years at HMS, I saw just about every conceivable human disease and how it was treated, but more importantly, our professors inculcated in us from day one a sense that it was a special trust and privilege to be able to care for patients. It may well be that medicine in America as a profession reached its apogee during these years or shortly thereafter.

The dean at HMS gave us a handbook on the first day called *The Care of the Patient*. The first sentence in that book read, "The way to care for a patient is to care about the patient." Another insightful and utilitarian piece of advice in that book was, "The way to make a diagnosis is to listen carefully to the patient. They will make the diagnosis for you." In other words, a careful and thoroughgoing patient history will often lead to a diagnosis. The HMS dean, George Packer, a Princeton graduate, said something else on our first-day orientation I will never forget: "Our job here at Harvard is not to make you an excellent physician when you graduate but to give you the incentive to continue to study for the rest of your life so that you will be a superb physician thirty or forty years from now." The dean also maintained that grades did not count at HMS, which I interpreted as meaning grades did count—and count a lot. I was correct in that conclusion.

Something else rather humorous occurred on that first day. I did not know who else from Princeton had been accepted at HMS prior to the first meeting. The dean's orientation was held in one of those typical amphitheater-like lecture halls. After I sat down, I noted way off to the side, slumped over and asleep and still wearing a rumpled tuxedo and white silk scarf, was a fellow I had known only slightly in college. What I knew about him was three things: first, he had his pilot's license pulled when he tried to hop beacons to get to Vassar to see a girl one night without filing a flight plan; second, he hit a New Jersey State police car in his Corvette head-on going around a traffic circle the wrong way at a high speed; and third, his father was in the same law firm as Richard Nixon. He was, therefore, the typical iconoclastic antihero in the mold of F. Scott Fitzgerald's Gatsby, whom many Princeton students probably secretly admired. My guess is that Mister Gatsby clone and man-about-town who drank deeply from the cup of life would have a very short bucket list at the end of his time because he had done it all. By some miracle, he eventually became a respected plastic surgeon practicing in a major eastern city.

Almost every teaching institution in the Harvard system had a storied history. The Massachusetts General Hospital (MGH) was where ether (anesthesia) was first demonstrated publicly in 1854 and where the Ether Dome is a designated national historic shrine. (Less well-known is that it is alleged that a surgeon named Crawford Long used ether in surgery four years before the MGH demonstration, but Long's work was never published and his work was known only to a small circle of friends.) Boston Children's Hospital was where Robert Gross performed the first heart surgery on a child—the ligation of a patent *ductus arteriosus*; Gross still served as chief of surgery at Children's in my student days. Boston Children's also is where the first children with leukemias were cured by Sydney Farber. Farber had trouble getting his first report on curing childhood leukemia published at the prestigious *New England Journal of Medicine*; the inside buzz was because he was Jewish. Many of us think he deserved the Nobel Prize for that work. The Peter Bent Brigham Hospital was where Murphy and Minot and Whipple won the Nobel for their treatment of pernicious anemia. These great hospitals are where men and women, who either had already made history or were making history at the time, were actively toiling in the vineyards of medicine, and most of them were either training students or residents or were lecturing at HMS or were doing both.

My third-year HMS counselor was assigned to the team caring for the preoperative nonidentical twin transplant recipients when clinical transplantation was just beginning at the Brigham. My third-year surgery instructor at the Brigham was none other than Joseph Murray, MD, who won the Nobel Prize in Medicine in 1986 for his seminal work on organ transplantation, which was just starting in patients when we were students. Two other Nobelists—John Enders and Tom Weller—taught virology and parasitology to our HMS class. Enders, Weller, and Robbins won the Nobel Prize for their basic work on culturing the polio virus in the laboratory, which made the polio vaccine possible. That is why the Harvard group was awarded the Nobel Prize rather than Salk or Sabin—because their work made the Salk polio vaccine possible.

As students during that time we were, as mentioned previously, present at the beginning of clinically useful organ transplantation. We saw the first nonidentical twin kidney transplant while I was a first-year medical student. My second-year mentor was in charge of the program to prevent rejection of nonidentical twin kidney transplants. To illustrate just how far medicine has progressed from those days, the way rejection in transplant patients was prevented was by delivering total body radiation to the recipients before surgery. This was accomplished by putting the patient in a device analogous to a rotisserie and turning them slowly 360 degrees while they were receiving high-dose radiation. Of course, the patient's white blood count became close to undetectable from the high-dose radiation, so the radiated patients had to be housed behind thick plastic sheets and an ultraviolet light barrier designed to kill airborne bacteria so they would not become infected in their immune-depressed state. We went to that area in the basement of the Brigham with our mentor on occasion, and it was something like an eerie Crichton or Cook science fiction novel. The patients and their containment area were bathed in bluish ultraviolet light, and the patient area was demarcated from the outside world by a thick, clear plastic barrier that extended ceiling to floor. You had to pull the plastic sheeting aside to enter into the patient area. All the personnel or visitors had to wear gowns and gloves, and hand washing was required. Students usually viewed the transplant unit's activities from afar or from behind the plastic barrier. This was the environment of early organ transplantation. The Brigham was alive with frenetic activity and intellectual excitement mainly because the physicians on the transplant team knew well they were making history. Of course, this program was a Nobel Prize in the making for Joe Murray (Nobel Prize 1986), who was a staff plastic surgeon and HMS professor who led the transplant effort.

We also had a member of our HMS class of '61, Michael Bishop, who won the Nobel for basic work in cellular biology and nucleic acid metabolism. There are not too many places where a medical student would have a future or current Nobel Laureate either as a clinical instructor or in the classroom, or both much of the time. Those experiences in such an inspiring and exciting atmosphere motivated the "Sons of Harvard Medicine" to go forth and at least attempt to do great things.

During our last two clinical years, when we left the classroom and went to the bedside, we divided into small groups of four for our clinical rotations and our dozen or so sessions in dog surgery. The groups were organized by the individual students. Tenley Albright, the Olympic champion, asked to be in our group of four, so when the group was complete, it consisted of myself; Curt Dohan, whom I knew at Princeton; Howard Carpenter from Rhode Island; and Tenley. In 1956 Tenley became the first American woman to win the Olympic gold in figure skating. In 1952 Tenley won an Olympic silver medal. Tenley became an Olympic champion while maintaining her class standing in Radcliffe, which qualified her for admission to HMS. She also won the US and North American championships to become the first triple-crown winner in figure skating up to that time. Tenley told me that since she was a child, she wanted two things: an Olympic gold medal in figure skating and to become a surgeon like her father—some goals for a child I'd say. Tenley was a delightful coworker and a natural surgeon. Almost every day you learned something about life outside medicine from Tenley. You certainly learned from her that at least in her life, success and sacrifice were interchangeable words. As Nathan Pusey, former president of Harvard, said quite correctly, "A Harvard education is everything you learn when you are not in class." Working with Tenley was one of the highlights of my Harvard experience.

During our fourth year, my wife and I were invited to the homes of some staff surgeons for a social evening. Our most memorable event was a visit to the home of the esteemed Oliver Cope, an HMS professor of surgery and MGH staff surgeon. It became obvious we were being looked over as possible house officers. Of course, the nervous HMS busy-bee students were abuzz with information about who had been invited where and what it meant. Most of the hard-nosed and driven students had a goal of a first rank residency, and they were tuned into even the most subtle signals that were being sent by the faculty relative to their future. They certainly did not want the upward trajectory of their careers to be altered by falling back to a less-than-ideal internship appointment. Frankly, I did not worry about such things because I had enough on my plate trying to balance my family and the demands of getting a full medical education that eventually included a residency.

In the final analysis, few students escaped the sense of obligation that was imposed on us by the history and traditions of the school. We left Harvard Medical School with a lasting sense of owing the men and women of the Harvard faculty of Medicine, who gave us the full measure of their devotion, knowledge, and mentoring while we were students.

Figure 5. Photo taken c. 1966 in the Ether Dome at Massachusetts General Hospital. Elwin Fraley, the author, sits in the far upper-right corner, second row, with his hand supporting his chin. Paul Dudley White, the famous cardiologist, sits to the far right in the front row.
Courtesy of Massachusetts General Hospital Archives and Special Collections.

TRAINING AT THE MASSACHUSETTS GENERAL HOSPITAL (MGH)

The Internship

The reputation of the MGH was such that it attracted many of the Harvard medical students interested in surgery. The staff was familiar with many of the students because we had monthlong rotations on various MGH services. The big day for anyone seeking a surgical internship was Intern Selection Day. That day was by invitation only. There were about 250 invitees, both from HMS and the other schools in the country, in attendance, competing for six slots.

In order to get an MGH surgical internship, one had to go through one last trial by fire. This was the Intern Selection Day, held by the MGH general surgeons, including the chiefs of all the surgical services, during which it would be thumbs-up or -down for a student, and the students knew it. The Harvard students and students from other medical schools arrived early one morning for their day of decision sometime in the fall of their senior year. In those days, an MGH surgical internship was akin to getting a US Supreme Court clerkship for the Harvard law students. Anyone who came for the day probably had MGH as their first choice. Many of those coming from other schools came with one of those "This student is the best I have ever seen and has my highest possible recommendation" letters, usually from a famous chief of general surgery. Also, many of those recommendations were written by former MGH trainees and should have carried great weight.

The day was structured as follows. Each applicant was potentially facing two interview committees. The first was a screening group of somewhat lesser lights, and the second or final committee was composed of the august chiefs of service.

There were several first-interview groups, which processed applicants efficiently in order to screen all the applicants in the early part of the day before selecting the ones to be interviewed by the final committee of chiefs. In retrospect, based on what I heard later at the MGH, I think they pretty much knew who they wanted, at least among the HMS students, well before the day began. We had to wait more or less in line for the first committee. Just ahead of me was a tall, handsome fellow with boundless self-esteem, who kept recounting loudly all the wonderful research he had done at Podunck U and how he was sure to be chosen. He went into the first interview just before me. When the door opened, he came lurching out from the interview looking like a candidate for the *Ghostbusters*. He was so drawn and pale as he staggered up to the secretary overseeing the process that I thought he might have taken ill during the interview. We all knew that if you made it through the first interview, you would be given a lunch ticket by the secretary because the second interview would be later that day, either in the late afternoon or even the late evening, as it was in my case. After checking with the committee for their decision, the secretary told Mister Wonderful it would not be necessary to stay for lunch, which translated to, "You are finished at the MGH, so you better look elsewhere for a surgical internship." Harvard students knew by the grapevine that if you did not get an invitation for lunch and an interview with the second committee, you were not going to be offered a job at the MGH. You had to make it to the second committee or else. All the HMS students were clued in about the day by the classes ahead of us. Mister Big Shot staggered off down the hall, probably devastated, at least on that day.

I found the first interview so easy I thought the fix was in one way or the other. When you were a medical student, you brushed up against a lot of giant egos, and you never knew who you may have offended, so nothing was certain in that rough-and-tumble competition. The first interviews were with a committee consisting in part of the younger stars or junior faculty of the MGH staff, or they were with faculty of MGH as well as faculty from other Harvard teaching hospitals like Boston City or the Brigham; they grilled us on everything from the history of medicine to current therapies. They also tested our knowledge about the very important papers they had written. Their papers were, in many cases, actually the same paper written over and over again, with any given version only slightly different from the others. It is alleged that Shostakovich once commented about Vivaldi: "Vivaldi had one good idea, which he repeated 385 times." When I was preparing for that first interview, I thought of that quote as I was reading papers by some of the MGH staff who I thought might be one of the first inquisitors on Intern Selection Day. As I learned later, the goal in academic medicine was to pad your bibliography with as many papers as possible to advance your career, and that is exactly what some of the interviewers had done. As Ron Malt, who comes alive later in this book as a mentor, once told me, "Search committees can count."

When the secretary came out with the decision of the first committee on me, she was all smiles and handed me lunch tickets and a projected time for my second interview, and I was on my way as I floated down the hall pleased with myself. In my mind, it was one more to go, so get ready to do your best.

The second interview was unforgettable. I was terrified before going in for what all students knew was a final judgment. In my mind, all was riding on that interview. Not all those who made the second interview necessarily were guaranteed an internship. We all knew more winnowing was yet to come. All the chiefs of service, most of them world-famous physicians, were sitting around an elliptically shaped table in a conference room paneled in the customary intimidating dark cherry or mahogany wood. The candidate was seated at the end of the table for all to see. Most of the surgeons were dressed in white surgical scrubs. Some of the staff underlings sat erect in straight-backed chairs against the wall waiting for instructions or some such from the chiefs. It seems powerful men or women like to have their underlings sitting along the wall behind them in important meetings while waiting on their every possible need. I guess such an arrangement projects importance and power. Visualize a congressional committee with the congresspersons in the big, soft and luxurious leather chairs, while the wannabes, who really run the show, are sitting dutifully behind them. In the War Between the States, it was common to have junior officers or troopers stand at attention holding the bridles of the horses of their superior officers while the generals or officers were in councils of war or otherwise occupied on a noisy battlefield. These officers or troopers were even derisively referred to as "horse holders" even when they were not so engaged. That tradition clearly persists today. All the people in that room on that day were superstars, even though some were positioned as horse holders.

I was surprised how friendly everyone was until they started dropping some difficult questions on me, most of which I answered, but some of which I had to admit I did not know the answer to. Some of the questions related to the history of the MGH, which I had down cold. I even knew the words John Collins Warren uttered when he finished removing a lesion from a patient's tongue under ether anesthesia. Warren turned toward the audience and said, "Gentlemen, this is no humbug." As the questions got tougher, at one point I felt like a contestant on the *Gong Show* must have felt, but the gong never sounded—thank heaven. As the interview wore on, they asked me why they should choose me among the hundreds of applicants; and as I came up off the edge of my chair, my answer was, "It is my intention to be one of the best surgical interns in the history of the hospital." What an opening I gave them with that crack. I do not remember for sure whether I slammed my open hand or fist on the table as I spoke, but I may have done so I was so keyed up. I do remember that, looking back, I was, to say the least, being way too forceful and presumptuous with the answer. One of the chiefs allowed that he had been an MGH intern and did I presume to think I would be better than he was. I paused for a minute, a long minute actually, and replied eventually, "My statement stands." That declaration brought a round of smiles and some glances back and forth, and things got easier after that. I could not tell whether easier questions meant I was in or out. Henry Beecher, the chief of anesthesia, asked me as a last question what I thought about socialized medicine, and I replied, "That is way above my pay grade, but intuitively I am against it."

My interview was late in the day, but I waited around after it was over for a friend so we could go for a drink at eleven o'clock at night, during which time we did a long postmortem of the day. We both needed a drink or two by the end of that incredible experience. We had a good laugh regarding some of the happenings, but mostly we were still uptight about our chances, even though we both made it to the second committee. The two of us knew that our future in medicine was being decided by a few people we barely knew other than as authors of leading textbooks.

Of course, if they had wanted to, the chiefs could have made that interview very uncomfortable for a medical tadpole like myself, as the first committee apparently did to the candidate who preceded me. That group of chiefs had plenty of savvy and experience, and if they had either not liked you or thought you were, as my grandfather used to say, a little too big for your britches so to speak, they could have had a little fun with the fish on the line. However, with me, they were all business and very professional. I left that interview completely spent, but sensing it had gone as well as I could expect, except for the one answer about being one of the best interns in the history of the MGH. Probably I should have upped the dose of my sedatives before that day—just kidding.

Students found out their internship assignments by gathering in the expansive foyer, with a beautiful marble floor, of Building A of the medical school a few months after their interviews. Sealed envelopes were spread out over a big circular table, and you had to sort through them until you found yours. A few students were unmatched, and that was dealt with by the medical school administration so they all got an internship eventually. Although I had been told by a mole at the MGH not to worry, I still was hesitant and a bit scared until I opened the envelope to find my assignment was—MGH in Surgery. That was one of life's highs; that envelope contained the reward for nine years of hard work. I called my parents and my wife with the news. My wife and I went out to a rather fancy Boston French restaurant that night to celebrate, but could only afford two entrees and one a la carte vegetable, green beans, which we shared—some celebration, but we had severe financial limitations. It was a celebration that was not based on what we ate but on what we felt having gained another career goal. My wife was very much a part of that triumph. A cynic once argued that behind every successful man was a good wife and behind her was another woman—not true for me.

I knew that envelope signified another step up a career ladder and that the MGH internship assignment was the capstone to my HMS experience. The relatively sophisticated HMS students knew their residency would go a long way in determining the level at which they would practice medicine the rest of their lives.

The Massachusetts General Hospital (MGH) is, of course, a Harvard teaching hospital. That means they have student rotations, as well as multiple intern and residency training programs. It is a privilege for any young physician to train at the MGH. That training provided some of the best surgical and urological training programs in the world at the time. I had two years of a surgical internship and junior residency in general surgery at the MGH and then entered the urology training program for three years under the renowned Wyland F. Leadbetter, MGH's chief of urology and clinical professor at Harvard. It is amazing that Wyland was not a full professor at Harvard, but Hartwell Harrison, the chief of urology at the Brigham, was. My guess is that Wyland did not want anyone telling him what to do, so he was happy to be a clinical faculty and therefore somewhat independent of HMS appointment and to be left alone to teach residents and earn a living.

MGH interns in surgery spent most of their time on a general surgery service, but we also had monthly rotations on other services, such as orthopedics, neurosurgery, and what turned out to be a game changer for me, a month on the urology service.

I remember well the day I reported for the first time to begin my internship. After ceremoniously signing in on a thick logbook, we were directed to a conference room on the west surgical service on White Building 7, where we were to meet the chief resident in surgery for orientation. The new interns, I remember, sat around chatting and sizing up our fellow interns while waiting for the chief resident. The interns were myself; Tom Hakala, HMS; Dale Wenlund, University of Minnesota (who left after one year to transfer to radiology at the MGH and who died in 1961 in an airplane accident); Brad De Long, Barnes; Joe Fischer, HMS; and Bill Abbott, UCLA or Stanford—I do not remember which. I do not remember the name of the individual who left in the middle of the internship year because he was alleged to have had the Baron von Munchhausen Syndrome; I was told you could not trust a word he said even about the simplest of things. You have to wonder how he slipped through such a highly selective process. Despite all this, it is my understanding he went on to a very successful career in another field.

We had not been seated long when the West Surgical Chief Resident, Ronald A. (Ron) Malt, entered the room. He was all business. He was a tall, erect, and imposing figure in what I noted was a recently pressed and starched white MGH house officer's uniform. I knew from experience as a medical student at the MGH that most house officers were always unkempt and the very definition of sleep deprivation and overwork and their uniforms reflected a certain state of detachment and disarray. Malt, by contrast, was a striking figure, looking much like the poster boy for obsessive compulsive disorder, with his stern visage and erect, military bearing. I noted that our intern slumps were replaced by cadet-like sitting postures as he spoke. Malt minced no words when he told us we were about to enter the best surgical training program in the world and that our endurance and knowledge would be tested to the extreme. He suggested, almost half seriously, that we might consider quitting before we started. In retrospect, Malt sounded like I imagine an orientation talk to new US Navy SEAL recruits might sound today. Finally, he pulled out a list of intern assignments, and my first rotation was West Surgical Service as Female Intern, with Malt. *God help me*, I thought. The only saving grace was that Tom Hakala received the same assignment on the male side. My fear and flight reflexes took over, and I had to exert maximum self-control to stay in my chair. We were given requisitions and told where to report to obtain our house officer uniforms. I asked Malt what time we should report for duty the next day, fearing the worst; Malt replied, "5:30 a.m. sharp." I arrived about an hour early that first day just to be safe. It was a habit that sports captains acquire—first on the field and last to leave.

Like most beginners, I screwed up to one degree or another on a regular basis, mainly in minor ways, but Ron was patient. I came to value early on that Malt believed in teaching and leading by example. The ward team knew that rounds always started on time, all conferences began and ended on the minute, and you were expected to use an economy of words in your presentations, either on rounds or in conferences. Punctuality is the ultimate way to show respect for others. This type of training, long on professionalism and efficiency, was invaluable to all of us for the rest of our professional lives. By the end of that month, the entire ward team had the highest regard for Ron. In short, he was the epitome of all that the MGH training program represented—the very best in American surgery. Everyone else was on a first-name basis by the end of the month, but despite protests from him, he was always "Sir" or "Dr. Malt" or "Boss" to me.

All MGH interns of that era were introduced to the scut board on day one. The scut board was the specific domain of the intern. Scut work is defined in the dictionary as follows: trivial, unrewarding, tedious, dirty, and disagreeable chores. The scut board consisted of an old, very low-tech clipboard that held a written list of all patients, with room for notes beside their names. As rounds progressed, the intern, like a good amanuensis, wrote down all of the tests, radiological exams, dressing changes, and so on that the chief or senior resident ordered for each patient. There were two interns— one male and one female—each of whom had thirty or forty patients to attend. By the end of the day, heaven help the intern if anything was left undone.

Well, after a very few days, I refused to carry the scut board because I thought I could train myself to remember everything of significance. So I was not surprised that Malt called me down to his little office for a "come to Jesus" meeting. He began by saying, "I n-n-n-noticed you were not using a s-s-s-scut board on rounds. P-p-p-p lease explain why." He clearly was not happy with me. I gave him my reason—namely, I was training myself to remember important information on patients without using that type of crutch. Furthermore, I asked him if I had yet failed to remember all or most of his instructions. He paused, reflected for a minute, almost smiled but caught himself, and said, "N-n-n-not that I can recall." I offered a suggestion: I would not be required to use the scut board until I failed to carry out one of his orders. Despite what I suspect were his instincts to the contrary, he agreed—reluctantly.

The rest of the month proceeded without incident, and I trained myself to remember essential patient-related information, a skill that I honed for the rest of my practicing life. It would have been very easy for Ron to insist I do it his way—the chief resident's word was, of course, law because any surgical training program has a military-like hierarchy with a strict chain of command, so he could have issued an edict that I carry a scut board and that would have been have been the end of any discussion. But he didn't, and that decision served us both well, then and thereafter.

Clearly Ron had his own ideas, but he was willing to listen, and when justified, he allowed us to stand on our own two feet and take responsibility. And that is why I remember this seemingly insignificant episode.

I also unlocked a secret in that meeting with Ron. Malt had at least a hundred or so immaculate uniforms hanging on a makeshift clothes rack cobbled together using small-caliber water pipes that stretched along one entire side of his office. I asked him how come so many uniforms, and he told me he had operated on the man in the supply room who doled out uniforms, so he could have as many as he wanted. Most of the intern mortals had six uniforms, two or three of which were always at the laundry because on any day on duty you were inadvertently covered with yellow liquid of a spilled drug like Furadantin® or various colored bodily fluids or ink or just plain dirt. I think, based on his appearance on most occasions, Malt changed his uniform two or three times per day, which was unthinkable for most house officers. Since the residents were paid only a few hundred dollars per month, you would have thought we might at least have been supplied with an adequate number of uniforms. By the way, as interns and later as junior residents, we did have the privilege of having our family join us on Sunday for the noon meal. Since, by this stage I had four children, I considered that a great deal in those days.

There were some interesting, even terrifying, moments during the two years on general surgery. To give a sense of what those two years were like, one of my most lasting memories is rolling out of the sack at 4:00 a.m. so tired that tears ran down my cheeks while I tied my shoes. We also remember, among other things, the long hours away from family, and I sometimes wonder today if it was worth it. I certainly would not have chosen the path I did if I were entering into the environment in medicine that prevails today.

Shoes and Sanity

During that first intern rotation, I became obsessed with Malt's shoes for some unexplained reason. Not only was his uniform always spotless, but he wore shoes that had both a white top and white soles. I pointed the shoes out to John "Red" Lewis, a senior resident on the female side and new friend, and told him I had never seen shoes like Malt wore. I asked Red if he knew where Malt got those shoes, but he said he did not but said if I found out where, he wanted a pair. I eventually discovered the shoes were worn by naval officers and you could get them at the Boston Naval Yard in Charlestown. Red and I each bought a pair and agreed that we would wear them to rounds the next day. Every morning the interns and residents all lined up in a semicircle facing Malt as he began to issue the orders of the day and OR assignments for the day. While he was speaking, his gaze fell on John and me, and he paused, looked us up and down, smiled just a little, and went on. We remained expressionless. Malt never commented on the shoes, but I believe he was pleased. But Malt referred to Red and me as Tweedledum and Tweedledee (the Lewis Carroll characters) thereafter, I think because of the shoes. These were the gotcha games we played, probably to keep our sanity. I kept those shoes until I retired.

Just after I left the West Surgical service the first time, I encountered a senior resident from another service in the hall and he said, "Do you people realize that everyone who was on the West service with Malt came off the service stuttering like he does—every damned one of you?" I had not thought about it, but after listening to myself later, I realized he was right. Speak about projection or identification with the aggressor per Anna Freud and her *Ego Defense Mechanism*. I promptly de-Malted myself and spoke as before, as did others eventually.

One of my major positive takeaways from my training was the experience of the Death or Mortality and Complications (D&C)

conferences. These conferences were held every month, and they dealt with any death or complication that occurred the previous month on patients from the ward surgical service. The MGH conference rooms were often small, so the conference was very crowded. The ward service was run by the residents, but there were staff visiting surgeons who came by the ward several times a month to review cases, mainly with the chief resident. It was a system where the residents had a great deal of autonomy in the management of the patients, including the doing of the actual surgical procedures. But on occasion, the chief resident might ask a visitor to scrub on a difficult case. The dirty little secret among the residents was that the chief resident occasionally was as good. Usually two or three senior visiting surgeons conducted the D&C conferences. They sat at a desk at one end of the room, like teachers at the head of the class, and they had a large logbook open on the table in front of them. Either the intern or a junior resident presented the case, even though they were not the responsible surgeon. After the narrative of the case and the X-rays (radiographs is the proper word) were presented and after everyone had their say in a discussion that often became rather heated, the visitors summarized the case and rendered their verdict on what went wrong in the case and why. They passed judgment on every case and thus on the responsible surgeon. The visitors entered their judgment into the logbook, which had the patient's name of each death or complication and also a brief note and grade for the surgeon's handling of the case. There were three E's for grading a resident surgeon's performance: error in judgment (EJ), error in management (EM), or error in technique (ET). Occasionally the judgment was patient disease (PD). PD meant no fault could be found with the management of the case. There was always a resident at a senior level who had operated on the ward patient, and he or she was held solely responsible for what went wrong. Residents were dispirited when the conference, with the concurrence of the visitors, gave them the dreaded three E's for their case: "error in judgment, management, and technique." They considered themselves fortunate to escape with one E. There was no, and I emphasize no, unavoidable as a judgment of a bad surgical result except on the rare occasions that the conference ruled that the complication was due to patient's disease (PD)—and PD was a very rare conclusion. That inflexible concept that complications or deaths were almost always caused by a surgeon's error was pounded into us every day. Thus, almost every complication or death was laid at the feet of one of the residents on the resident-run ward service—more often than not, the chief resident. These conferences kept the residents under some measure of control, and they were very, very emotional experiences for those on the hot seat, who in most cases were getting E'd. Despite all that, these conferences were essential teaching and learning sessions. I should have mentioned that many of the private visitors on the service were often world-class surgeons like Sweet, Bartlett, or Claude Welch. Welch was called by the Vatican to operate on the Pope.

The MGH was a place where history was made quite frequently. I just happened by chance to be in the emergency ward one night when the police came crashing through the emergency room doors with a young boy on a gurney in tow. Someone in the crowd following the gurney was carrying an oblong object wrapped in a sheet that turned out to be an arm. The patient, Everett Knowles, had his arm amputated near the shoulder when he fell under a train while attempting to hitch a ride to a ball game. After some arguing and heated discussions, we placed the arm in ice and began to run cold saline through the vessels—into the brachial artery and out the veins. Malt, whose service was covering the ER that night, was contacted, and he agreed with some urging that it was worth an attempt at reimplantation of the arm. Ron assembled a team of assorted specialties, and they indeed succeeded in reimplanting the arm during a surgery that lasted many hours. There were six or seven specialties scrubbed in on the case all the time, so those of us who were responsible for getting the case done in the first place could not get anywhere near the operating table. This was the first reimplantation of a completely amputated limb in medical history. Malt became world-famous for this surgery, and when he was interviewed by the media, he spoke flawlessly. It took a year before Knowles began to move his fingers and almost two years before he moved his wrist.

Stress in the Bulfinch

There are, of course, many incidents during the internship that we all remember, but one was important because it had a direct bearing on a situation I confronted early in my Minnesota career. We were finishing rounds one evening, and Malt called me aside and told me to grab a surgical kit and some tracheotomy tubes and go to Bulfinch 3 (medicine service) to do a trach (tracheotomy). I organized what I needed and headed for the medical wards in the Bulfinch Building, where the Ether Dome is located on the top floor. The medical wards were always dimly lit, a drab gray in appearance, with chipping paint, probably containing lead, and the patients were placed close together in the old metal beds with metal guardrails that made a loud rattle-like racket if the patient shook with a chill. The beds were adjusted with hand cranks at the foot or by using so-called wooden shock blocks to elevate the head of the bed. The MGH wards were little changed in the last hundred years before then. Needless to say, the internal medicine ward amenities were *de minimus*.

Except for the depressing atmosphere, the patients received excellent care. I thought at the time, if I were really sick, the medical or surgical wards were where I would like to have been cared for. The private rooms were nicer, but the intensiveness of care was better in many cases on the wards.

When I arrived on the Medicine ward, the medical intern took me to a bed that had curtains that were pulled around it, but behind those curtains was a sight to behold. The female patient weighed well over three bills; she was short, gasping for air, and she was cyanotic. She turned and looked at me in a haze, like some sort of animal in distress. I was terrified. Doing a tracheotomy in the OR with good lighting and skilled help would have been difficult enough in this obese woman with a bull neck, but doing a tracheotomy on the ward was another matter—I thought this had the making of an intern-caused surgical disaster. Nonetheless, perceiving that the woman was about to die, I opened the surgical kit and dumped the trach tubes on the sterile field, then did a mini-scrub and put on mask, gown, and gloves.

After preparing the neck and draping the field and gowning and gloving, I infiltrated her neck at the putative incision site after establishing the surgical landmarks that would help place my transverse incision over what I hoped was the trachea and not the thyroid gland. The two lobes of the thyroid are connected by a band of thyroid tissue overlying the trachea, and it needs to be avoided during a tracheotomy because it can be the source of profuse bleeding. I was about to start the incision when I heard the snap, snap of rubber surgical gloves going on with the help of a nurse, and Malt appeared suddenly across the field sans gown and mask opposite me. "W-w-w-what's up?" Malt asked. After he assessed the neck, we put a pillow behind it to open the field better by hyperextending the neck—which was something I, the lowly intern, forgot to do in the heat of battle. That little maneuver helped save the day. Next, Malt asked me to indicate the location of the incision. "F-f-f-fine," he said, "let's g-g-go." In short order we had a tracheotomy in that women, and her breathing was relieved and her normal color returned. We finished up by suturing the trach tube in place and partially closing the wound.

On the walk back to our ward in the White Building, Malt indicated, "Something t-t-told me to come to B-B-B-ulfinch because the medical intern sounded d-d-desperate and f-f-f-flustered." He said he really admired my willingness to proceed alone because the woman would never have made it to the OR. Just before we parted he said, "Have that patient transferred to our south wing [that was the wing on the ward for the extremely sick] because I d-d-d-don't want to go b-b-b-back to the B-B-Bulf-f-finch in the middle of the night because a bunch of 'f-f-fleas' can't manage a trach tube." I do not remember for sure, but there may have been another F-word in front of "fleas." *Fleas* was a term of endearment (or derision) used by surgeons to refer to all medical types. No one knows the origin of the appellation, but a different surgeon told me, "Fleas are the last to leave a dying body—we call their stethoscopes flea collars." I always wrote the use of the term fleas off as friendly banter between two groups with an entirely different approach in most instances to medicine and patients. I got the feeling early on that some fleas would go so far as to lie down in front of the OR door to prevent patients from having surgery.

When Minutes Counted Next Door in Minnesota

The Bulfinch episode had a direct bearing on an episode that occurred years later in Minnesota. A short time after arriving in Minnesota, I was just settling down in the bedroom at the far end of the house very tired after a long day in the OR. I had fixed a drink, but fortunately as it turned out had not touched it. There was a door at the end of the hall that opened onto a three-season porch. Suddenly the inside hall door to the porch burst open, and one of the neighbor's sons said pleadingly that I had to come quickly because his sister was dying. I was barefoot but off I went through the porch and out into the yard, with the son running toward the house next door.

I found his sister, a ten-year-old girl—designate her LH—lying unresponsive on the bathroom floor with labored breathing. I lifted her eyelids, and her pupils were slightly dilated and unreactive. She was not responsive to voice or stimulation. LH had had a shot of penicillin at her pediatrician that afternoon and never got a reaction to the drug until evening. It was clear she had severe angioneurotic edema (the trachea's or windpipe's equivalent of hives) and that her trachea and pharynx were closing down due to edema or swelling in the lining of the airway.

About this time both my neighbor on the other side, Roger B, who heard about all the commotion in the neighborhood, and LH's pediatrician appeared simultaneously. I immediately dispensed Roger for any type of light he could find. I informed the pediatrician that I was about to attempt a jungle-surgery tracheotomy on the bathroom floor because the child was dying; I was told by others the pediatrician fainted, so someone dragged him feetfirst into the living room out of the way while I was in the kitchen looking for something sharp. I rummaged through the kitchen drawers until I found a box of new razor blades. The kitchen lights had long stringlike pull cords, which I cut and recut with scissors so they could be used for vessel ties if there were bleeding. I did not know whether the girl would bleed because I was not certain that she would still be alive by the time I got to her.

Roger arrived from somewhere with a light that had a flexible light source that could be directed as needed. Roger was a real yeoman because he held the light where I needed it while I did the procedure. I know he had never seen anything like an operation, so watching what I did was tough for him. Thank heaven he did not pass out.

Most preadolescent girls are somewhat obese and their tracheas are small and soft so their tracheas can be hard to identify in an open wound. I used a transverse incision in LH's short, pudgy neck, and I had no anesthesia but she never moved during the whole procedure. I kept checking surgical landmarks as I cut down to the vital neck structures. When I got to the trachea, I felt several times for the carotid arteries before opening into the trachea. I could not feel a pulse in the carotids because her heart was probably contracting inefficiently at that moment. I knew she was still alive because there was some dark, almost black bleeding during the operation. When the trachea was opened, LH coughed and expressed a plug of something and some liquid that I thought was vomitus. I found a plastic straw in the kitchen, and I directed the straw down the trachea toward the lungs. All the time, I was sucking liquids and food particles out of the trachea until she began to breathe better, and soon thereafter she woke up—to a degree.

The next thing I knew, LH and I were in an ambulance headed for the hospital. The ambulance exited from her house over the lawn, and as we got to the end of the street, we met her parents returning home by car. Of course, all the lights were on in their house and there were numerous neighbors milling around both inside and outside their home as we left for the hospital. I rode all the way to the emergency room beside LH breathing through the straw to make sure her trachea remained open.

When we arrived at the ER, an anesthesiologist could not pass a trachea tube through the mouth down the trachea because the upper airway was so edematous. The same individual made a crack when we first arrived that I should have waited until we got to the ER, where an endotracheal tube like the one used for general anesthesia could have been inserted, which implied the tracheotomy, although rather dramatic, was unnecessary. This comment was made despite his having just been unable to pass such a tube. Someone restrained me from going after that genius, because I was in a highly emotional and agitated state after what I had just been through. So, LH had a formal tracheotomy in the OR, where a permanent tracheotomy tube was placed. The surgeons were able to use the incision and trachea entry point I made.

The ending to that story is that LH grew up to become a happy, productive citizen. Over the years, she would send an occasional thankful remembrance for being alive.

I have never felt so drained in my life as I did for a long time following that episode. By this point in my life, I thought I was a pretty mentally tough surgeon, but this experience stressed me to the limit. However, the episode next door was not a contrived fake episode on a television program like *ER*—it was real life in real time for me. My thought at the time was, *Thank God for my MGH training and the great men who trained me.* The MGH'ers would have expected no less from me than what I did. I also called Ron Malt to thank him, which was the last time I spoke to him for any length except in passing at a surgical meeting now and then.

BACK TO THE SURGICAL INTERNSHIP

I tried to be on the ward before anyone else when I was an intern even on rotations through services other than general surgery. I was sitting on the urology ward about five thirty on the first morning of my urology rotation reviewing all the urology patients' charts. Urology was on the eleventh floor of the White Building, so you got there via the elevator. The chief of urology, Wyland Leadbetter, MD, had to walk from the elevator past the ward patient chart area to get to his office. I heard the elevator ding open about five thirty-five and saw Wyland walking briskly by the ward, apparently fully occupied. I recognized him from the Intern Selection Day interviews. Later I noted that his door was open, with the light shining out into the dark hall. The second morning I arrived at 5:30 a.m., but this time Leadbetter's door was already open and he was in his office. The next morning I arrived a little after five o'clock, and Wyland arrived about fifteen minutes later. I saw him glance at me briefly as he passed through the ward. Well, this little charade went on for a couple of days, and the time for both of us kept getting earlier and earlier. So eventually I went to Wyland and told him I was the current surgical intern assigned to urology, and further, I always attempted to get to the ward earlier than any of the other residents.

So I offered that if we were both going to get some decent sleep, we should both agree to arrive at 5:00 a.m. or thereabouts. He pretended to keep on working, but briefly looked up with a little smile and muttered that was fine. He never asked my name. I was sure he barely knew who I was because the urology interns and junior residents had little interaction with Wyland except at the weekly urology service sit-down that we referred to as our grand rounds. Remember, I was a lowly intern entering into a potential conflict with an MGH chief of service. In those days as an intern, you were made to feel that you were the lowest form of life, kind of like a West Point plebe or worse, and the MGH motto was: "No tern should go unstoned." The Medicine hierarchy in those days was much like the German *Geheimrat* system, where any chief has absolute power in the hospital, especially with interns.

While I was still an intern on urology, I was doing a cystoscopic procedure on a Saturday morning when the chief stuck his head in the procedure room and motioned for me to come with him. I followed him down the hall—the cysto room was on the same floor as the ward and staff offices—wondering what I had done wrong, and he guided me into his office. I thought he might be upset about our early morning confrontation. He closed the office door behind us. He was still in his operating garb, with an untied mask hanging down and a surgical cap on, and he leaned back against the door and said without prologue that he wanted to offer me a job in his residency program. Furthermore, he said I would always have a job with him in his practice when I finished should I need it. He finished up by saying curtly, "Think about it!" and departed back to the OR, leaving me standing in the middle of his office. My first instinct was to faint, then I gathered myself; I decided I was going to change careers and accept the offer after discussing it with Jeanne—that is, if she agreed. Prior to that interchange with Wyland, I had planned to go into thoracic and cardiovascular surgery; I had given no thought to a career in urologic surgery although I did in fact enjoy the work and surgery in urology. But then the great Pied Piper worked his spell. Until he called me into his office, I did not think Professor Leadbetter had taken any notice of me, or as stated previously, even knew my name. He was a forceful although somewhat reserved man, so it was in fact hard for me to read him all the years I knew him.

The Urology Residency

Professor Leadbetter decided to expand his training program the year I started in urology, but he forgot to tell anyone, including the hospital administrators. Therefore, when I arrived to sign in and start my residency, there was no slot for me because another first-year resident, Frank Carlton, had already signed in the hospital's book. Frank was a slow-talking southerner, who, in retrospect, reminds me of James Carville. Everyone liked Frank because of his calm and cool approach to things. One consequence of this oversight was my four children and a wife had to be supported with no salary for a couple of months or until the hospital finally approved the expansion. Fortunately, Wyland reached into his own pocket and helped us until my salary started. My first check was retroactive, allowing me to pay Leadbetter back. The MGH paid a total monthly salary to a first-year urology resident of about $200 per month, and Wyland, the flinty, frugal New Englander, took back the loan. Wyland owned enough Maine timberland that he had a trail and a lake named after him, so he really needed the lucre.

As residents in urology, our weekends off began when the Saturday operating schedule—that is right, Saturday operating schedule—was finished, often well into Saturday evening. (At that time, America was on a five-and-one-half-day-a-week work schedule.) Leadbetter especially delighted in scheduling a radical cystectomy (removal of the urinary bladder), a six-hour case in those days, to begin late on Saturday afternoon.

On one of those late Saturdays when we were toiling away on some difficult case that had no end in sight, the chief looked up, sighed, and said wistfully, "You know, it is so great operating on Saturday when the phone isn't ringing!"

Professor Leadbetter loved operating until we and he were ready to drop. The MGH operating schedule was several printed pages long every day, including Saturday. The operating room served as Leadbetter's heaven on earth, and those late Saturdays were like going to vespers for him. At the time, most residents thought to themselves, of course: "Sure, Boss, you love staying here all day because you do not have a young family waiting for you at home like most of us do." But residents had no choice but to salute and do what was expected of them.

Leadbetter had at least one major flaw: he was no administrator. The last thing he wanted to do was push papers around. Consciously or unconsciously he passed that attitude on to some of his trainees, including *moi*. In fact, they almost had to cut a hole in the ceiling of his office when his inbox got piled too high. I asked him about that legendary inbox one day, and he said, "If you wait long enough, most problems solve themselves." How true in those days. Incidentally Churchill had similar thoughts about deferring administrative decisions during peacetime. As a matter of fact, if MGH had fired Wyland, he would never have seen the written notice. Alice, his secretary, said it "was one way to keep your job."

Figure 6. Wyland Leadbetter, one of urology's
great chiefs, and six of his residents
Photograph taken at *Locke-Ober* Restaurant in Boston, at the
time of Dr. Leadbetter's retirement September 11, 1969.
Top row, L to R: Frank Carlton, Elwin Fraley,
Jay Howard, and Lamar Weems.
Bottom row, L To R: Don Halverstadt, Professor
Leadbetter, and John Donohue.
Four of these men became chairmen in urology: Donohue (Indiana),
Fraley, Halverstadt (Oklahoma), and Weems (Mississippi).
[The dinner was held in one of the small private upstairs
dining rooms, where Jack Kennedy planned his campaigns,
including the one for president of the United States].
With thanks, Lamar Weems, MD

Wyland could be a mercurial individual at times, and he had a
ferocious temper that was often lit off by a discussion of money.
When Wyland's cousin, Guy Leadbetter, who was a partner in
Wyland's MGH practice, asked "the boss" to lend him a couple of

dollars for lunch, Wyland became uncontrollably irate and delivered a fifteen-minute, in-the-face, spittle-laced, foot-stomping tirade to Guy, backing his cousin up against the wall as he went off on him about how financially irresponsible Guy and his wife were. It was truly a Joe Kennedy-type performance over a couple of dollars. Maybe Wyland was serious, or maybe he sensed that his partners Guy and Ted were about to ask for a raise and that was the way to head it off. Needless to say, from that time on, Guy asked the residents when he needed to borrow money to eat, as he often did. I hasten to add, it was also not unusual for "the boss" to ask the residents for a loan to buy lunch. Maybe this is a New England trait of some sort, because JFK was also famous for never carrying any money.

(Incidentally, my secretary in Minnesota loves to tell about my inviting residents to lunch and having no money. The residents knew the drill and always collected from my secretary, who in turn nailed me for the money.)

Winston Churchill once told a servant, possibly a chauffeur, who objected because he believed Churchill had mistreated him, "I am entitled to treat you any way I so choose because I am, after all, a great man." I often thought Wyland also may have harbored some of the same thoughts, although he always was kind to the residents and almost always treated us with respect unless we made a mistake, which justified alternative treatment. He was most likely to tear you apart if, as a resident, you presented a case you thought was a real triumph. As mentioned before, the MGH surgical tradition was a *zero tolerance policy* when it came to making a mistake that harmed patients.

There were no residency review committees in those days. If such a committee had existed, it would have attempted to tell Leadbetter how many residents he could have and how to train them. One thing I have observed over the years is that when a political hack (cipher) gets appointed to a committee and is granted some power, he or she almost immediately loses any perspective on his or her own inadequacy. Think about it: imagine a bunch of "lessers" (bureaucrats) telling Wyland, one of the greatest trainers of men in the history of urologic surgery, how to conduct his business. I can assure the reader of one thing: Wyland Leadbetter did not have the time or the inclination to deal with such outfits. Leadbetter kept busy fighting diseases in the trenches and training great surgeons. Minnows have been nipping at whales throughout history, often to no avail to the benefit of civilization.

One thing I learned about myself, when I finally became chief resident, was I enjoyed teaching surgery to the younger residents as much as I did doing the surgery myself. As a consequence, I gave away many of the cases that I should have done to juniors. I remember one case in particular—a horseshoe kidney that was forming stones in both collecting systems. Horseshoe kidneys derive their name because the lower poles are connected by a bridge of tissue that often obstructs urine outflow of one or both kidneys, so stones form in the renal pelvis of the obstructed kidney(s). The goal of the surgery is to remove the bridging tissue and rotate and place the kidney(s) in a more cephalad position so they will drain better. Also the goal in such cases is to remove the stones. I took the late Ben Gittes (later became professor of urology at the Brigham) through that case even though I had never seen one or done one before. I turned the MGH mantra "See one, do one, teach one" upside down in that case. I decided, based on that case and others during which I was teaching another resident how to perform the required surgery, I wanted to be a teacher and a professor, rather than just go into private practice.

Another disadvantage to MGH surgical training was that we all knew, or at least thought, we were the best. We were encouraged to believe there was nothing we could not handle in the operating room. So we were, in a sense, the medical equivalent of "the masters of the universe." As one wag put it, "There is nothing more arrogant than a Harvard man with a C-plus average."

In some instances, our hubris worked to a patient's disadvantage, as occasionally unsupervised residents tried to perform surgeries they were not capable of doing, and also, sometimes to our disadvantage later in our professional lives, the MGH atmosphere encouraged many of us to become out of touch with the real world of medicine and see ourselves as arrogant beyond belief. Ironically, such hubris did not prepare me well for dealing with the likes of many of the private practitioners I encountered early on in Minnesota. Fortunately in the great scheme of things, that was a minor failing, though a great irritation to them and to a lesser extent, me.

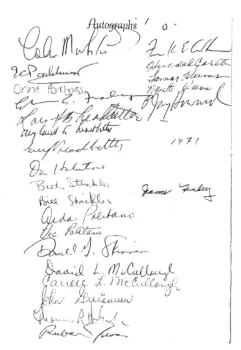

THE

WYLAND F. LEADBETTER

SOCIETY

MONDAY, MAY 17TH, 1971, AT 6:30 P. M.

JOHN HANCOCK CENTER

SUITE 4, 59TH FLOOR

CHICAGO, ILLINOIS

Figure 7. Autographs from the first Leadbetter Society meeting. There were eight future professors and chairmen, all trained by Leadbetter, signed on that program. Note the signature of Victor Politano, who, in collaboration with Wyland Leadbetter, developed the surgical technique for ureteral reimplantation to correct vesicoureteral reflux in children.

National Cancer Institute of the National Institutes of Health (NIH) (Surgery Branch)

After I finished my residency, and following a short time on the MGH staff practicing with Wyland and the other members of his group—Guy Leadbetter and Ted Parkhurst—I left Boston for an appointment for two and one-half years as a senior investigator in the Surgery Branch of the National Cancer Institute (NCI), a division of the National Institutes of Health (NIH), in Bethesda, Maryland. The NCI appointment carried with it an officer's commission in the United States Public Health Service. I felt I was at a dead end in Boston and expected that my academic aspirations would die a slow death there if I did not radically change direction. The NIH gave me the chance to develop a laboratory program and write papers almost completely free of clinical obligations. I saw the NCI appointment as the proverbial golden opportunity for a young academic surgeon.

How I obtained the appointment at the NIH is a story the theme of which should be *Persistence Pays Off*. As I was finishing my MGH urology residency, the Vietnam War was heating up, and physicians up to the age of thirty-five were being drafted almost without exception. It was possible in those days to obtain an appointment at the National Institutes of Health, where, if you chose, you could serve at the NIH as an officer in the United States Public Health Service. If you served for two years in that capacity, you fulfilled your military obligation. I was thirty-two years old, now with six children, so I was desperate to avoid going to Vietnam because I was concerned about my family. We were, of course, in debt from my long education, we had no life insurance, and the government death benefit was five thousand dollars. Never before in our nation's history had anyone in their thirties with a large family been subject to the draft—not even at the height of World War II. I was neither a draft dodger nor a coward. In fact, before I entered my urology residency, I tried to enlist in the US Army while I was a first-year surgical resident so as to discharge my military obligation before starting my specialty training, but I was told by an army representative in Harrisburg that, because of the size of my family and my age, the military would "never call me in a thousand years." Sure—and no wonder I don't trust the government.

In any event, I found out about appointments in the Surgery Branch at NCI and made an appointment for an interview with the chief of the NCI surgical service, Alf Ketcham. Ketcham told me his branch was staffed by one urologist, and the other staff were board-certified general surgeons. He allowed that he did not need another urologist because he already had one. I asked him if he would mind if I checked back from time to time to see if a position had opened up; he agreed to take my calls, and he even gave me his home phone number. After I got back home, I called Ketcham every few days until it got to the point where I could tell he was getting irritated. Then one day, my phone rang in Boston and it was Ketcham. The conversation went something like this: "This is Alf Ketcham at the NIH. My urologist just walked in and quit, so I need someone right away. Since you have called me more than my children do, yours is the only goddamned name I could remember. Do you still want the job?" I accepted the offer immediately and asked for instructions how to get the appointment done. I went down to the NIH to fill out the paperwork and secure the appointment in the Public Health Service with Ketcham's help. I knew from someone on my local Pennsylvania draft board that they were about to lick and send my draft notice. All that was left to do at that point was to tell Wyland, pack our bags, and sell our Newton house. I often thought I obtained the NIH position by attrition, but who cares?

As Ketcham informed me, the NCI staffed the Surgery Branch mainly with general surgeons, many of whom went on to distinguished academic careers after they completed a three- to four-year tour of duty at NCI. In those days, most of the physicians that served at the NIH were commissioned officers in the United States Public Health Service, which also fulfilled their service or military obligation. For my family and me, this was a godsend because it meant that I could not be drafted and sent to Vietnam.

There were actually two levels of physicians at the Surgery Branch: the senior investigators, who were boarded surgeons, and the more junior clinical associates. The junior associates had, for the most part, interrupted their careers as surgical residents in training to go to the NIH as an alternative to serving in the military. Those junior clinical associates were a wonderfully talented group, and two of them, Dave Paulson and Jean deKernion, eventually became urology chairs at Duke University and the University of California Los Angeles (UCLA) respectively. I had the privilege of working with Dave Paulson in my NCI laboratory for almost three years. We wrote several papers together, and among other things, the work won two American Urological Association first-place prizes for research. Those prizes were not a big deal because, at the time, there was little competition. In fact, our submissions may have been the only in the Research category that year. The other clinical associates went on, in many cases, to ranking positions in either general surgery or one of the surgical specialties. One of them became a factor in the Najarian fiasco mentioned later herein.

I had an interesting experience relative to Dave Paulson. When Dave came into my laboratory, I knew he was planning to go into urology at Duke. But somehow, and I do not remember exactly how, I heard by the grapevine that Dave had had some personal problems with someone at Duke and that the chief of urology, Jim Glenn, was not going to accept him for a residency. I knew firsthand that Dave was a highly intelligent fellow and a hard worker who deserved that residency and was far from some kind of incorrigible, so I decided I would try to intercede on his behalf. I drove to Durham to meet with Professor Glenn. Glenn was a delightful guy, but he kept me waiting for several hours in his outer office before he deigned to see me; I was probably a nobody in his eyes. In our meeting I told Jim how I knew Dave well and had worked with him and told him not taking Dave was a huge mistake. Glenn sat there looking at me and probably wondering, "Who in hell is this cheeky bastard who is trying to tell me how to run my department?" I left Durham quite discouraged with how the meeting with Glenn went. However, not long thereafter, Dave came bouncing into the NCI lab all smiles and announced he had a job a Duke, but it would be a year later to start than he wanted. Dave spent that extra year in the lab at the NIH with me. I don't think Dave understood why he had to wait an extra year, but I am sure it was because it took until then to create another slot for him. Dave became professor and chairman at Duke several years later, and he was a great chairman. And Jim Glenn lived to see Dave's ascendency to the chairmanship.

Although I learned several things during that time, one of the most important was about leadership, as exemplified by Alf Ketcham. I share more details about lessons learned from Doctor Ketcham later in this book.

I provided the foregoing as a summary of the educational and professional experiences and people who in large measure shaped my concepts of how you train young surgeons and also how you train and prepare individuals for academic leadership positions in a surgical specialty.

My Surgeon's Hands[7]
By John Ott, Jr., and Posted by Terri Norris

Lord, bless his hands,
And keep them steady, for my life,
And make them do whatever,
He does ask.

---

[7] Ott, J. Jr. Ott is a sister to Terri Norris. He wrote this song and poem on September 20, 2005, as he faced gastric bypass surgery. Terri Norris posted Ott's poem on her website at http://allpoetry.com/poem/2213621-My-Surgeons_Hands-by-Terri-Norris. Retrieved on September 9, 2011.

CHAPTER 1

FIRST CONTACT FROM
MINNESOTA—MAYO CLINIC

MINNESOTA LOOMS: THE ROAD TO
A CHAIRMANSHIP—MY FATE?

In late 1967, I received a phone call at the NIH from Ormand Culp, MD, head of the Section of Urology at Mayo Clinic, during which Culp indicated that Mayo might be interested in recruiting me. Culp learned about me from his good friend Professor Leadbetter. (This is an example of the old boys' network in action—the academic medical "grapevine." Thus, thanks to Culp, I received my first call from Minnesota.) I went to the Mayo Clinic in Rochester, Minnesota, for a recruiting visit that could best be described as a mini-disaster, the details of which are best left untold. Suffice it to say, Mayo made me three offers (two while I was in Rochester and one after I returned to Maryland), none of which were acceptable financially. To the Mayo's dismay, I turned them down and left no further room for negotiations. In a word, I was unhappy that Mayo placed such a low value on my abilities. As I told Culp, who called me after I got back to Maryland, "You have told me what you think I am worth, but I have children to educate so I need to find a better-paying job." Culp was very upset, which was reflected in the following comment of his: "Those damned businessmen in administration really screwed up, and I am sorry." I told Culp, "I see no need for further negotiations, but I do appreciate Mayo's offer." Culp was an extraordinary man, and I always enjoyed his company in the years that followed. I also met the late Dave Utz, who was staff under Culp but who obviously was a class act destined for big things. In fact, Culp indicated Utz would be the next chief at Mayo when he stepped down, and he was.

Nevertheless, even though I was not going to Mayo, I observed that Minnesota was a friendly, clean, tranquil, and very beautiful place. Mayo was a spectacular enterprise that was known to deliver high-quality patient care. Despite my short visit, I came away impressed that Mayo deserved its glorious reputation in every respect. I have had a lot of second thoughts about turning the Mayo down, but there is no rewind function for the "tape of your life." I write more about the Mayo Clinic later in this story.

One of the other reasons for demurring at Mayo besides the salary was because I really wanted an academic appointment in a university-affiliated medical school, where I could teach and train residents. Mayo did not have a medical school at the time. I did not want to stay in the Washington DC area any longer. We had just experienced the Martin Luther King, Jr., post-assassination riots, and during that unrest, I stood on the roof of Building 10 at the NIH and watched downtown Washington DC as it burned. I simply did not want my family to be in an environment with the potential for that type of violence during the rest of my professional life. In addition, there were minimum academic opportunities in my field in DC because of the lack of major academic medical centers in the area, except for George Washington and Georgetown University medical centers. I interviewed at George Washington prior to going to Mayo and was offered the job by the dean at twenty-four thousand dollars per year. I asked the dean whether he was kidding. His rejoinder was that the offer was more than I was making at the NIH. My response was anything would have been more than I was earning at the NIH and that was one reason I was leaving. That was the end of those negotiations.

Of course, there were "rumors" that it was cold in Minnesota on occasion, but that fact did not change my overall favorable impression of the state as a place to live, raise a family, and work. My subsequent experience has convinced me my judgment was, for the most part, correct.

SECOND MINNESOTA CONTACT—THE UNIVERSITY

Shortly after my Mayo adventure, Don Morton, the illustrious oncologic surgeon and a fellow NCI senior investigator at the time and good friend, came into my office-lab at the NIH late one afternoon with an exciting report. Morton told me he had just had a long conversation with John Najarian, the chief of general surgery at Minnesota. Furthermore, Don said Najarian "is looking for a new head of his division of urology."

Figure 8. Donald L. Morton, MD

At that time, urology was still a division in general surgery at Minnesota. Don Morton and Najarian were pals since their San Francisco residency days. That residency program had, under its chairman Leon Goldman, produced several giants in American surgery: Morton, Blaisdale, Najarian, and Bill Silen among others.

It was not clear to me initially why Don had mentioned his talk with Najarian until, as Don walked toward the door, he paused, turned, and with a wry smile told me he had given Najarian my name as a potential candidate. Don knew, of course, I had been interviewed for several chairmanships around the country and that I was, therefore, "on the make" academically, so to speak. As I reflected on the fact that two positions had surfaced in Minnesota in such a short time, I began to wonder if Minnesota was meant to be.

Several months went by before Professor Al Michael, MD, a professor of pediatrics and world-renowned pediatric nephrologist (children's kidney specialist), called and invited me to come to Minnesota as a candidate for the urology chairmanship. At the time, as urology was still a division in the department of general surgery, the appointment was controlled by Professor Najarian.

Things moved with glacial speed in Minnesota in those days, especially in the summer, so I heard nothing more for several months. In the interim, I learned that the division of urology had been without leadership because its chief had been ill for more than a year. It did not occur to me until later that a department without a head for so long should have been a clue as to the level of priority urology held in the grand scheme of things at Minnesota. I disregarded or rationalized away that information because I needed a job so I could take care of my family.

The most common method by which a medical school and its hospitals recruit new staff starts with the dean appointing a search committee. The search committee is normally composed of six to ten leading faculty members, whose responsibility it is to scour the country to find the best candidates for a position. The committee's faculty members thus essentially become headhunters, a role they often are too pressed for time to discharge properly. (As time went on, my impression was the Minnesotans took recruiting very seriously and acted diligently.) Search committees usually tap into the network of existing chairmen in the field in which they are recruiting to see who among their trainees would be suitable candidates. Sometimes these chairmen will recommend one of their own trainees or faculty, while on other occasions, they will suggest someone trained by one of their colleagues who has impressed them somewhere along the academic circuit.

It is the responsibility of the search committee to come up with final recommendations to the dean. The dean usually has the last word in making the appointment. But that was not exactly the Minnesota protocol in all cases because, as it turned out, the dean played no role in my appointment.

So once again, I headed back to Minnesota for trips up and down the runway of "the academic recruiting fashion show." I first visited the University of Minnesota in August, probably because that is a time of the year when Minnesota is at its best, or at least its warmest. Professor Richard Varco met me at the airport gate, which was unusual, and believe it or not, he immediately offered to carry my bag. (It was my custom at that stage, being young and driven, to carry at least two briefcases stuffed to overflowing with current papers in progress.) I thanked Professor Varco, but carried my own bags.

Figure 9. Richard Varco, MD
Courtesy of University of Minnesota Archives, University of Minnesota—Twin Cities

Varco's offer stunned me. I was in the presence of this short, rotund, high-energy guy with pool-of-oil-like dark eyes and bushy eyebrows, truly an Edward Teller look-alike, who was known to me only as the world-famous surgeon who, along with C. Walton Lillehei and John Lewis,[8] had pioneered open-heart surgery in Minnesota and the country. It is an understatement to say that the fact that this giant of surgery wanted to carry the bag of a thirty-two-year-old nobody left me impressed.

---

[8] As I reviewed the history of the Nobel Prize in *The Physiology of Medicine,* I was amazed to learn that a Nobel Prize had never been awarded for the development of cardiac surgery. But I did learn that one of the "Fathers of Heart Surgery," C. Walton Lillehei, MD, of Minnesota, was in fact recommended *several times* for the Nobel Prize based on the fact that he and John Lewis, MD, did the first heart operation under hypothermia. There is no doubt in my mind if the same work had been done at Harvard, the Cantabs would have been awarded a Nobel.

This was taken from a book review of G. Wayne Miller's *King of Hearts*: "If there had been a Nobel Prize for cardiac surgery, it would have been awarded to half a dozen surgeons, starting with Gross and Gibbon and extending to Starr or Favaloro. In the middle of this list would have been C. Walton Lillehei." NEJM< 342:2004. June 29, 2000.*The problem with this analysis is that the rules of the Nobel Prize state that no more than three people may be awarded a single prize.*

During the ride from the airport, Varco showed himself, at least to me, to be a friendly and warm man with great presence. He chatted away about this and that, but at the same time, obviously took my measure by asking a few penetrating questions, some of which I was in the middle of answering when he interrupted my answers by asking his next question. Patience is not common in great surgeons. One question I never forgot was, "What do you want to accomplish as a chairman?" My answer was straightforward and without pause, because I had thought about the question of what I wanted to achieve as a chairman for at least a couple of years: "First, establish a training program that would provide MGH-level clinical training for residents and fellows. Second, establish an extensive basic research program in urology." (Almost no urology departments had a quality research program in those days.) "Third, create a developmental program within the department that would produce future academic leaders in the specialty (department chairmen)." After a very few minutes, Varco looked at me intently and said, "I hope you will take this job. We really need someone."

"How can you say that?" I asked. "You barely know me."

Although Varco never answered that question in any detail, I learned later of course he had already vetted me extensively with Wyland and the NIH and a few others in surgery and urology at the MGH. Varco also had the information Najarian learned from Don Morton, whatever that was. Richard Varco, along with Najarian, had one of the last words on policy in the medical school and department of surgery at the time. I was sure that if you failed to pass muster with Varco, the first trip to the university would have been the last.

As time has passed, I have concluded that Richard Varco was one of the most outstanding individuals I ever knew. I could write a book about Varco alone. Varco stories, as I understand it, reverberate among the Minnesota academic surgeons even to this day.

By the way, that little episode of Varco asking me to consider the job reminded me of my very first medical school interview at Jefferson Medical College in Philadelphia. It ended with the interviewer saying, "You're admitted."

"How can you say that?" I asked, very much taken aback. "Because I am head of the admissions committee," he answered matter-of-factly. Touché. (My encounter at Jefferson certainly changed my perception as to how difficult it was going to be for me to gain admission to medical school.)

What led up to that pronouncement by the director of admissions was a little quiz I had to take. The interviewer had a library along one wall of his office, and on the top shelf were several native drums that looked like primitive bongo drums. These were covered top and bottom with separate animal skins held together by some sort of leather ties to draw them taut. Just after I sat down, he asked me from where I thought the drums originated. I looked at them very carefully and noticed two or three faded black and white stripes on the corner of one of the skins. My answer therefore was, "If those are zebra skins, the drums must be from Africa." I assume the answer was correct because we quickly moved on to other subjects, and before the interview ended, the interviewer told me, speaking as director of admissions, I was accepted. In any event, I was interested in Jefferson because my father-in-law and Jeanne's brother were Jefferson graduates. The other point about Jefferson was that it was unpretentious and clinically oriented. The school was famous for producing good clinicians and practitioners. At the time, I wanted only to be a good physician and to be able to provide high-quality patient care.

The August weather was pleasant, and the scenic drive along the Mississippi River from the airport to the medical school was beautiful. Varco, who chose the route, was probably thinking along that old cliché, "You only have one chance to make a first impression." I did say to him at one point, "I see you chose the scenic route to the medical school." He just smiled.

Later that evening I met some of the giants of American clinical medicine of that era at a dinner party at Varco's large, rambling 1930s *Little House on the Prairie*-style home. Here I shook hands and conversed with Owen Wangensteen, Richard Varco, Bob Good, John Najarian, Mike Paparella, Al Michaels, and Bob Vernier (pediatrics). I also met John Moe, one of the world's most famous scoliosis (spine) surgeons; Lyle French, the neurosurgeon who was president of the elite neurosurgical *Cushing Society* at the time; and several other medical luminaries. I had no knowledge of whether I impressed them, but they certainly impressed me.

However, I noted there were no community urologists present and no one ever mentioned Don Creevy, the retiring chief of the division of urology. I knew of Creevy from the preliminary due diligence I had done on the division before coming to Minnesota. I had talked to Colin Markland, the assistant professor in the division of urology, whom I knew from MGH days. Markland served on Creevy's faculty so I looked forward to meeting both Professors Creevy and Markland on their home turf, although that did not happen on the first visit.

The people at Varco's home were evaluating me as they would any candidate, probably with two main thoughts in mind: first, of course, they wanted to make sure I could actually lead a department, given my young age—and they wondered if I had the requisite surgical skills to teach others and take proper care of patients. Second, and perhaps even more important to them, they wanted to know if such a young, inexperienced fellow, a virgin chairman so to speak, understood the importance of preserving the existing university private practice plan. They, of course, worried whether I could be co-opted by the dean and others who wanted the university physicians to form a group practice. They may have suspected I might be a romantic idealist right out of the East who knew little about the economic facts of life. These men knew how important their practices and economic freedom were in maintaining and developing their departments. They were well aware that the state would not provide enough funds to maintain a viable, competitive medical school, so their monies from patients were essential to maintain the high standards of the clinical arm of the medical school.

Dick Varco had prepared a wonderful meal for us: everyone knew he was a gourmet cook. His surgical career had been cut short when a champagne bottle he was opening exploded and severed the tendons and nerves in his wrist.

The Varcos had a large dining room befitting a gourmand. A large, circular "stinkwood" table dominated the center of the dining room. That grand table accommodated everyone present, some twenty to twenty-five individuals; it made me think of what it must have been like sitting at King Arthur's roundtable.

Varco served a sumptuous dinner topped off by a towering pyramid of ice cream balls served on a long-stem cake platter. Atop the ice cream he had ladled all sorts of goodies and crowned it all with a sparkler. Varco was not only a gourmet but also a showman.

We adjourned to Varco's big living room after dinner for a question-and-answer session. The very first question was, "What do you think about private practice?" I am unsure who asked it, but I will never forget it was the first question asked. The room fell silent. Everyone's ears were on receive, and the eyes of Minnesota were upon me (apology to the Texas longhorns). As I reflect back, that was one of those few moments in life when it is all on the line, and I sensed it was then or never in Minnesota. "Well, why do you ask?" I retorted. "Is there any other kind?"

My response stopped the show. I heard lots of chortling and saw looks of relief and furtive glances back and forth among the group, and there was some electricity in the air. I suspect that answer at least helped clinch the job offer, but of course I'll never know for sure. At the time I had no idea how important that question was or what it portended for the future of all physicians at the university.

I did not discover until later that at the time I was being recruited, an intense battle raged between the medical school dean and his allies and the rest of the practitioners at the university over the private practice monies. The dean's allies were the relative financial have-nots (medicine and pediatrics, primarily). Other staff told me the have-nots wanted to wrest control of the private practice monies away from the financial haves (the surgeons, and the other big producers, like orthopedics, otolaryngology, cardiology, medical oncology, and lab medicine). The have-nots and the dean, of course, wanted at least some of the money earned by the haves because that would "only be fair," or so went their mantra. We are all now recognizing the old fairness gambit, and forty-five years later, I have had fairness up to my keister, as have most of the real producers in this country.

Somewhere in the murky background of this tableau playing out behind the scenes, I heard that Owen Wangensteen, the world-famous former chief of general surgery at Minnesota, had thrown in with the collectivists—of course after he retired. In the eyes of Wangensteen, however, due to his advanced age, he had become a spent force to some degree in the politics of the medical school, or metaphorically one of those "burned-out volcanoes" that Churchill occasionally referred to when speaking of those *older* men who were out of power and past their primes. Even at a distance, however, I learned the great Wangensteen name and voice occasionally still parted waters in not only any one of Minnesota's ten thousand lakes, but in Minnesota medicine.

At that time, the haves were so strong that they were able to resist any attempted takeover of their practices. The departments that counted financially did their own recruiting, and they appointed individuals who received the dean's rubber stamp, *pro forma* approval. The department chiefs in those days held all the cards because they, not the dean, had the money to support new faculty, at least until they were able to build a practice. In a sense, the state legislature tied the dean's hands, thereby limiting his influence through the pittance appropriations it made to the medical school.

The strong departments, therefore, kept appointments under their control so they could recruit those who they were reasonably sure would hold the line on retaining the private practice within the medical school and produce resources (money). The chiefs knew from experience that individuals with the incentive to achieve, and who controlled their own financial resources, had the most success building and sustaining Minnesota's great clinical departments. The university and the state legislature made an unwritten pact with the clinicians to the effect that the physicians would be free to generate money through fee-for-service medicine that was theirs to control as long as they maintained a first-class academic department. This policy created winners on all sides and provided Minnesota with a high-quality medical school on the cheap. The efforts and generosity of the physicians provided a great benefit to the state. (I will explain this arrangement in greater detail later in the book.)

In a sense, the school leaders had built the medical school on a foundation equivalent to the San Andreas-like financial fault line. The school depended almost entirely on patient care revenues to sustain many of the clinical departments, and even to some extent, the basic science departments. When there were needs in the basic sciences, the clinicians would cough up money to help the dean meet those needs. No one explained this system to me at the beginning, and I was neither experienced nor savvy enough at that time to understand the situation on my own. The full-time geographic arrangement for the clinical faculty at Minnesota was unlike any arrangement in the other major medical schools with which I was familiar. The established practices generated plenty of money, so there was no prospect that things were about to change, certainly not in those pre-HMO and pre-government interference days. None of us could know at the time, nor did any of us imagine, the massive economic changes that were about to impact medicine as a whole and private practice at the University of Minnesota.

The University of Minnesota president, James Morrill, with advice from leading citizen consultants, created the full-time geographic private practice system that was in place and functioning when I arrived. Morrill appointed Minneapolis attorney Kenneth Anderson to a panel of outside advisors who were charged to design a practice plan for the medical faculty that would help the university establish a "world-class medical institution." One thing you can say without reservation is that the best people in Minnesota thought big. Attorney Anderson shared those exact words of President Morrill about creating a world-class medical center with me long after I moved to Minnesota.

Attorney Anderson advised President Morrill to allow and encourage flourishing private practices by the clinical faculty at the university. Anderson and his committee believed allowing private practice inside the clinics and hospital would both attract very high-caliber physicians to Minnesota and provide funds for the university hospital and clinics and the medical school. Anderson recommended that the academic medical practices should be governed by so-called *Regents' Rules of Practice.* The rules would set limits on physician salaries, and their economic activities would be monitored. Thus, the school appointed an attorney to monitor the practices, and therefore all the physicians reported their incomes and tax returns to the monitor at least once a year, and the monitor would, in turn, report the data in summary form to the central administration of the university and the dean of the medical school. The financial arrangement worked exceptionally well for everyone, so it came as no surprise in "progressive Minnesota" that the collectivists at the university could not tolerate it over the long, long term. Minnesota's left-of-center government, growing incrementally ever so much stronger and more acquisitive, began to see the physicians' private practice arrangement as a target. It took the takers several years to figure out how to seize control of the private practice monies.

It is no coincidence that the private practice system produced precisely what it was intended to produce: a world-class medical institution. The school's success provides a clear demonstration of the difference between policy based on sound economic principles, human nature, and the free market, as compared to an institution or enterprise built on good intentions or the egalitarian, coercive utopian theory of the "progressive masterminds." As proof, consider that the world recognized the University Hospitals as among the top ten in the country during the 1950s and through the 1970s. Also, the medical school became a training ground for many physicians who went on to become leaders in their disciplines. Medical academicians saw the university's many departments as in the first rank of similar departments in the world. The medical profession knew most of the clinical faculty members as national icons, such as Owen Wangensteen, Walt Lillehei, Richard Varco, Leo Rigler, Lyle French, Bob Good, John Moe, Mike Paparella, and many others.

The medical school counted, among its many specific clinical achievements, trailblazing work in open-heart surgery, immunology, and pediatrics. For example, as a result of the heart surgery program, the university featured the very first hospital in the world—the Variety Club Heart Hospital—that was completely devoted to the diagnosis and treatment of cardiovascular disease: The Variety Club Heart Hospital building still stands on the bank of the Mississippi River, but I do not know what it is used for these days. Unfortunately, it is no longer the epicenter in the world for the diagnosis and innovative treatments of cardiovascular diseases.

In the 1950s, even the cardiac surgeons Michael DeBakey and Denton Cooley, the two now world-famous Texas heart surgeons, often came to Minnesota to watch Lillehei, Varco, Lewis, and their associates operate on hearts. The University Hospitals constructed special observation rooms (domes) so that individuals could watch its surgeons perform their breakthrough heart surgeries. The medical school built the observation rooms specifically as a response to the large number of visitors to the heart program. When I first arrived, some of the dome rooms were used to store files. I wonder if the observation domes even still exist.

Today, thanks to Doctors Cooley and DeBakey and other farsighted, free market-oriented Texans, the Texas Heart Institute in Houston flourishes as an internationally known cardiovascular center, where kings and queens and world leaders have their surgeries or other cardiovascular-related procedures. Sadly, the names of Varco, Lillehei, and Wangensteen do not echo through the halls of the Texas Heart Institute, even though the Texans owe them so much.

Meanwhile, back in Minnesota, the timbers of the former heart hospital are being assaulted by cellulose-eating microorganisms (rot), and its weathered exterior has seen better days. Legend has it that ghosts in long white coats that, for a time, wandered the halls and former wards of the Variety Club Heart Hospital to inspire young physicians have even now abandoned the site, so I am told.

The Heart Hospital in Minnesota still has "heart" in its name, at least in the minds of the few who still remember, but the greatness that once was is long gone. The now so-called heartless building is a tribute in large measure to mismanagement and a lack of vision—or you might say heart on the part of university bureaucrats, who by and large are more occupied with who has control of whom than they are in creating wealth and greatness. Someone once described the sclerotic bureaucracies of some universities and state governments as often having the vision of a blind man with cataracts standing on a hill trying to see through the fog, a disease sometimes referred to by many of us as "bureaucratitis." Or as Buchwald wrote, the university medical school and its clinical arm became the victim of *administocracy*.

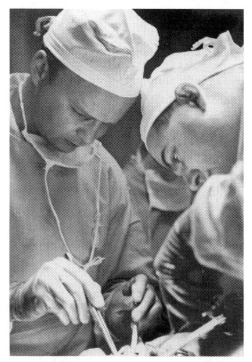

Figure 10. Drs. Lillehei and Varco in the dog laboratory.
Courtesy of University of Minnesota Archives, University of Minnesota—Twin Cities

CHAPTER 2

FREEDOM AND AMERICAN EXCEPTIONALISM

In case the reader thinks the concern about the loss of economic freedom in America in general, and at the University of Minnesota Medical School in particular, is misplaced or exaggerated, here is a citation from the Heritage Foundation on the subject of economic freedom in our country:

> "The Heritage Foundation annually ranks the world's economies in order of freedom. Last year the United States fell to number eight, now classified as 'mostly free' rather than 'free.' Canada's economy is now rated as freer than ours." Along with that freedom came the finding that Canadians are, for the first time in history, wealthier than Americans. [9]

Actually the battle for control of private practice at the University of Minnesota Medical School probably reached farther back than the previous chapter indicated. Although I am not certain of the exact details, sometime prior to World War II, the university's central administration attempted to take over at least part of the practitioners'

---

[9] Radia, Andy, *The Global Mail*, July 17, 2012

medical practices. As a result, the university physicians bolted for downtown, where they founded the Nicollet Clinic. Their exodus cleared the deck for the university to formulate new rules for private practice.

Soon thereafter, University President Morrill appointed Owen Wangensteen as chief in general surgery and Cecil Watson as chief of internal medicine. This set in motion the rebuilding of the medical faculty. Wangensteen was only twenty-eight years old when he was appointed.

This period saw the beginning of changes that propelled the University of Minnesota Medical School and hospital to the front rank of American medicine. A key element that drove this success was the private practice structure established by Ken Anderson and President Morrill.

Allowing faculty to practice private medicine within the medical school led it to a "golden age of greatness," and this stature of the medical school accrued to the entire school and the state of Minnesota. Exactly what occurred way back then is deserving of more research on my part. In the end, however, whatever the dustup was all about, it led to revitalization of the medical school and hospital under Morrill's practice plan. But that was a different era.

The United States, unlike most other nations, chose to rely on a private health-care system. To know why America is (was) unique or exceptional in so choosing, I refer you to Paul Starr's *The Social Transformation of American Medicine*.[10] In this day especially, Starr's book is really worth a read, as we witness the government's aggressive attempt to gain control of the medical profession and. indeed, the entire health-care system.

---

[10] Starr, Paul, *The Social Transformation of American Medicine*, Basic Books, 1983.

The attempt by university administrators to control private practice money and the personal freedoms of the university physicians reminds me of the genesis of such titanic battles as are reflected in a passage from *The Memoirs of a Superfluous Man,* by Albert Jay Nock.[11] By the way, the Ludwig von Mises Institute at Hillsdale College has dubbed Nock's book as one of the most important books ever written on economics. The institute ranks it just below Friedrich Hayek's *Road to Serfdom* in importance, and Hayek's book ranks among the most important books on economics. along with Adam Smith's *Wealth of Nations.* Nock wrote:

> If a regime of complete economic freedom be established, social and political freedom will follow automatically; and until it is established, neither social nor political freedom can exist. Here one comes in sight of the reason why the State [*in any form*] will never tolerate the establishment of economic freedom. In a spirit of sheer conscious fraud, the State will at any time offer its people "four freedoms," or six, or any number; but it will never let them have economic freedom. If it did, it would be signing its own death-warrant, for as Lenin pointed out, "it is nonsense to make any pretense of reconciling the State and liberty." Our economic system being what it is and the State being what it is, all the mass verbiage about "the free peoples" and "the free democracies" is merely so much obscene buffoonery.

Physicians and patients must realize that without autonomy and economic freedom, they will suffer reduced professional and personal freedom. Physicians will find that their loss of freedom eventually will impact their ability to properly care for patients, just as it has with top-down government-run medicine around the world.

---

[11] Nock, A. J. *The Memoirs of a Superfluous Man:* See Suggested Reading

There are those who argue, including President Ronald Reagan, that top-down government-run medicine is the "IV" that, once inserted, is the beginning of complete government control over the lives of not only physicians but also private citizens. In fact, the consequences of government control have already begun in the United States with Medicare patients. Be forewarned: A government system, if it follows the lead of most government-run medical plans, eventually will limit the number of physicians, it will tell them where physicians will practice, it will determine what fields within medicine they may enter, and the government will tell physicians what treatments are suitable for a patient of a given age. Life tables will determine the care Medicare patients will be allowed to receive, just as it does now in Great Britain, and those tables will become more impactful for those patients than medical science. This type of care is treatment by numbers; it is not treatment of the whole patient based on medical indications. In addition, government-run health care will limit patients' options as to which physician they will be able to see. Patients will learn anew the experience of waiting for an appointment with any physician, and especially with a specialist. Patients will also have to wait for time in any procedure room, including for open surgery.

The government has failed to demonstrate that it can run anything more efficiently or better than the free people of the United States (with the possible exception of the military). Some argue that the Egyptian pyramids were the last successful government project. I would argue it was the GI Bill after World War II, which provided assistance to returning veterans to pay for their education.

Those physicians among the readers who understand the threats imposed by government-run health care need to inform your patients of the consequences resulting from their physicians' loss of autonomy and freedom; eventually it will severely impact patient care.

In short, physicians may become little more than implementers of policies formulated by bureaucrats, who have no knowledge of either the science or art of medicine. Giving bureaucrats control over medicine would be like giving one of my teenage granddaughters (no Amelia Earharts, they) the right to pilot a helicopter without any license or training. The disastrous results for all concerned would be absolutely predictable in either case.

> The loss of economic freedom presents a greater problem for our county as a whole. The loss of economic freedom is tied directly to a decline in standard of living and even longevity. Excellent discussion of the importance of economic freedom can be found on the web site.[12]

> "Leftists have sold socialized medicine to various populations on the fraudulent premise that government-run health care can do the impossible: reduce costs while simultaneously providing all the care one wants, especially in one's old age. The reality has been entirely different. Socialized medicine has resulted in spiraling costs and reduced services, much like government-run post offices."[13]

Someone once said, "History doesn't repeat itself, but it does rhyme." The following is an excerpt from a 1949 letter written by Alexander Fleming,[14] the Scotsman who won the Nobel Prize for the discovery of penicillin: "Here the doctors are up in arms against the threatened state service (national health service). They want to be doctors, not civil servants. The state takes over hospitals on July 5th next. It will not affect us much here as we are a teaching establishment but it will make a difference to a lot of places."

---

[12] www.economicfreedom.org. Retrieved on June 5, 2014
[13] www.powerlineblog.com/archives/2012/03/annals-of-government-medicine-9.php Retrieved on June 5, 2014
[14] In author's personal collection.

Of course, Fleming was terribly wrong. The United Kingdom created the National Health Service (NHS) in 1948. Few professionals, and especially physicians, who have been associated in any way with medicine in England have prospered. UK patients traditionally face long wait lines for treatment. Decisions made by the UK's National Institute for Health and Clinical Excellence, euphemistically abbreviated as NICE, consistently has denied lifesaving treatments to patients simply because of cost. As a result, today the private health-care sector is the fastest-growing segment in the health-care industry in Great Britain. Not only have UK's patients suffered, but the whole enterprise of British medicine has been diminished, with drastic cuts in research.

Remember, England, like America, has a history as a wellspring for medical science advancement. UK and American medical scientists earned credit for unraveling the structure of DNA, the discovery of penicillin, and advances in basic immunology that have extended the life of transplanted organs

These are but a few examples of British medical advances. Sitting at the headwaters of medical progress are the academic and teaching centers in both Britain and the United States: I fear the headwaters are drying up, and this will choke off future medical advances in Great Britain to the detriment of everyone.

In terms of patient care under the UK's National Health Service, the stories of neglect, denial of care, poor treatment results, and squalid conditions are common. A recent report by a whistleblower stated that older patients were having their mouths taped so they could not bother the caregivers in one hospital.[15] The British press consistently reports the NHS's failings. Recently, for example, British media reported that the pediatric heart unit in Bristol had a death

---

[15] www.irishtimes/com/news/crime-and-law/courts/nurse-who-taped-patient-s-mouth-given-probation-act-1.1772749 Retrieved on June 6, 2014

rate in their surgeries of twice that of the norm.[16] Apparently as this information leaked out, it caused an outrage in Great Britain. Investigation of that unit's performance is underway even as I write this narrative. However, no sensible person would have confidence that the NHS or any British government agency investigating itself would produce an unbiased analysis of the situation.

If government-run health care is so poor and if the UK experience shows it, why do we not hear the same horror stories about the Canadian health-care system? (Actually, these stories are becoming better known, thanks to books like *Health Care Reform: The End of the American Revolution?*, by Canadian-born physician Lee Kurisko, MD.[17])

Public opinion surveys in Canada regularly indicate that most Canadians are satisfied with their health care (I have documented this with limited numbers of interviews with Canadians). One explanation for the apparent difference in performance of government-run medicine in the two countries might be that the United Kingdom is more strapped for resources than Canada.

Canada, as everyone recognizes, has a minimal military force and essentially lives under the American defense shield or umbrella. At last count, Canada had fewer than 120,000 men and women under arms.[18] As a consequence of such a small military budget, more money is available for social welfare programs in Canada than in the United Kingdom.

Most health-related money in Canada goes directly into patient care. Canada has no extensive health-care research infrastructure such as

---

[16] Circulation. 2001; 104:e9011-9013, doi:10.1161/hc3201.097067

[17] Kurisko, Lee, *Health Care Reform: The End of the American Revolution?* 2011. See Suggested Reading

[18] www.globalfirepower.com/country-military-strength-detail. asp?country_id=canada. Retrieved on June 5, 2014

exists in the United States. Canada also does not maintain numerous centers of teaching and training excellence, as are common in the United States. But the Canadian medical education system did give us Charles Krauthammer, who is a proverbial gift that just keeps on giving.

Canada spends very little on research and development of new drugs or medical instrumentation. I am not aware of a single new major drug, other than the LH-RH inhibitors so useful in managing cancer of the prostate, having been developed in Canada in the last decade. There are probably some others but less widely known Canada-developed drugs for patients. According to the Pharmaceutical Marketing Association of America, the United States spends 80 percent of the world's budget for pharmaceutical research, while Canada spends less than 1 percent. Today it costs 1.38 billion US dollars just to bring a new drug to market.[19] No wonder new drug development is stymied in many countries.

Finally, if you push Canadians hard enough, most of them admit they would head for the United States if they had an urgent or complex medical problem; in fact, one of their provincial premiers did just that recently when he needed advanced cardiac surgery. The British, and most of the rest of the world, do not have the luxury of a short trip to the United States over an open border to receive medical services that are unavailable or inadequate in their own countries. A recent study from the supposedly nonpartisan Fraser Institute reported that over 40 thousand Canadians seek treatment in the United States annually.[20] The United States is Canada's health-care safety valve, especially for its politicians and the wealthy. Mark Steyn, the brilliant Canadian pundit, author, and blogger, said his emergency room was in the closest town in Vermont. Steyn has

---

[19] The Pharmaceutical Industry and Global Health. Facts and Figures 2012
[20] Fraser Forum. May/June 2013 p17-19

written and spoken forcefully about why America should not install government-run medicine.[21]

Knowing that American medical care is easily available to them may explain why Canadians are not more dissatisfied with their health care. Besides, Canada does a reasonably good job with primary care, although more than 4 million Canadians struggle to find their own family practice physician.[22] This makes it more difficult to see a specialist, as the family physician is the gatekeeper on referrals. When someone needs critical care or an advanced diagnostic test, he or she too often sits on the floor for a long time on wait lists.

Canada researchers should redesign their surveys about Canadian health care. They should divide the survey into two groups: one group would be Canadians who have never had a major illness, while the other group would be those who had been treated (or attempted to be treated) for a major, life-threatening illness in the Canadian health-care system. It is easy to like a health-care system you have never had to use, or a system the quality of which has never been tested by you or your family for its ability to treat potentially fatal disease.

---

[21] Steyn, Mark, Our Sick State. Jan 2012. www.steynonline.com/4783/our-sick-state. Retrieved on June 5, 2014

[22] Family Medicine in Canada-Vision for the Future. College of Family Physicians of Canada. Ontario. Nov 2004

CHAPTER 3

SECOND RECRUITING VISIT TO MINNESOTA AND JOB OFFER

Although I am now getting ahead of the story, it was not until late in the second visit that I met Dean Robert Howard, but it was a very brief meeting. The dean had not even sent me a letter inviting me to Minnesota to consider a major position in the medical school. Instead, all of my contact with Minnesota early on had been with a member of the search committee by phone or the Varco interaction.

By the time I assumed my position as chairman the following summer, Dean Howard had already lost the battle for control of private practice, as well as his position as dean. I went to the dean's office to meet him because Howard had signed the job offer letter that included details about the university's financial and space commitments (e.g., laboratory space, seed money, etc.) the school made to entice me to come to Minnesota. When I arrived in the dean's office, a sign painter was meticulously removing Howard's name from the outer door. I asked the painter what he was doing, and he looked up and said something to the effect that Howard was no longer dean so he was removing his name from the door. I thought that was at least better than what happens in business when they just place tape over the previous guy's name on the phone and write your name in ballpoint pen on the tape. I stood there with my letter in hand, mouth open, and was panicked because the man who made all the written commitments on behalf of the university and the medical school was no longer dean. Neither the dean nor anyone else had informed me that he was leaving.

The cashiering of Howard told me the Minnesotans, like most people with a lot on the line, know how to play hardball if necessary when it comes to money.

What followed was the first of many waves of terror that went through me in the early days. Feeling more than a little desperate, I went to the late Lyle French's office, who at the time was head of the Department of Neurosurgery. He heard me out regarding the dean and other issues while still sitting at his desk looking up over his half glasses. Then he said, "As far as the dean is concerned, we fired him." About the financial commitments the dean had made to me, French said, "Give me that letter from the dean and I'll take care of it."

I knew the conversation had ended, but I had no way of knowing if he or anyone would "take care" of anything. Over time, however, French and others did take care of it—for the most part. My takeaway from that brief encounter with Lyle was: be careful, pal, or we will also have you fired. I realized right then and there it was good-bye to the idealism and the romantic concept I had of academic medicine; it was, rather, welcome to the hard reality of the real world.

Everyone at the medical school knew and respected the fact that Lyle French was all powerful. When you stood in his presence, with his silver hair and erect soldierly bearing, you knew you were in the tall grass with the big dogs. Lyle was a truly great man, and I would learn even more how substantive he was as I watched him in operation.

Figure 11. Lyle French, MD
Courtesy of University of Minnesota Archives, University of Minnesota—Twin Cities

The movers and shakers in the medical school at the time besides French were John Najarian, Dick Varco, Fred van Bergen (anesthesia), and Don Hastings (psychiatry). The haves fondly referred to them as their "financial front five." These five men kept a wary eye on the dean and the administrations of both the medical school and university. Just as importantly, they were well connected with the state legislature. With Lyle French leading the way, the whole group was capable of some vigorous political high-sticking when necessary, which Dean Howard learned to his disadvantage. French seemed to know and be known and liked by everyone who was anyone. He had the advantage over the rest of us of being a lifelong Minnesotan. French had connections in state government at all levels, and as a result, many of the state's leading politicians became our patients. Before I retired from the university, I had taken care of five governors or former governors, a couple of United States senators, and one vice president of the United States. Remember, this was the era of the great Minnesota Vikings defensive front four: Page, Eller, Marshal, and Larsen, the purple people eaters. The clinical front five could easily have been named the five dean eaters.

Most of the front five have since moved on to their final reward, so I will probably never know how Dean Howard was fired. However, I have the impression that John Najarian, a shrewd character and good man in every respect, stood aside in these matters and let others do the "wet" work. Najarian had only been chairman a short time when the dean was fired, and he was at the time focused on building his department. My guess is that Lyle French wielded the ax in the cashiering of Dean Howard.

In those days the front five clearly had the same view of medical school deans that Owen Wangensteen had at one point in his career when he said, "the only Dean who was good for anything was Kipling's regimental water carrier, Gunga Din (pronounced dean), because at least he gave you a drink of water."[23]

MY SECOND RECRUITMENT VISIT

Now back to the chronological narrative: During my second recruitment visit, I played out the usual Polish minuet of academic recruiting: spinning, approaching, and then spinning away without touching. I only remember two main things about the second visit: unlike my August visit, this time the weather was bitterly cold. The second memory resulted from finally meeting the former head of the division of urology, Professor Don Creevy, at a cocktail party at Lyle French's house.

---

[23] Quoted by Henry Buchwald *Cancer:* 124 (4)-p. 595, 1998

Professor Creevy had been the chief of urology and he had become ill, so he had to step aside prior to my visit. He suffered from lung cancer and had had a lung removed. Creevy smoked for most of his life, and his long smoking history and surgery left him dyspneic. He spoke in short phrases and got directly to the point. Creevy studied me before talking. Then he gasped out a few sentences spoken through purple-tinged lips, interspersed with rapid, shallow breaths. "If you come here, you are on your own [gasp]. So do not expect any help from me [gasp]."

Creevy then turned away abruptly, and with his oxygen tank in tow, left me standing alone in the middle of the room, badly in need of some of his oxygen. What was remarkable about this interchange was that I had never met or spoken with Professor Creevy prior to that party, and I spoke to him only once briefly thereafter. I have wondered if perhaps one of his faculty saw me as a rival—maybe knew me from Boston?—and maybe that individual gave Creevy some negative input before Creevy met me so his chief would help him torpedo my candidacy for the urology chair. Don Creevy remained true to his word. To this day I have never been absolutely sure what prompted Don's pronouncement that night. If it was not instigated by someone in the division, Creevy may have already decided to leave the university and enter downtown private practice. I wondered if he thought he would position himself as an adversary to anyone at the university, thereby attempting to improve his standing or compatibility with the antiuniversity crowd among private practitioners. But I reasoned that was unlikely because he was already in very good standing with the private urologists, having trained many of them.

The offer came initially by phone. Professor Al Michael made the call that provided me with a verbal job offer. Michael served as cohead of the search committee with Dick Varco and Bob Vernier. All three of the individuals were of the highest standard. I received the call shortly after I had returned to the NIH. I said, "Before I give you my answer, I would require the offer in writing." Ron Malt served as my mentor at the MGH as long as I stayed there. I knew Malt as a sophisticated and urbane general surgeon and an adroit medical politician. The "Malt Rule" said to always get a job offer in writing before beginning negotiations about what it would take to recruit you—in movie parlance, first the hook and then the sting. Malt explained that if the school got the sense a candidate's requirements were unreasonable, the written offer would never come.

Figure 12. Ronald A. Malt, MD

Of course, the institution's goal is to recruit a candidate by expending as few resources as possible. As in any negotiation involving money and resources, "fair" is defined as how much an individual can negotiate. Most candidates judge how much a school wants them by the amount of resources the school is willing to expend to recruit them.

Aspiring academicians must understand that it is also important to get a job offer in writing just so if they decide not to accept the school's offer, it will be clear who turned whom down. That offering letter prohibits anyone, such as a future competitor for a job, from circulating the rumor that the school turned him or her down.

It becomes a rough game at the leadership level in medicine, and competitors for the next good job are not above starting such rumors.

Academic medicine recruitment operates almost exclusively by word of mouth. Anyone who is anyone can always find out information about a potential candidate through another physician who either trained with him or her or who knows someone who did. Most young academic aspirants never realize that, in surgery, the reputation you make for yourself at the intern and resident level follows you throughout your professional life. In fact, there is no place to hide your stinky feet in the upper echelons of American academic medicine. Finally, candidates for a headship of any stripe are likely to get more from the institution trying to recruit them if they first make the school commit to wanting them.

As indicated previously, Dean Howard sent me my official letter of a job offer. I believe this letter was sent in part to create the impression that he actually had some relevance in the affairs of the medical school's department of surgery. During the recruiting process, I negotiated space and money in large measure with Najarian, not the dean. As a result, the department of surgery and other clinical departments eventually came through with the requisite space and seed money; as a consequence, I was headed to Minnesota.

My main recruitment requests focused on lab space and seed money to equip a cell biology laboratory. One of my main research interests was working on cell lines derived from human and not mice cancers. I thought the practice would take care of itself, since I was confident I could attract patients. I should have, in retrospect, paid more attention to the clinical facilities, but I assumed them to be more adequate than they turned out to be.

Thus, when I arrived that first day, I knew little of what I should have learned about the division and the urology clinical service before taking the job. I certainly did not know that fixing urology in Minnesota would make the labors of Hercules seem like pickup sticks or jacks.

OTHER AREA PROGRAMS

Before I officially accepted the position in Minnesota, there was one other important prerequisite needing attention. On my recruiting visits, I learned that there were four—that is right, four—urology training programs in the Twin Cities: Hennepin County Hospital (three residents), the VA hospital (seven to eight residents), St. Paul Ramsey Hospital (three to four residents), and the University of Minnesota (four residents). I saw this as an intolerable situation, especially considering the fact that all of these programs were turning out, at least by my standards, poorly trained urologists. None of the programs offered any significant academic activity, including the university program.

As a prerequisite, then, the university administration was told they would have to combine the Minneapolis VA Hospital and university urology residencies before I would agree to come as chair. I wanted someone else to set this up other than me because I knew it would be controversial. The candidate maintains some leverage prior to accepting a position, but once you agree to accept an offer, that leverage rapidly diminishes. Honeymoons don't last as long for chairmen as they do for a US president.

I had broached the subject of combining programs to the staff and residents at the VA during my second recruiting visit, but they adamantly opposed the move. They wanted to remain separate but unequal was my view, and I could not have tolerated that. I dropped the idea at the time, but adopted an end-run technique, using the school as a bodyguard of subterfuge. A Catholic prelate told me once, "It is sometimes necessary to be a bit devious to do God's work."

I did not care about competition from the Hennepin and Ramsey programs because I thought they would eventually collapse on their own. However, the Minneapolis VA had tremendous resources, especially in the research area, and a wealth of clinical material. The VA Hospital was a mini-NIH, with tremendous potential for academic development. Over time, I used the headship of the VA service and labs we developed there with the support of the VA as an academic incubator for several academic surgeons who eventually became professors of urology and department heads. As it turns out, academic urologic surgery and our department owed the VA system a great deal for the resources it provided for our entire department and the residents by the time my chairmanship ended.

When the university finally agreed to have the VA and university programs merged, I was Minnesota-bound. Because the university had met all my requests, backing away from the offered appointment would not have been an honorable way to conduct business.

NEED FOR TRAINING WHEELS AND RULES WOULD HAVE BEEN HELPFUL

It is a crime that no one makes training wheels for department chairmen. Unlike some academicians, I never held a junior position under a wise, senior department chairman who could teach me "the ropes." I could have especially used training in the art of finessing difficult people and situations—like my dealings with Creevy. For me, from the beginning, I had nothing but on-the-job training, which had both its upside and downside for all concerned. Therefore you could say I was a virgin chairman.

No one from either the medical school or central university administration bothered to conduct a new chairman's orientation session for me. I had been told that all physicians practiced under a set of rules called "Regents' Rules of Practice." The University Board of Regents set those rules for determining our compensation from private practice. Strangely, however, although I was told about such rules, I never saw a copy of them during my first several months on the job. The private-practice monitor (an attorney the physicians had hired) with whom we met regularly to review and report our salaries (we gave him copies of our federal and state tax returns) could never tell me precisely what the Regent's Rules said or how much we were allowed to earn. The monitor reviewed our tax returns and reported to the dean that we were all in compliance, whatever that meant. I should have been smart enough to drop the subject, but I had a sense all was not right with that system and that it left all of us vulnerable. Was I ever right!

Sometime later I decided the time had come for me to review the Regent's Rules. I went to Dick Varco's office and asked to see them. No one else, including the monitor to whom we reported, had a copy. After some effort while fumbling around in a couple of filing cabinets, he produced an undated and unsigned copy; I still wonder how many of the university physicians had ever read them.

It turned out that we had to guess the best way to set our salaries. It seemed strange to me at that time that no one from central administration or the medical school administration seemed to have much interest in what we were doing about salaries. It was very much a live-and-let-live environment.

I, however, could not be satisfied with guessing, and did a national survey of salaries in similar departments across the country. Then I set the salaries in urology so they would be competitive with like institutions nationwide. To ensure I received good data, I only spoke with people with whom I had trained and knew well. In summary, salary-setting was a very slipshod arrangement, and somewhat of a metaphor for how the university did many things in those days in the medical school.

CHAPTER 4

MINNESOTA, THE STATE, IN 1969

There is more to taking a job in a new part of the country than just coming to work one day. In many instances it requires acclimation to a new way of life, one that is sometimes quite different. And though one might think it is trivial in terms of what I faced at the university, knowing the local culture and traditions is a key element of building a successful program that must exist within that culture. Hence, I share here some of my initial observations of my adopted state, Minnesota, land of ten thousand lakes, five thousand fish, and a billion mosquitoes the size of waste disposal trucks. In fact, I learned quickly that if you kill one of those mosquitoes, about a hundred come to the funeral.

House hunting in Minnesota began soon after my appointment was confirmed in writing. Minnesotans decorated their homes quite differently from many of those in the east. There were plenty of oak gun cabinets with a surfeit of guns and ammunition in almost every home, and there was a lack of quality artwork (as an Easterner saw it). Minnesotans seemed to prefer the wildlife scenes of the Les Kouba genre. But there are just so many ways you can depict mallards landing in a marsh or deer walking across a snowy field.

Also, several Minnesota houses still had elaborate bomb shelters left over from the 1950s. One in particular had multiple steel doors interrupting the passageway to the shelter. The doors had eye-high small openings with little doors that slid back. If you stood behind one of the big doors, you could peer back down the hall from which you had come. As it turned out, the realtor told me, with cool detachment, that those little openings were gunports that allowed you to shoot your neighbors if they tried to force their way into your shelter in times of an emergency. I would offer that was not exactly "Minnesota nice."

Shortly after arriving in Minnesota without the family, I was unloading the dishes in the kitchen of our new home in Edina, trying to ready the place for my wife and children. The little countertop TV, which was turned away from me, blared as I worked. I paid little attention to it, being otherwise occupied and very tired. Then I heard the reporter mention something about a possible Russian plan to nuke China over a border dispute. The mention of a potential nuclear attack aroused my interest. I thought, *Did I just hear what I think I did?* Incredible, so I wanted to hear the details. Yet in short order, the story moved on to the vote on sewer bonds in Coon Rapids. I rushed to the TV, but by then, the reporter had moved to yet another local story, something about a fire department trying to get a cat down off a roof or some such.

I called a friend in Washington, DC, and learned that the local stations were broadcasting an hour-long special during which some of the highest officials of the US government were bloviating on air about the aforementioned dangerous developments between China and Russia. By then, the Minnesota news had moved on to sports; welcome to the land of Midwest isolationism. It has been argued that the reason Ron Paul is so popular is because 40 percent of Americans want as little as possible to do with the rest of the world.

In Minnesota in 1969, you could not get same-day home delivery of the *Wall Street Journal*, the *New York Times,* or the *Washington Post*.

We discovered quickly that Minnesota restaurants had similar menus. I wondered if someone maintained a central kitchen, with conveyer belts going out to the outlying restaurant kitchens. How else, I questioned, could all these restaurants serve these identical meals? With a little effort, you could order dinner out with your eyes closed. Nonetheless, Minnesota restaurants served some of the best beef in the world.

I found one exception in restaurants: *Charlie's Café Exceptionale* in Minneapolis. Charlie's was one of the most elegant eateries of all time. Besides the great meals I ate there, I became close to many of Charlie's longtime employees, some of whom also became my patients. One day, however, those employees came to work only to find the place locked and their job gone, without explanation. The lot had been sold to the Lutheran Brotherhood Insurance Company. I felt bad at their loss, but worse at mine, as it forced me back into the city's bland cafés. Today there are a number of quality dining spots in the Twin Cities, as the city has grown and become more cosmopolitan.

Minneapolis's tallest building in 1969 was the thirty-two-story Foshay Tower, the first "skyscraper" in the Midwest. The state eventually sent Wilbur Foshay, for whom the building was named, to prison after the 1929 stock market crash. The government convicted him of running a Ponzi scheme, somewhat like Bernie Madoff perpetrated. Eventually, President Truman gave Foshay a full pardon. Legend has it that Foshay committed suicide by jumping from the upper floors of his tower, but his death was nothing so dramatic: he died unceremoniously in a nursing home in Minneapolis.

As we hunted for the perfect house, we saw very few two-story homes. Most of the houses were one-story ranch-style homes, and many had wet basements. We pined for the beautiful colonial-style houses common to the East Coast. Not so soon after we moved to

Minnesota, that situation began to change, as new two-story eastern-style houses were built all around us.

The best news, however, is that most of the people outside of the university whom we met initially, although somewhat reserved, were kind and eventually welcoming, and some became lifelong friends. "Somewhat reserved" may be an understatement of that Scandinavian personality trait. One wag said that a Minnesotan of Norwegian heritage was so passionately in love with his wife that he almost told her so. These people were, for the most part, all "old Minnesota": hardworking, decent, materialistic, and honest.

At the university I met an eclectic blend of dynamic, brilliant, and driven men and women. Many of them accomplished great things. Some of their names appear throughout this book, and they deserve the greatest of respect

One thing that was particularly attractive about Minnesota was if you were reasonably well connected, the Twin Cities were small enough that you were able to meet many or most of the famous Minnesotans. (Incidentally, the Twin Cities refers to Minneapolis and St. Paul, two cities proud of their independence, but happy to be recognized as linked together.)

To be sure, I do not want to leave the reader with the wrong impression. Our family grew to love our adopted state and its people, and most especially, the great accomplishments achieved due to an outstanding group of associates at the University Medical School.

CHAPTER 5

MINNESOTA'S POLITICAL CLIMATE: 1969 TO PRESENT—CHALLENGES TO FREEDOM

In 1969, the Minnesota medical milieu differed greatly from that of Boston or most other Eastern medical centers, and the difference had to do in part with Minnesota's cultural DNA. Back then, Minnesota's private practitioners placed less value on excellence and supporting the regional university medical centers than did their Eastern US counterparts.

Every locale has a somewhat unique herd or pack mentality. In Minnesota, it dictated that it was better to stay within certain boundaries and not act like you wanted to change the world. A former president of the University of Minnesota actually said, "Nothing plays as well in Minnesota as mediocrity. Minnesotans just love mediocrity as long as it is done well." But that cynical statement was made just after he was fired for making outlandish expenditures on remodeling the home of the university's president. When those costs were made public, the legislature went postal and the president was fired.

Despite the strong gravitational pull of the alleged mediocrity, many Minnesotans rose to a high level of creativity and excellence, especially within the medical school and parts of the university.

Physicians and medical academicians across the world respected Owen Wangensteen and the cardiac surgeons, and later, John Najarian and his merry band of transplant surgeons. Some of the other university graduate schools—the Institute of Technology, the Law School, and the Business School (now the Carlson School)—also enjoyed stellar reputations.

Minnesota society has what is to me a troubling strain of "prairie populism" (socialism) underpinning its private and public institutions. It is certainly more left than right politically. This populism promotes the attitude (policies) that the state and federal government's roles are to take from what successful people have produced and give it to others who have "less"; this they do in the name of "fairness." In many ways, Minnesota is trying to prove itself to be the experimental laboratory for egalitarianism or secular progressivism in the United States.

The Minnesota populist mind-set occasionally gives rise to what I see as electoral disasters, like the first act of a new Minnesota Senator when he refused to shake Vice President Bush's hand. Prairie populism also served to some extent to energize the Najarian affair, when vicious allegations by his detractors drove him from his chairmanship. More of that disgraceful episode appears later in this book.

In summary, Minnesota is truly a complex society that can elect conservatives like Governor Tim Pawlenty and Congresswoman Michelle Bachmann, and then also send Al Franken, a hard-core liberal, to the United States Senate.

The aforementioned egalitarian mind-set was and still is very prominent in, but not restricted to, the Iron Range in Northeast Minnesota. It is also dominant in the urban areas, which include the university and a number of other educational institutions and their left-leaning faculties and their liberal students. I mention this because this populist or socialist political bent drove the multiple attempts we encountered to bring down the private practice system at the medical school. The idea that academic physicians could earn professional-level salaries offended some Minnesotans' idea of what it means to sacrifice for the greater good. This "idea," however, made it possible for the university to attract some of the best and brightest, and retain them on the medical faculty just as those who set up the practice plan had postulated.

Needless to say, the populist culture and politics in Minnesota meant great adjustments for lifelong easterners and conservatives like our family. Of course, that Minnesota culture—for lack of a better descriptive term—obviously was not always necessarily helpful for someone trying to do what our entire faculty attempted to do. As it turns out, neither was it conducive to supporting a prosperous and successful academic university medical center in the long run.

Conservatism is driven by fact and logic, while liberalism is driven by emotion and empathy and good intentions. Results do not matter to liberals as long as the motivations are well intentioned. Former Congressman Jack Kemp defined compassion as "helping the unfortunate to gain independence from the government." The true conservative also believes that our country should have exactly as much compassion as we can afford; otherwise you end up, heaven forbid, trillions of dollars in debt. These same liberal elitists—or the ruling class, at least for now—are fiscal profligates, so is it any wonder then that so many states, especially the larger ones on the coasts (with surprise, surprise, the highest taxes and the strongest government unions), are now bankrupt? At the time this book is being written, California is $111 billion in debt—that is, *B* as in billion. Even Wisconsin, our neighboring state, is $3.4 billion dollars in debt, making it the second-highest state indebtedness *per capita* in the country. Wisconsin has a rich heritage of socialism, thanks to

Norman Thomas et al. States all across the nation have overspent and now face wrenching budget and tax decisions. The recent election of a Republican governor in Wisconsin and the battles he won against public sector unions may restore sanity, at least in Wisconsin.

In short, the new intellectual class has worked for decades to change the cultural DNA of America from center-right orientation to "statism" or "progressivism." Their ideal would be to have America resemble more the social democracies of Europe, even if it leads to a total implosion of American society and its capitalistic, free enterprise financial underpinnings.

Therefore, right now, the only thing holding our beloved country together, in my opinion, is "flyover country" and much of the south. Eric Hoffer, the longshoreman turned philosopher, said, "It is outrageous that the ideas of many intellectuals can be so outlandishly asinine without damaging their reputations." Nowhere is that statement truer than in today's public policy arena.

The statists love to play ideological camouflage in that they try to conceal their true nature by calling themselves "progressives," rather than socialists and statists or even liberals, which are appellations that more accurately describe them; of course, some of them are so far left they most resemble communists. When I think of the dreaded C-word, it is not cancer I have in mind.

Some have dubbed these battles for the soul of America our national "culture wars." The outcomes of these battles will determine how medicine is practiced and how patients are cared for because, in the last analysis, these arguments concern the allocation of diminishing resources.

God help us if all or the majority of America's heartland areas ever turn politically liberal, as are the east and west coasts. Even

Minnesota, a left-leaning state, occasionally elects a conservative senator like Rod Grams or governor like Tim Pawlenty. And it even, on occasion, elects a senator who is masquerading as a Republican, like Dave Durenberger, or it elects a governor masquerading as a Republican, like Arne Carlson. But if Minnesota transitions to a permanently liberal state by electing purebred liberals and Easterners begin to view Minnesotans as "sophisticated," Minnesotans will be poorer due to exorbitant taxes and profligate spending (and the state eventually will be in bankruptcy's neighborhood and less free).

Minnesota recently elected Mark Dayton, a liberal Democrat, as its governor. During his 2010 election campaign, it seemed as if Dayton, a candidate with a significant amount of personal problems, made the gravamen of his campaign "tax the rich more." As Minnesotans are wont to do, while sending Dayton to the governor's office, they elected a conservative Republican legislature. Furthermore, so far, Dayton has done a reasonable job as governor. The ultimate outcome regarding state indebtedness remains to be seen, but even under the Pawlenty leadership, a conservative chief executive who tried to hold down spending, Minnesota faced a projected significant budget shortfall in the coming years (a $6 billion projected deficit for the next biennium, but that depends of course on the economy and rate of government spending).

The actual record on state government spending in Minnesota is as follows: for every biennial budget since 1970, state spending has averaged a 21 percent increase every two years at a time the state experienced low single-digit economic growth—talk about unsustainable. And by the way, Governor Pawlenty cut that rate of increase every two years to 2 percent during his governorships. And he did this without raising taxes. The governor's critics claim that he left a several-billion-dollar deficit in the coming years, but such a deficit would have occurred only if the Minnesota government returned to massive increases in spending.

Since 1978, Minnesota has experienced a split government, usually with a GOP governor and Democratic legislature, except for six of eight years during the Rudy Perpich administration (1982–1990), during which the Democrats dominated both branches of state government. If, however, Minnesota's "progressives" take over all branches of government anytime soon, Minnesotans eventually will be plunged into a gray, joyless, mindless collectivist (progressive) existence in any iteration, and the functioning of the state will end up having been crippled by its citizens being forced to pay for the *compassion and coercive utopianism of the left.* As Winston Churchill said in 1945, "The inherent vice of capitalism is the unequal sharing of blessings. The inherent virtue of Socialism is the equal sharing of miseries."[24]

If Minnesota moves completely to the left in upcoming elections and if Minnesota fails to maintain some political balance, subsequent generations of "Gophers" will have a diminished experience with any of the following: happiness, freedom, and solvency. They may be in the cradle-to-grave progressive environment, but they may have trouble even getting to the cradle what with all the abortion mills busily taking the lives of the unborn.

The choice is up to Minnesotans, and I wish them divine speed because many of them, for lack of a better description, are still truly "salt of the earth." The human body, being what it is, I am realistic enough to know I will not be here to see what happens, but I know that what happens will have a profound effect on medicine and the great medical centers of the state.

The outcome of the battle for the mind and soul of America, even though it appears to be a separate battle from health care, is in fact one and the same. How that fight resolves itself will eventually

---

[24] www.nationalchurchillmuseum.org/socialism-quotes.html. Retrieved on June 5, 2014

determine how medicine is practiced, and thus, in large part, the quality of life for physicians and their patients. For a preview of the results of the direction of today's health-care reform effort, we need only to look north to Canada and across the pond to the United Kingdom and most of Europe, precisely the direction that progressive America's elitists are determined to take our country.

CHAPTER 6

THE UNIVERSITY AUGEAN STABLES

Modern university athletic departments beg for, and usually win, first-rate training facilities and arenas. Coaches know that to attract the nation's best athletes requires first-rate facilities. Apparently this idea skipped past the medical school, at least in 1969. The urology facilities in which I had to work made my challenge far greater than I expected when I signed on to the job. Building a world-class medical department included fighting for more space, equipment, and modernization, a task sometimes more difficult than performing intricate surgery.

It took but a few days to realize that the urology academic facilities and outpatient clinic were unbelievably cramped and decrepit. As one consequence, we had no space to add faculty, which would have to wait until the medical school built a new hospital years later.

Once we had the new hospital, we could transfer patients to it from the old Station 57. But a new hospital remained several years in the future in 1969. The main urology station, Station 57, was right around the corner from the cystoscopy suite, the urology academic offices, and the outpatient clinic on the fifth floor of the Mayo Building. Eventually we were able to expand the department's office space into what had been the old Station 57 patient-care area, once all the beds were moved to the new hospital.

The urology division's quarters were so outlandishly bad at the beginning of my tenure that one new outpatient of mine, a former missionary in Africa, looked around and opined, "I saw better medical facilities in Sierra Leone."

Each exam room had a radiological table. This doubled as an exam table during outpatient visits. I winced each time I saw patients get on and off those tables, worried they would bang their heads on the overhead radiographic machine, which they often did, or that in the dismount they would fall.

One time a patient sat waiting in an exam room and heard a loud noise. He looked down only to see a large drill bit had come up through the floor, fortunately between his feet rather than through one of them. Cement dust lay all over his pants and his shoes. He let me know he was not only terrified, but very unhappy.

The sorry condition of the university hospitals in those days presented another problem. The downtown hospitals, against whom we had to compete for patients, were modern, up-to-date, clean, and welcoming. In contrast, the university inpatient facilities had become very much "out at the elbow," and some of the rooms were shabby and depressing beyond belief. For example, patients had no reliable television reception in their hospital rooms. We found ourselves having to wrap tinfoil around the rabbit-ear antennas, and show the patients or their families how to keep manipulating the antenna to watch the limited number of stations available to them.

It bothered me greatly that the university hospitals were also unkempt much of the time. Walking down the hall one day, I saw a small mound of dirt stretching the width of the hall. There was a mop leaning against the wall just beyond the pile of dirt that was abandoned by the janitor, who was nowhere to be found. He apparently just stopped right where he was at the very minute his "break" time came or his shift ended, never even bothering to push the dirt to one side. (Imagine if surgeons took a "patient be damned" break every two hours, just because their contract said they could.)

During the early years, several out-of-state patients checked in, looked around, and left without a word. Once they saw the facilities on the urologic surgery patient station in the Mayo Building, they were unwilling to risk their health care to us.

The first day I went to the hospital to begin work, I tried to enter through the Mayo Building's front door. Mayo housed the hospital, as well as many of the clinician offices and some of the basic science departments. As I walked to the door, I looked up and saw the name Mayo Building. I thought, *Those Mayo brothers were certainly shrewd, so it is no wonder they did what they did.*

Imagine a patient having the same experience I did. I encountered a heavy revolving door that, even for me, was hard to push around. Someone on crutches or in a wheelchair had to struggle to enter the hospital through that revolving door. I have often wondered if possibly the Mayo Brothers also designed and donated that door. If they did, the only thing they overlooked was to print directions to the Mayo Clinic on it, because many people who tried to enter would probably have preferred going somewhere else. Once I transited the door, I charged into the hospital director's office, not far from the front entrance on the first floor, and demanded this problem be fixed. This is when I learned that "demanding" did not fly in Minnesota. Those doors remained the same for years. A recent visit by me confirmed that area of Mayo has been remodeled and that old door is gone.

As our practice grew, we looked around to find more space. I found a large bathroom next to urology, and from it I meant to enlarge the patient waiting room. The bathroom sat just down the hall from Dr. French's office. After the remodeling began, Lyle French stormed into my office, protesting that "his bathroom" had been compromised. I suggested we should put in pay toilets and have our departments split the revenues. French failed to appreciate my humor and stomped out. Lyle had a lot of great qualities, but a sense of humor was not one of them.

I regret never taking photographs of the "sty" in which we worked and practiced all those years.

Those conditions were decrepit beyond most people's imagination. During my tenure, those facilities never did improve significantly, and the final disappointment came when administrators cut out the new urology department we were promised in the new hospital for the second time because of alleged financial constraints.

During the early 1970s, when I was still new to the job, we had our first chance for new facilities. The university was finishing buildings B and C (the Phillips-Wangensteen Buildings). That building program represented a major expansion for the health sciences in general, but especially for the medical and dental schools and their clinical departments, most of which were housed in the old Mayo Building before the expansion. Planning for buildings B, C, and D had gone on several years before construction began and before I came to Minnesota. When I found out there was no new space for urology, I complained vociferously, but to no avail. Someone, possibly Lyle French, showed me a letter that Creevy had received in the planning phase. Creevy was asked to participate in planning new space for urology in the proposed new B and C buildings. He scrawled, "No interest, Creevy," across the bottom of that letter and sent it back. I tell this story to set the context in which I worked to build a world-class department. In his defense, Don Creevy probably had no incentive to get involved in the planning of facilities he knew he would never use. Possibly I would have done the same thing under similar circumstances. I learned early the lesson that if urologic surgery did not look out for itself at Minnesota, no one else would do it for us.

Chapter 7

ARRIVAL IN MINNESOTA JULY 4, 1969

"All accomplishment in this world is
relative to where you start."
—Grandpa Harry Fraley

At the risk of repetition, I came to Minnesota almost entirely unprepared for what I found, both with respect to patient and divisional resources, as well as the atmospherics related to the private practitioners. I did not expect the intense town-gown hostility that existed between the private practitioners and university physicians because I had never heard of such a thing. I learned a critical lesson the hard way: before I accepted the job, I should have done more upfront due diligence—my bad.

I arrived in Minnesota to take up my position on July 4, 1969. Since all my worldly goods followed behind me in a moving van, I went straight to the hospital. There I discovered no urology resident was to be found. Furthermore, the staff man covering the clinical service could only be reached by one-way radiophone to his boat on the St. Croix River, more than fifty miles away.

Within the next few days, I met the four university residents, one of whom was a morbidly obese Pickwickian who never bathed, in the best European tradition, and as a result, quite plainly stank.[25] After a short discourse with the others, I quickly determined they were not residents of the intellectual quality one would expect to find in a major university training program. For example, one barely spoke English, which was very unusual for American surgery residents forty-five years ago.

I was younger than three of the four residents—in some cases by several years. One day they had the temerity to ask me what they should call me. I replied without hesitation and with a straight face, "Your liege would be fine."

There were two staff men whom my recruiters apparently had kept out of sight during my recruitment. The first was Dan Merrill, a highly intelligent young man who was fiercely competitive and driven in a way I had seldom encountered in the profession. For example, Dan decided to become an accomplished classical pianist late in life, and he did. He sat for hours at the piano, pounding away at some very difficult scores with a metronome ticking to the beat, until he became quite accomplished. This was absolutely amazing given his age and the demands of his profession. However, if political correctness, like matter, had an antipolitical-correctness counterpart, Dan Merrill was it.

Dan had many admirable qualities, not the least of which was an uncompromising honesty. We both eventually concluded that Dan

---

[25] Obesity hypoventilation syndrome is also known as Pickwickian syndrome. The syndrome is named after a character in a Charles Dickens novel, *The Pickwick Papers*, who seemed to show some of the traits of this disease, a condition in which severely overweight people fail to breathe rapidly enough or deeply enough, resulting in low blood oxygen levels and high blood carbon dioxide (CO_2) levels. Many people with this condition also frequently stop breathing altogether for short periods of time during sleep (obstructive sleep apnea), resulting in many partial awakenings during the night, which leads to continual sleepiness during the day.

had no place in the type of academic department I wanted to build. It is not unusual, of course, for an incoming chairman to want to bring in his own people with him. For example, a new departmental chairman at Harvard Medical School forced my sponsor in the laboratory to leave, and it disrupted my lab time during my senior year. I had to follow my sponsor to Hopkins, where I spent a month or so finishing my laboratory project on transport mechanisms in the walls of lymphatic vessels. Dan came to understand that he needed to move on, and eventually went to California, where he had a very successful career. I was delighted because I liked Dan a lot.

The other staff man was Colin Markland, a tenured associate professor who had been passed over for the chairmanship. As time went on, Colin decided to be helpful rather than an adversary, as too often happens in these situations.

Ironically, Colin had been my chief resident (boss) in urology at the MGH when I was an intern in 1961. My main recollections of him from that time in Boston were that he let me do a lot of cases, which is all a surgical intern cares about, and that he had an unusual but engaging personality. I also recalled that Wyland Leadbetter, his chief and later mine, closed the urology ward service down for a time after I left urology as an intern because Colin began having too many surgical complications—at least that was what I was told. That Leadbetter had closed a ward service is quite significant and unprecedented at the MGH, where resident autonomy is sacred.

With that background in my mind, just before my first recruiting visit but after I had been invited to do so, Colin invited me to breakfast at the annual Spring American Urological Association meeting in Miami. We had breakfast in the coffee shop of the original Fontainebleau Hotel, which was decorated in blue of all shades—and I dislike the color blue intensely. Colin told me the university planned to name him as the next chairman of urology. Given this understanding,

Colin said he wanted me to come and join his department after his appointment was official. Specifically, he wanted me to head up the urology service at the university-affiliated St. Paul Ramsey Hospital, a clinical service over which he would never have had control as chairman at the university. To this day, I do not know what could possibly have been going through his mind in that regard. Although I was reluctant to tell him at first, I reasoned he would find out soon in any event, so I advised him that I had already been asked to come to Minnesota to be interviewed, not for St. Paul Ramsey Hospital headship in urology, a very minor position, but for the chairmanship at the university. My news stunned him: he apparently did not even know a search committee in urology had been appointed. The expressions of surprise and dismay on his face were unforgettable.

I felt sorry and somewhat embarrassed for Colin in his disappointment of the moment, so I reassured him that the visit would probably come to nothing. After our breakfast, Colin wandered off in a daze, having learned what was afoot. I paid for the breakfast to which he had invited me. Probably soon after breakfast Colin burned up the phone lines back to Minnesota. Of course, as it turned out, he had reason for concern.

Part of the booting up of a department requires the leader to assess all of the personnel to determine whether they can be useful and productive department members going forward. With respect to Colin, it took some time, but I came to value him, especially for his diagnostic acumen. In addition, I often enjoyed his company because he was a delightful person socially during the first few years we worked together, and he was a more-than-capable surgeon. Colin had some serious personal problems later on that caused him to leave Minnesota for another institution. Unfortunately he often followed a young Barry Goldwater's axiom: "Shoot, ready, aim!" Thus I learned, as time went by, it was not out of character for Colin to be claiming unrealistically that he would be the next chairman before he had the job nailed down. Also, some of the town-gown problems I inherited had their origin in conflicts between Colin and some of the private practitioners. On this score I cannot judge Colin too harshly because it was impossible for me to avoid the same type of problems as the department grew. I still remember Colin with great fondness for the early years.

DOWNTOWNERS

By 1969 the University of Minnesota Medical School (and other academic centers around the country) had trained so many residents that a large number who chose to stay in the Twin Cities went into practice "downtown." These were physicians who were trained in all the modern advances, and they competed for patients with the mother ship at the university. These practitioners were almost entirely patient care- and income-driven, and they insisted that the downtown hospitals really cater to patients to assist the growth of their practices. The university was above—in fact, way above— catering to patients in those days, mainly because for years they had not needed to do so.

The downtowners were very shrewd and constantly cultivated the idea, especially among the well-to-do, that they gave the best care. They actively fostered the idea that a patient should avoid the university, telling patients that at the "U" they would be nothing but "guinea pigs." Or at least that is what many patients said they had been told by a practicing downtown urologist when the patient requested a second opinion at the university. All this back and forth was fostered by the competitive environment in an area where a university no longer dominated medical practice. If there were such a thing as "frequent bandwagon rider miles," I had the impression there would never be many such miles awarded to these people for riding my bandwagon.

By 1969 the private practitioners in urology, almost all of whom were the products of the aforementioned Minnesota culture, were growing in strength to the point that they controlled an increasing number of patients. Many of them saw the university as a threat because it sat in their backyard. They thought that if they referred a patient to the U, it admitted to a sign of weakness and a threat to their livelihood; in a sense this was understandable. I recognized quite frankly that if I had been in their shoes, I might have had the same attitude. These men had a lot invested in their education, and many of them had families to provide for.

In essence, these U of M graduates and their colleagues turned their relationship with their own university into a Hatfields-versus-the-McCoys-like situation. Yet by some twisted logic, the downtowners saw no problem sending patients to the Mayo Clinic, a place that was indeed exalted and remote, with plenty of mystique. I came to see that at least some of these practitioners did not care a whit about tradition or the Creevy legacy, the viability of their profession over the long term, or having people properly trained at their own university. They may have been in the minority, but there were enough of them to impede the growth of our department. In addition, they felt that any resident who had at least learned the basics could become fully trained by them as an apprentice after residency, so the quality of their training really did not matter. Their attitude adversely affected what I was attempting to do at the U, as the practitioners wanted to show the trainees how things should be done once they arrived downtown. As a result, poorly trained residents would have been at the practitioners' mercy. Sadly, private practitioners across the country hired many of these unsuspecting individuals with the idea of using them as cheap labor for five years, after which they denied them partnership status. The practitioners saw them as replaceable, and the cycle could be restarted after they left. I observed, however, that this nefarious practice certainly was less common in the Twin Cities than it was elsewhere in the country. I also learned that the practice of exploiting graduates of professional schools with the disingenuous carrot of partnership was not unique to the profession of medicine.

By the early 1970s, the private urologists had reached such an exalted state of hubris they thought they were capable of "training" residents from the start, though none of them had any academic or teaching credentials—but neither did I when I started in Minnesota. If the practitioners had had their way, their choice for chairman in urology at the university would have been a timid Caspar Milquetoast, someone happy to divide his time between the mouse lab and pushing papers around while administering his nonprogram. Better yet, the practitioners would have asked the Milquetoast to be a professor in name only, thus being self-delusional enough to convince themselves that they were doing something important. It is a good thing no one asked that of me, for such a situation truly would have been death by a thousand cuts and therefore intolerable. I did not become educated and trained to the extent I was to be a figurehead or a so-called placeholder. Rather, I intended to drive my department to a national standard of excellence if I could. If it did not work out, there was the escape valve of private practice back east.

In the first few months on the job, I learned, to my great disappointment, that most of the private practitioner urologists were unwilling to do even the simplest things to help their own university training program. In fact, they liked to have "clinical" appointments on the faculty only because that gave them priority for football tickets, not because they were helping the department. For example, they even refused to bring cases to our weekly grand rounds, something that would have been extraordinarily beneficial to the residents, fellows, and students. As a consequence, I decided reluctantly that courting the downtowners was a waste of time. I concluded that my energies could be spent more productively building a department in spite of them. My feeling was that if I were too solicitous of them, it would only have been interpreted as weakness.

As our program eventually began to achieve national standing, some of the practitioners wanted back in, but like Evita, I kept my distance. Accordingly, I never opened my kimono to them. My experience with the downtowners reminded me of the attitude of Ted Williams, who decided he would never tip his hat to the Boston fans because they booed him repeatedly during his early years—and he almost never did except on his last day. These early experiences forced me to realize that if I were going to be successful, I had to not care what my critics were saying about me. Once I came to that point, it gave me tremendous freedom to act according to my own dictates. In retrospect, I wish the atmospherics relative to the private sector had been different, but they weren't. I had to work in the environment I had inherited, and find solutions to all or at least most of the problems. I have never agonized over the situation long-term, and I have zero regrets today over the way my time as chairman played out.

I knew I was no Will Rogers, but also knew I could train academic and practicing urological surgeons to the highest level with or without the downtowners, and that was what I really cared about and what our department did over the subsequent years. As I told my academic trainees when they were going off to be a chairman or a section head somewhere, to paraphrase President Truman, "If you have the need to be loved, get a dog." The Fraley corollary to that admonition is, "Be sure it's a small dog because it may turn on you."

There were a few practitioners well outside of the Twin Cities who were very good to us and sent some interesting and challenging patients. They surely helped the department become what it did; we were all grateful to them for that contribution. Despite the attitude and practice of some of the downtowners, we did find a few supporters in the Twin Cities' practicing community: Bob Geist, George Garske, and Gordie Strom, among some others. We are also thankful for that support.

Relative to the town-gown situation, the following encounter says it all. I arrived in Minnesota in July 1969 and learned that the North Central Urological Association was meeting in Detroit in the fall. I decided to attend because it was a gathering of many practitioners in my geographic area. As I wandered around in the exhibit hall shortly after arriving, I saw an obviously hostile fellow, arms flexed and pumping like a power walker as he swiftly approached. "So, you are Fraley," he snarled through gritted teeth. (Later I learned he was a Twin Cities' practitioner.)

"That's what the name tag says," I replied, looking down at my chest. "Why do you ask?"

He promptly declared without any verbal foreplay and with an air of certainty, "We want you to know *we* are going to run you out of town." And then he hustled away abruptly, without as much as a by-your-leave. I saw this as the first shot on Fort Sumter, and the real civil war (or uncivil war, as the case may be) was on.

After my confrontation with that physician, I thought, like Hercules, that I had just met the Nemean Lion, the Lernaean Hydra, and the Erymanthian Boar all rolled into one. He also bumped up against me while he hectored, reminding me of stories of victims of shark attacks. Apparently, according to experts, sharks often bump up against their victims several times before deciding whether or not they are going to eat them. "Bump, bump, bump," replayed through my thoughts for weeks after that encounter, but there was no doubt in my mind that particular shark was not ambiguous about his intentions of eating me. At the time, I thought the guy was a little unbalanced, but I learned over the next few months he was perfectly serious and sane, and he had plenty of coconspirators willing to go after the brash young interloper from the east. One thing that still leaves me puzzled, however, is how anyone knew I had arrived in Detroit, or that I was almost alone in that exhibit hall during the meeting.

I still wonder if that encounter had been possibly choreographed by someone within our department, someone who knew my plans and approximate whereabouts and whose interest would have been served by my leaving Minnesota. (Academic departmental politics is another minefield through which the chief must negotiate.)

From this experience I learned of another mistake I had made. Overconfidence prevented me from taking potential enemies seriously. Believe me, that is, or at least can be, a fatal mistake for anyone in a responsible position. But I am getting ahead of the story.

The contest with the downtowners was tough enough, but I learned of more bad news in that the attitude of many of the university clinical departments toward their patients was incompatible with how I had been trained and planned to practice medicine. Many of the university physicians had grown complacent and lazy, and clearly were living in the old days, when the university had little competition and when patients chose the institution simply because it was there. The clinical physicians failed to recognize the new era had arrived, in which they were in competition for patients by well-trained—thanks to them—private practice physicians. By contrast, the departments that did reasonably well financially looked after their referring physicians and promoted their services to them, especially to those with the most to gain by doing so: the surgeons and surgical specialties. Rich Lillehei, the brother of C. Walton Lillehei, was an energetic young general surgeon who taught me a lot about how to look after referring physicians. If Rich referred a patient to you, he wanted a copy of the letter you sent to the primary physician. Rich was, and I mean this in the best sense of the words, one of the original overweening mother hens to his patients and referring physicians; I really admired the man.

The lack of interest in patient care of many of the other university clinical services was atrocious. Many patients on some clinical services did not even know their physician's name. Some of the patients with whom I spoke as a consultant seemed only aware that a mostly anonymous group of physicians in white coats appeared in their room every day. The patients, even though they had no relationship with anyone except the residents and nurses, in most cases assumed they were getting adequate care because they were at the university. (Just try that approach in today's competitive market.) Nurses, not physicians, answered most of the patients' medical questions. The fact that patients on some services could not identify their treating physician by name caused me to launch a two-year-long battle to get the patients' physician's name(s) placed on their plastic identification wristband upon admission. Believe it or not, certain service chiefs—one of whom I saw as a consummate fraud as a physician—fought that effort to the very end. It appeared to me that the last thing some staff physicians wanted was a personal relationship with any of their patients.

Not all departments were the same in terms of the level of personal care they provided. B. J. Kennedy and the medical oncology staff looked after their patients with caring and compassion in every sense. That may have been because B. J. and his staff were financially independent from the internal medicine department, so he and his associates had an economic incentive to cultivate and maintain a large practice. In addition, B. J. trained at the MGH and knew how to care for patients; his motivation was not totally financial. Professor B. J. Kennedy was a very, very great man and a compassionate and skilled physician. Giants like B. J. come along maybe once in a generation under the best of circumstances. However, it is less likely that the world will see his likes again in the new era of medicine by the numbers; may he rest in peace. The sadness caused by his death lingered a long time in my emotions.

Cardiology is the other group in internal medicine that practiced in a manner similar to medical oncology. I believe this is related to their historical link back to the university's famed entrepreneurial cardiac surgery program. Internal medicine as a whole should have been a great source of referrals for us, but it was not, probably due to the leadership of the department.

DEALING WITH RESIDUE FROM THE PREVIOUS CHAIRMAN

Early on there was one surprise or new discouragement after another. I often felt so morose that just a month after arriving during that 1969 summer, I packed up my family and headed to a cabin on Minnesota's Crow Wing Lake, where we retreated for a week. I used the time to contemplate my future. All I could think of initially was that line from *The Wizard of Oz*: "Toto, we are now a long way from Kansas [substitute Pennsylvania, my home]."

At the cabin, my first thoughts centered on whether I could possibly build a ranking department and train at least a few academic urologists while supporting a family of seven dependents, given the condition of the division. However, as I thought more and more about the problems, I realized that I was not the first leader to face what might seem to be overwhelming difficulties, and many of those leaders prevailed over their situations. I called on my readings of history, specifically those about Lincoln, and realized my problems were so-called small potatoes by comparison. Remember, Lincoln faced a divisive war, the constant hatred of so many citizens both north and south who called him, among other things, "an ugly baboon," and the emotional turmoil caused by his wife and the death of his sons. I decided keeping my petty problems in perspective was important.

I knew not to expect help from Creevy from his own pronouncements, and furthermore, he had left by the time I arrived. Creevy went downtown into private practice with Baxter Smith, a prominent private urologist in Minneapolis. Creevy had also gathered up all of his teaching slides and donated them to the VA Hospital urology training program (before I came to Minnesota a separate training program), allegedly to gain a tax deduction, and he took most of his patient records to his downtown office. He sent letters to all the patients stating that he was entering downtown private practice. The letterhead from the Baxter Smith practice featured the Creevy name prominently at the top. In fact, Creevy's name stayed on that letterhead long after he died. Not only did Creevy take many of the department's patient records; he made sure to give all the former patients his new phone number. The only thing he left, and I mean the *only* thing, was the department's phone number, a number known to referring physicians throughout the region. Forgetting to transfer that phone number may well have been an oversight on Creevy's part based on his other actions. Or possibly he did it as a small goodwill gesture—I'll never know.

Creevy gave me little reason to think kindly of him. Other than the brief encounter at French's home, I never met him or spoke to him again. He came from a different cultural, urological, and surgical orientation, so we had little in common. I assume that his goal during his last years was to survive and to accumulate enough money to have a decent retirement, and as mentioned previously, he had been very sick. He clearly had no love for the university, and in fact, at one point in his tenure, he pulled out of the university and went downtown for a short time, but eventually came back to the university. Furthermore, after the first meeting and his subsequent actions in leaving, I lacked the wisdom to turn the other cheek so that I could court him and possibly bring him inside the tent where, using the LBJ metaphor, he would have been "pissing out of our tent instead of being outside pissing in." I had neither the time nor the savvy to at least attempt to make him a friend rather than an adversary, and that was my misjudgment. (A word to the wise among you: as a chief you should build alliances whenever possible, even with your detractors. Or as the Godfather said, "Keep your friends close and your enemies even closer." There were other things Creevy did later on that furthered the conclusion he was not a friend, and I should have been able to prevent that from happening.

In all fairness, Don Creevy gave long service to the university and he advanced urology in his time, so he deserved to be treated with more deference by everyone, including me. I must say, however, that I heard the university never treated him much better than I did, which was, or became, par for the course for the university's treatment of its medical faculty in general. I cracked at a clinical chiefs' meeting a few years later, "If we were on fire the administration would not even piss on us to put the fire out." For reasons that will be detailed later, I eventually even came to the conclusion that if a medical faculty member had discovered fire, the university administration would probably have used it to burn him or her at the stake.

Creevy was a tough "flinty" Minnesotan, but someone I sensed who had great integrity, and for reasons that are not entirely clear to this day, the locals revered him. During Creevy's chairmanship, America was a more civil and genteel place, so one did not attack or speak ill of their betters—usually. Creevy's career spanned the time before the competitive town-gown problem arose, so he did not threaten anyone. It helped him that he had trained many of the private practitioners who were active when I became chairman, so it was no wonder they all adored him. There must have been good reasons why those he trained held Professor Creevy in such high regard. For one thing, he may have been a bit of a martinet at times, but he was honest, took good care of patients, and was not pretentious according to those who knew him. I would handle Creevy much differently today, if for no other reason than he could have helped with at least some of the downtown urologists. "Too bad," as Shaw said, "youth is wasted on the young."

How I dealt with Don Creevy was only one of many mistakes I made during the next twenty-five years. Pencils may have erasers but life does not. I hope someday to be able to apologize to Don for being less than gracious and respectful if he would apologize for his egregious conduct relative to his former division; such a tradeoff would be fair.

I add one more bit of Creevy lore to this history. Despite his austere exterior, he had a great sense of humor. As departmental legend has it, every time Milton Reiser, his longtime associate in the division of urology, attempted to sit down with the boss and ask for a raise, Creevy would pause, and then reach into his desk drawer and pull out an ivory-handled six-shooter. He placed the revolver firmly on the top of his desk and then resumed the conversation thusly: "As you were saying …" Unfortunately, you would probably be jailed for a stunt like that today, even though the intent was to bring some levity into the conversation.

CHAPTER 8

DECIDING PRIORITIES

Shortly after arriving in Minnesota, I called a number of department chairmen around the country to listen to their reflections and thoughts about their jobs and to seek their advice for a neophyte. I did this because I had no experience in even being in an academic department or division of urology, let alone running one.

The MGH urology program focused strictly on the clinical, with no academic pretense. The MGH setting in the 1960s, therefore, most resembled a big hospital, with an emphasis on patient care—and little else. Today, that institution has taken on the character of more of an academic medical center, with more emphasis on basic medical research. I was therefore an academic neophyte and needed all the input I could gather to run an academic department.

As I conferred with other department heads, most of them seldom mentioned their residents or how they wanted to help some of them become tomorrow's leaders. I found this especially true of Wyland Leadbetter's former residents, some of whom, like me, were already chiefs. I found some of their attitudes especially odd given that one of Wyland's main contributions to medicine was the men he trained. As it turns out, the perspective I picked up during my conversations with them was accurate: none of them who went into academic urology ever trained, with one or two exceptions, a single substantive leader or department chairman. Sadly the Leadbetter legacy of producing leaders might have died if perpetuating that legacy had been up to most of them. Most of these individuals are or were outstanding physicians and surgeons, and their attitude toward giving back illustrated how differently people react to a given situation.

When I ended the process of talking to other department chairmen, thanks to their guidance and my intuition, I had identified more than twenty separate areas in which a medical school and its administration expected a surgical chairman to contribute. These included teaching residents, students, and fellow urologists, and participation in the administrative and governance functions of the medical school and the hospital. Chairmen also were expected to attend innumerable local and national meetings of vastly different stripes, some of which had little to do with either teaching or imparting scientific advances in the field. I asked myself if these meetings should be a priority—were they really so important? Did they serve my training program, or were they more about promoting my own image nationally? These were important questions, and to this day I don't know whether some of my decisions and chosen priorities were correct.

I concluded that no one, including myself, could contribute in all the aforementioned areas and still have any time for their family or themselves. Straightening out the urology division at the university was, by itself, very demanding and time-consuming. Thus, I set priorities, and those were in order: family, caring for patients, the care and feeding of the residents and students, establishing a basic research lab program, and mentoring the putative academicians, hoping that the department could develop at least one or two substantive leaders in the field. It seemed to me that anyone wishing to build any organization would be well advised to go through this same process of setting priorities and planning just how the program could be developed.

No one brought up the importance of keeping a diary. Memories and dates go into the glimmering of time, never to be recalled with precision. If one accepts my argument on the importance of history, it is important for leaders to keep a record of their lives. I failed to do that, much to my regret. I was encouraged in talking to the new urology chair at the university that he is keeping a diary.

Probably I should have done more on the national stage, but I calculated that if I had gone to all the national meetings that I was expected to attend, I would have been gone from Minnesota approaching 40 to 60 percent of the time. If I had committed to so much travel, I felt sure it would become a destructive habit. Frankly, the lack of adequate financial resources early on, combined with my less-than-enthusiastic like for such an "escapism" travel schedule, would have meant being away from my own family and the program far too often. Besides that, we were meticulous about publishing what we were doing, so we had extensive contact with the outside academic world through journals and the speaking engagements of our faculty.

All leaders must know their strengths and use them to guide their department and the people in it. For me, other than family time, I felt most comfortable at the bedside or in the operating room with the residents or trying to direct the laboratory. As a result, those areas are where I ended up spending most of my professional time and where I decided to plant my chairman's flag.

Most, or at least many, of Leadbetter's trainees, and especially the dozen or so chairmen he trained, always felt Leadbetter's influence on their decisions, especially relating to patient care, for the rest of their lives. The description of our training earlier in the book goes a long way to explaining why. Wyland's influence certainly had a lot to do with whatever success we had in Minnesota, and I am eternally grateful to him.

Thus, what I cared about most professionally was the residents and our patients. These priorities explain my approach to the department, which was uncomplicated and had well-defined goals. I set out to train future professors and competent practicing urologists who could function as urologists at whatever level they chose. History will judge any leader's decisions, but as President Reagan said, "History depends on who writes it."

No one can be everything to everyone, so I did not try. I more or less took a lesson from the Isaiah Berlin fable of *The Hedgehog and the Fox*. I assumed the role of the hedgehog, who knows one or two big things in depth, as opposed to the fox, who knows many little things superficially. In my opinion I was in good company in one sense, in that Reagan, who was clearly a hedgehog, summarized his complex, multifaceted strategy of how to deal with the Soviet Union with the formulation "We win—they lose." Such is the reasoning of a brilliant hedgehog.

I approach the end of my life well satisfied because I did my best and I did at least as well, mistakes and all, as most individuals would have done as a chairman in Minnesota at the time, considering where the division started in 1969. It is precisely that starting point that most people have forgotten or of which they have no knowledge. I have chronicled the record of accomplishments of what became of the department of urologic surgery at Minnesota toward the end of this history, and that record is a *res ipsa loquitur*. I hope history will render its judgment based on the facts.

CHAPTER 9

AMERICAN ACADEMIC MEDICINE: A SHORT BUT IMPORTANT HISTORY—THE FLEXNER REPORT

I interrupt this narrative to provide some additional background on America's medical academic teaching and research centers, since the story is set in one of these institutions.

Most Americans have little understanding of how these great research and teaching hospitals came to be during the last century, or little appreciation for the reasons they are so important, not only to this country but to the world.

My story occurred in one small corner of such an institution, but I believe it is worthwhile to share some historical context regarding America's academic medical research and training centers.

At the turn of the twentieth century, physicians received teaching and training in large measure from proprietary for-profit schools of medicine unaffiliated with any university. These schools—really trade schools—had no standards for admission and few standards by which to judge the quality of their curricula. As a result, many of these so-called medical schools were nothing more than "diploma mills" that, for a fee, were churning out poorly qualified graduates with "doctor of medicine and surgery" degrees. At that time, states licensed most of the medical school graduates as physicians and surgeons, even though the "doctors" had very meager knowledge of either general medicine or surgery.

The surgeons of this era were just a cut above the bloodletting "barber surgeons" of earlier times, who bled patients as their main form of treatment. After they graduated from "medical school," older physicians trained the young physicians clinically as apprentices. Early on, there were no formal training programs equivalent to the modern specialty residencies of today. Consequently, there was no nexus between our great universities and medical education. We learned at least one thing from the eighteenth century's medical experience: *making the same mistakes day after day is not good training, nor is that process conducive to a patient's longevity.*

During the late 1800s or early 1900s, the famous educator Alexander Flexner (under the sponsorship of the Carnegie Foundation) undertook a detailed study of American medicine. He intended to produce recommendations to improve the overall quality of medical schools, as well as the postgraduate education of physicians. Flexner's now-famous report called on American medical schools to enact higher standards for admission and graduation, and to adhere strictly to rigorous scientific standards in their teaching and research. Furthermore, he recommended all medical schools should be affiliated with a university.

Thus, the Flexner Report of 1910[26] is the predicate upon which our modern university-based academic medical enterprises were developed.

Flexner set the table for the subsequent development of America's many great medical training and research centers. Institutions such as Harvard, Johns Hopkins, and others, responding to the Flexner

---

[26] Carnegie Foundation, Book Four. www.carnegiefoundation.org/sites/default/files/elibrary/Carnegie_Flexner_Report.pdf.

Report, established the first of what later became a vast network of coast-to-coast university medical centers. Research and innovations in medicine have flourished at these institutions, which also became the hub of both medical student and postgraduate medical education. These centers eventually became the driving force that made American medicine the envy of the world.

Abraham Flexner was one of the most important and farsighted educators in history. Flexner also helped found the Institute for Advanced Study at Princeton. The Institute is a private, independent academic institution located in Princeton, New Jersey. It was founded in 1930 by philanthropists Louis Bamberger and his sister, Caroline Bamberger Fuld. Past faculty included Albert Einstein, who remained at the Institute until his death in 1955. In addition, there were distinguished scientists and scholars such as Kurt Gödel, J. Robert Oppenheimer, Erwin Panofsky, Homer A. Thompson, John von Neumann, George Kennan, Hermann Weyl, and Eugene Wigner.

Today, approximately 90 percent of all medical research and clinical advances in the world come from US academic medical centers and from America's great pharmaceutical companies. Sadly, these facts are apparently unknown to the irresponsible politicians who want to tear down our superb medical profession and all of its components in order to gain further control over our lives and to fulfill their own bureaucratic blood lust for power.

For many years, academic physicians such as Osler, Hallstead, and Welch at Hopkins, and others like the stars at Minnesota (Wangensteen, Lillehei, Varco, Good, et al) were considered to be among the *crème de la crème* of American medicine, and they were heroes for many of us. Little known, however, outside of medical professionals is that the progress that resulted from the efforts of these individuals and their colleagues came, in many instances, at a tremendous cost to life, limb, and reputation.

For example, the individuals who developed the whole field of radiology in this country suffered greatly from constant exposure to radiation (electromagnetic radiation, or in common parlance, X-rays), since in the beginning it was not known how to protect against its harmful effects. One of America's first radiologists, Frederic Bejater at Hopkins, suffered from multiple cancers. *Some of his fingers became so damaged by radiation they actually fell off*, and he had severe radiation-induced dermatitis, a lifelong debilitating condition, all the result of unprotected and prolonged exposure to radiation. Bejater's story was not unique in his field.

A urologist, Werner Forssmann, created an important breakthrough in the field we now know as interventional cardiology. Forssmann passed a catheter retrograde into his heart (right atrium) through an antebrachial vein in his arm. By so doing, he proved that access to the heart was possible via a closed technique using arm veins as the conduit. Forssmann and two others received the Nobel Prize for his potentially life-threatening stunt, and the other two Nobelists (Richards and Cournand) for their many other contributions to cardiology.

Figure 13. Werner Forssmann, MD, Nobel Laureate
With Permission: Museum and Archives, DGU, German Urological Society.

As modern medicine expanded its reach with ever-increasingly advanced surgical techniques, many of the surgeons had to endure high mortality and complication rates in their patients. Surgeons like Charles Bailey experienced professional obloquy because of the complications associated with his pioneering attempts to operate on blocked coronary arteries.

Professional medical societies expelled a urologist, William Herbst, Jr., in Washington DC in the early 1940s for treating patients with advanced cancer of the prostate with estrogen (female hormones). Eventually the medical community exonerated Herbst, and he received many awards from his colleagues after Huggins received his Nobel Prize. Bill Herbst examined me when I sat for my urology boards, which I could not do from the NIH, and the first question he asked me was whether I knew what he was famous for; I regurgitated his whole story and added how much I admired him for his work—that was a genuine sentiment because I knew I did not need to curry favor with anyone to pass my boards. That was the only question he asked me, and as a little tear ran down his check, he said, visibly glowing with satisfaction at my comments, "you pass." How I felt at that moment in the presence of a great man who knew he was remembered and honored by the next generation is difficult to set to paper. I know I never forgot that very emotional moment, and I hope that neither did he until he passed.

Some years after Herbst's ordeal, Charles Huggins, MD, an academic urologist, received the Nobel Prize for showing that modifying the hormone environment of a patient's cancer by interfering with hormone signaling could alter the growth or progression of his or her cancer. The Nobel Committee gave no credit to Bill Herbst for his early observations and efforts—another case of Nobel injustice.

Figure 14. Charles Huggins, MD, Nobel Laureate
With Permission: The AUA William P. Didusch Center for Urologic History.

And so it went, the price of progress brought about only by determined and courageous academic physicians and surgeons affiliated with university medical schools. Still today, surgeons make progress at similar potential risks. Two examples: transplant and other surgeons are constantly exposed to a variety of odd diseases, not the least of which is hepatitis, and of course, those treating AIDS can contract the disease as a result of various types of mishaps.

In summary then, modern American medicine as we know it originated in the great academic and training centers, and that is why such institutions became national and world treasures, as well as examples of American exceptionalism. Many responsible and informed citizens, and I am among them, believe these institutions must be preserved at almost all costs. If these centers disappear, all humanity will be the loser, and progress in medicine will be impacted negatively.

Today, there is no prospective replacement for America's academic medical institutions and the benefits they continue to create for mankind: they cannot, nor will they, be replaced in any other nation on earth. This is true because only the United States of America has had the resources for such an undertaking, and of the world's residents, only Americans place such a high value on the sanctity of human life—or at least they used to.

When one writes or speaks about reforming the American health-care system, it is essential to remember that the network of our academic medical centers that stretch from coast to coast are an integral part of health-care delivery, and more importantly, upon their various activities rests the world's future progress in medicine.

CHAPTER 10

RUNNING BETWEEN THE
RAINDROPS: FINANCIAL REALITY

One final first dose of reality awaited me. Having discovered that the urology clinical service was a near-disaster, I learned in my first meeting with Neal Gault, the new medical school dean, that the divisional finances were also in disarray.

In order, I learned these tough facts: if the division of urology had been a department, it would have had the lowest budget in the medical school (incidentally, that never changed in twenty-five years, even after we became a department); two of the residents were being paid on a federal training grant, and use of that grant for that purpose was not authorized, which made me very uneasy; and finally, the division budget only paid for one and one-half secretaries. Since the divisional secretaries were responsible for enhancing the academic productivity of the faculty, it made it nearly impossible for me to recruit faculty, since it was common practice for each faculty member to have a secretary.

The budget paid two faculty base salaries: mine at around $20,000, and another at a slightly lesser amount, which when I arrived went to Colin Markland. If the school did not increase the urology budget quickly, the division would be out of 0100 money—state money from the medical school—by April of any calendar year. It was perfectly clear to me that to grow and increase the scope and standing of the division meant finding our own way to generate the required financial resources—that is, from patient care fees and possibly federal grants, but I knew that grants would only come after we had established a laboratory program.

After reviewing the department budget, I wondered in which pot of budgeted money would I find funds to pay two residents and faculty if the training grant went away? Neither I, nor anyone else, could answer that question, mainly because additional university (0100) money did not exist, at least not for urologic surgery. The school had moved on after they recruited me, and any loose money was going to recruiting additional faculty.

The shortage of "hard," or 0100, dollars was common. The state never adequately funded the school, and as a result, medical school administrators always tried to squeeze the clinical departments for additional money to run the entire school. The administration also saw our clinical departments as a way, at least in part, to fund the basic sciences, which were as weak in many instances as the clinical departments were strong.

Basic scientists prefer living in places with warm climates, mainly because they can. Scientists gravitate to universities that have plenty of money and where famous names in cutting-edge science reside; I certainly do not blame them for doing so. Minnesota was, at that time, not such a place.

I had a second question, one that directly affected my ability to recruit top physicians. Why were the hospitals not paying us for all our residents, as was the practice elsewhere in academic medicine? (Finding adequate salary money for residents, secretaries, and junior staff remained a daunting problem throughout my tenure.)

My mind and emotions were in turmoil when I left the dean's office the first time. Fortunately, Dean Gault, a physician, turned out to be a great man and a friend in need, especially at one critical point in the future. So as I began my chairmanship, I found that the division, not yet a department, was replete with financial problems that could only be resolved by the medical staff and a private practice that would generate the needed funds.

At the time, I concluded that the medical school collectively had misrepresented the situation in the division during the recruiting process. Having done so, school officials never seemed to have a sense of shame over what they had done, and certainly no sense of obligation to make it right. The moral turpitude shown by the university at the beginning was not the last time I saw a feckless central administration, medical school administration, or Board of Regents exhibit similar behavior.[27]

I should have drilled down much more into some of these matters before accepting the chairmanship. My decision to take the job in Minnesota "as is" put my family and career in jeopardy. It is true that you can lose a good opportunity by overanalyzing a situation, but it is equally true that you can get yourself into a hell of a mess, as I did, by under-analyzing a job opportunity. Until I went to Minnesota, my career moves were almost perfect, but that was negated at least temporarily by going to Minnesota.

---

[27] By and large, this is the same crew that lacked the smarts, the will, and the organizational skills to support the physicians so that they could keep Minnesota's cardiac and general surgery programs at the head of the world's pack. In short, the university and state bureaucrats eventually blew it to the extent that Minnesota does not lead any part of those fields today. The leadership Minnesota had in those areas is gone, more than likely never to return. And was anyone held accountable? Was anyone held accountable for 9/11 or the Bernie Madoff debacle? The answer to all three questions is "no."

My pathetic excuses for not having made a better analysis of the division of urology in Minnesota were youth and inexperience. It is not surprising, therefore, that I subsequently concluded that extreme care should be exercised before anyone thirty-three years of age should be appointed to a major academic surgical post. (There are always exceptions. Minnesota appointed twenty-eight-year-old Owen Wangensteen as chief of general surgery at Minnesota, so it works on occasion.)

Academic leaders, besides myriad other responsibilities, must deal with the politics of bureaucracies. Remember this: most government or institutional bureaucrats have two main goals: 1) to expand their power, and 2) to preserve their jobs at any cost. As a result, bureaucrats constantly and necessarily deflect blame to others, like President George W. Bush, for example, if anything goes wrong in their sphere of responsibility, just as they did later as the university ALG program fell apart (more about this in a later chapter). That episode relative to ALG was bureaucratic CYA on steroids. Furthermore, it usually ends up that the victims of bureaucratic malfeasance are blamed for whatever went awry. Never do we hear that the programs of the bureaucrats were poorly conceived or incompetently administered because that would be an admission of inadequacy by the bureaucrats. Responsibility and accountability are to most state or federal government bureaucrats like crosses and garlic are to vampires.

Many of the university bureaucrats reveled in making as many of the medical faculty as possible miserable by imposing on them a long list of petty rules and regulations, which bureaucrats invent out of thin air. This assault on the physicians did not start in earnest until the economic situation began to deteriorate for the physicians and the position of the physicians became more and more untenable. To a functionary, nothing is as exhilarating as being able to function (especially with the "force" (guns) of government behind them). Or as a friend said, "There is nothing like minions that minionate."

These nasty functionaries or mandarins will protect their jobs at all costs, even if they have to behave like cuttlefish expelling their ink of confusion to, above all, avoid any responsibility or accountability. Most of these people could not remain employed outside their civil service sinecures. Boutros Boutros-Ghali, the former secretary-general of the United Nations, said it best: "The way to deal with bureaucrats is by stealth or sudden acts of violence." More about these bureaucrats later in the book.

As young physicians, we could never imagine falling prey to the directions and whims of such creatures. Things have, however, evolved to the point where the John Galt and Howard Roark equivalents in medicine, as generally foreseen by Ayn Rand, are headed for subservience to deplorable little squishes like the Rand character Ellsworth Toohey in *The Fountainhead*. As bureaucrats and their regulatory ruinous recipes continue to evolve, some of the giants, innovators, and producers in medicine will just stop trying, while other people like them will never enter the profession in the first place. Thus, the long-term consequence of the bureaucratic attack on medicine and physicians is that it will choke off the young and driven from even considering medicine as a profession. If that happens, the fish will rot from both the head and the tail toward the middle. Again, to be fair, there were many bureaucrats at the university and in the dean's office who were conscientious and hardworking and who had the interests of the medical school as a priority. To this point, a physician panel of a dermatologist, a cardiologist, and a family physician was asked, "Would you encourage your children to enter medicine?" They all answered that they were discouraging young people across the board from entering medicine. This will be one of the unintended consequences of the type of health-care reform that has been passed into law.

(By the way, the Buchwald paper listed at the end of the book under suggested reading ("A Clash of Culture—Personal Autonomy Versus

Corporate Bondage") presents an elegant and creative exposition as to how these said bureaucrats function and the "commandments they live by"; it is very worthwhile reading.)

The following anecdotes illustrate even better the potential fate for physicians in a bureaucrat-dominated world:

A young Scottish house surgeon told me that when he first arrived at his new government-directed National Health Service post, he found there was a single sixty-watt bulb in his sleeping quarters. It provided so little light that he had difficulty seeing well enough to read. He went to the nasty little mandarin who was the government administrator for that medical district and requested a more powerful lightbulb. The official looked up at him from behind his desk and said with a snarl, "You shouldn't be in your room reading; you should be on the wards taking care of your patients." Yes, the world is changing, and the future for physicians and patients is currently being constructed under the guise of health-care reform.

That true story also reminds me of another, about a union soldier who had been a slave before joining the Union Army. He sat alongside a road, resting for a few minutes as guards marched a group of southern prisoners past him. The soldier looked up, and to his amazement, recognized his former owner and slave master among the confederate captives marching by. He jumped to his feet and shouted, "Well, mas'er, it look like da bottom rail is now on da top." I'd say that is a pretty elegant metaphor for a supposedly uneducated slave. Sadly for physicians and unsuspecting patients, it is indeed becoming a world where a lot of bottom rails (bureaucrats) of all stripes are ascending toward the top.

Faced with what I had learned from the dean about division finances, I met with several other clinical heads. I sought input from the other department chairmen on how to solve the problems of the urology division.

I also met with Owen Wangensteen, the *eminence griese* of the school. Wangensteen kept an office in the history of medicine section in the medical school library after he retired. Little did I know that Wangensteen, besides being a great man, was, in a nice way, the personification of general surgery arrogance, who probably thought urology was something you contracted in the army. (If I had achieved what Wangensteen did, I might well have been even more arrogant than he was.) It may not have helped my cause to have taken over one of Wangensteen's fallow laboratories, which I had converted into active productive space doing cell biology; I heard later this had displeased him. I asked Wangensteen to explain the origin of the town-gown problems, but he never responded to the question. I am not sure he was even aware what town-gown meant. Wangensteen had operated in an era when the all-powerful university and Mayo Clinic dominated medicine in the Twin Cities and the state—even the entire upper Midwest. He never had to compete with the private practitioners as we did. My guess is that as far as he was concerned, they were just there and not a problem for him or his program. In retrospect, I am very glad I had face time with a truly great chairman of surgery. Incidentally, Dr. 'Arnie' Leonard has just written a book that is, in part, a Wangensteen hagiography and is worth a read.

Figure 15. Owen Wangensteen, MD
Courtesy of University of Minnesota Archives, University of Minnesota—Twin Cities

Two departments, orthopedics and gynecology, had reneged on the amount of seed money they committed to provide for urology before I accepted my position. I found that they had little interest in helping urologic surgery further or even talking to me.

In the beginning of my tenure, after I learned of many of the downsides of the job, there were times I thought I might not last any longer than Pope John Paul I, who was poisoned thirty-three days after he became Pope. It seemed that every day I could hear ice cracking and preparing to give away beneath my feet; after all, I was in Minnesota. At this point, I made a critical decision. I concluded, for reasons cited previously, the time had come to shake away the despair and negativity and to start running fast enough to dodge between the raindrops. Some might argue that I was driven onward in part by the realization that the Little Bighorn and its history was close by and that I had no inclination to become a Custer.

As indicated before, we had our bags packed, at least mentally, on numerous occasions in those early days, mainly because we knew there were unlimited opportunities at attractive salaries in private practice in the east, especially for anyone trained by Leadbetter. My family was always first on my priority list, and I had already moved the children twice in four years, so I wanted them to put down some roots. Thus, I finally decided Minnesota was it, for better or worse, unless it became truly intolerable.

Leaders are competitors and often have an ornery edge to them; some would argue that description fit me perfectly. In the last analysis, I determined that no one would run me out of anywhere. I resolved that if I ever did leave, I wanted to say that I had made every attempt to secure the rigging and caulk the hull of the urology ship before exiting stage right. Such an exit would have been on my terms, not someone else's.

After the encounter in Detroit with the bombastic Twin Cities' urologist, I remembered the famous Churchill 1941 Ottawa speech, when Winston said, "Hitler said he would ring Britain's neck like a chicken; some chicken, some neck." That encomium of Churchill's kept recurring in my thoughts during those early days until the tide began to turn. Then, and only then, did I know with certainty that it, in fact, had been for me and the department "some chicken, some neck."

In summary, after I had been on board at Minnesota for a couple of months, I learned I had inherited the following nimbus clouds on the horizon:

- a terrible town-gown situation
- inadequate departmental academic facilities
- a decrepit inpatient hospital station
- negligible faculty or secretarial support money (and no endowment)
- few, and for the most part only marginally qualified, medical and resident staff
- a near paucity of patients and no system to generate referrals

Furthermore:

- I found that some of the major departments, like internal medicine, had faculties that seemed to care little about either practicing medicine or patient care.
- In addition, the former chief of urology had stripped the department bare and had gone downtown to set up shop in direct competition with the enterprise he formerly led.
- Finally, I had taken way too much on faith and had not done sufficient due diligence. I had assumed, wrongly as it turned out, that an institution of Minnesota's caliber would have had sufficient resources and facilities to support any and all

departments within the medical school. Let this be a caution to all aspiring leaders: do your homework, and make sure you understand the situation you inherit before accepting the job.

Wyland Leadbetter once told me, "If you take an academic job, go to a place that is down and out and build it up, because that is the only way you will ever get any credit." Minnesota's urology division at the time met Leadbetter's standard perfectly: the division of urology most certainly was down, if not actually out.

However, on the positive side, the university, whether by design or by default, gave me the most important gifts possible: economic and personal freedom—freedom to tackle the problems and build the practice and the department, and freedom not to have to account to bureaucrats on a regular basis. I found freedom and opportunity at Minnesota, America's foundational first principles in action, and in that sense, I was lucky.

There was one other asset available to me, and that was the overall excellence of the clinical faculty of the University of Minnesota School of Medicine. The university's reputation for excellence, at least in some areas, such as medical oncology, pediatrics, cardiac surgery, gynecologic oncology. otolaryngology, neurosurgery, and transplantation, helped to make its hospital a viable clinical center in the early 1970s.

CHAPTER 11

CREATING AN INCUBATOR FOR ACADEMIC SURGEONS

"You will be the same person in five years
as you are today, except for two things: the
people you meet and the books you read."
—Charlie "Tremendous" Jones

I am an avid reader. I found joy in marinating my mind with the ideas and philosophies expressed in the great books of the ages. Books are a way of learning from the collective wisdom of those who lived life and accomplished something. I read the classics first because I remembered what Hemingway once said to a young writer: "If you want to be a writer, read the classics because then you will know what you are up against." I knew I would be doing a fair amount of writing in an academic career.

The most influential books and authors that on reflection had a direct bearing on my career and chairmanship were the Bible and the Bard, followed by the aforementioned classics. I relished books by Clausewitz, Sun Tzu, Ulysses S. Grant (his memoirs), Ayn Rand, and Adam Smith; and the writings of Jefferson as set forth by Dumas Malone, *Academica Microcosmoraphica*, Albert J. Nock's *The Memoirs of a Superfluous Man*, Mark Twain, William F. Buckley,

Jr., Irving Kristol, Friedrich von Hayek, John Derbyshire, and Carl Sandberg's *Lincoln*. I enjoyed books about Vince Lombardi, such as *When Pride Still Mattered* by David Maraniss, and many others of a similar bent. But there was one little work I especially valued. A. P. Wavell, the famous British World War II general, gave a series of lectures at Cambridge in the late 1930s entitled *Generals and Generalship*. The Wavell lectures were published into a hardcover booklet.[28] The copy I own (not a reprint) is the only one of two I have ever seen. The gravamen of these lectures was that it did not require much "generalship" to win battles when the leader had superior numbers and matériel, but that the great generals were the ones who were outnumbered and facing defeat and who even lacking sufficient resources could rally their forces to turn the tide of battle and eventually win. George Washington was such a general and leader.

My experience as a resident and staff member at the MGH and as a senior investigator at the NIH, of course, also shaped my approach to the division/department and its developmental environment. I had been in practice with Professor Leadbetter at the MGH for six months prior to going to the NIH, during which time Leadbetter charged me to develop a laboratory program; surprisingly, none existed in urology at the MGH (or anywhere else in urology). Since MGH urology per se had no space or research money, Ron Malt in general surgery took me into his basic science laboratory (molecular biology). Malt's lab was MIT-affiliated, and this is where I received excellent laboratory training.

---

[28] Erwin Rommel, the great German general of World War II, thought so much of the Wavell lectures that he had a copy of them leather-bound. Rommel carried the book with him throughout the war. After the war ended, Mrs. Rommel made a special trip to England to present her husband's dog-eared copy of Wavell's lectures to Mrs. Wavell. That little book is now in the British War Museum. Wavell's hobby, like Patton's, was writing poetry, and he published a beautiful anthology of poetry (*Other Men's Flowers*).

I soon learned in my time with Malt that you cannot mount an effective lab effort if you are being interrupted every fifteen minutes or so to take care of trivial clinical problems, an all-too-common occurrence when I was practicing with Wyland and his associates. Remember, these men were clinicians with no pure academic inclinations, and they set their daily goal to care for a large number of patients. Wyland even told me once that the only reason he ever wrote a paper was to bring him more patients. Wyland was a truly great man, but he had no understanding of what it took to be successful in the laboratory; greatness, too, has its limits. However, Leadbetter, to his credit, was one of the first of his generation to at least recognize that urology chiefs in the future probably would need to have more than just a clinical dimension. I remember telling him one day that Johns Hopkins School of Medicine had just hired a neurochemist to head the clinical department of psychiatry, not a medical doctor psychiatrist. He thought a minute and said something like, "Well, that is the direction of the future." Wyland was a deeper thinker than some gave him credit for, and irrespective of all that, Wyland gave his trainees so very much, for which all of us have always been more than grateful.

During the time I tried to serve "two masters" at the MGH, I became convinced that an academic urologic surgeon needed protection to be free to develop a credible laboratory program away from everyday clinical demands. I saw that such a commitment to the laboratory would take at least two years of full-time effort after finishing a residency. Later on after I became chairman, I conceived of and proposed that an American Urological Association scholarship or fellowship program be created and funded by the AUA that would provide academic support for young, academically inclined urological surgeons. I knew it took time to develop academic surgery, and I knew they needed to be supported adequately during their development so they could refuse the blandishments of a lucrative private practice.

At the NIH, I learned from the chief of the surgery branch, Alf Ketcham, that the job of a chief was to support the staff and stay out of their way and let the young people get credit for what they did. That is not to say that a chief should be the proverbial invisible hand in the shadows. I saw Ketchum kick the occasional butt when it was necessary. Alf Ketchum was a great leader and a great man, who made a monumental contribution to general surgery and the surgical specialties through the men he helped flourish in the laboratory while they were at the surgery branch of the NCI (NIH).

An unlikely source inspired some of my other thoughts about how an academic department should be structured. We lived on Wolf Tree Lane in Rockville, Maryland, while we were at the NIH. The street took its name from a tree that grows primarily in the east and especially, for some reason, in Maryland. The tree's name reflects the fact that its elaborate root system and large crown are so extensive that nothing grows in its shadow. As I thought about it, I began to analogize between the wolf tree and several department heads I had observed even before I went to the NIH. These included some of the professors I met as a job applicant at the end of my urology residency at the MGH or had heard about from others.

These aforementioned professors were so driven by self-aggrandizement and fragile egos that they could not tolerate good people around them, nor could they give others credit for what they did. I remember, in particular, a job interview (more like an audience at the Holy See) I had with a professor of urology at a major medical center in New York City. This interview came after I had almost finished my residency, but before Dr. Leadbetter officially offered me a job as he had promised. This individual had set his desk on a platform that lifted it twelve to fifteen inches off the floor. Thus, when he sat behind his desk, he looked down from "Olympus" at anyone sitting before him. Very few people ever made me as uncomfortable as that professor did during my interview, which, of course, probably was his intent. In war, when the enemy fires down on you from high ground, it is referred to as "plunging fire," and is almost impossible to defend against. What Professor X was all about, namely him, was very clear to me. I cut the interview short with some excuse because I knew for certain that I had no intention of working for him. Private practice would have been a better alternative. As it turned out, history proved me right. Professor X never trained a single academician of substance despite having the vast resources of an elite university and medical center at his command. He probably made as little impact on our field relative to the resources at his disposal as anyone in the history of the specialty.

In contrast to the Professor X's I met during my career, the successful chairmen I observed have recognized that their young trainees not only need protection, but also they must get credit for their work. Ketcham at the NIH was anything but a wolf tree. Leadbetter, at least as judged by his inclinations, was a little less so.

Although I was not entirely familiar with the training program in general surgery at Minnesota that Owen Wangensteen had established before I came to the university, I soon learned after I arrived that he had a philosophy about training residents and academicians that was very similar to my own. For example, Wangensteen was one of the first surgical chiefs in the country to require that his residents spend time in the laboratory, and many of them even pursued advanced degrees based on their laboratory experiences. Some of Wangensteen's residents earned PhDs as a result of the lab program. Cardiac surgery evolved from studies on cardiac physiology that were begun in Minnesota's surgical laboratories. That same laboratory work carried over to the development of heart transplantation pioneered by two Minnesota trainees, Norman Shumway and Christiaan Barnard. Much of the initial work that led to clinical heart transplantation actually started in the surgical dog labs by residents in training at Minnesota. Maybe this concept of training and the results it produced are the reasons why history has judged Owen Wangensteen to be one of the five most important figures in American (medicine) surgery of the twentieth century.

I had an additional debt to Wangensteen. Many of the best residents we recruited early on had come to Minnesota to study with Wangensteen. So even our program in urology had a connection to Wangensteen and his greatness.

One more historical fact regarding the Minnesota heart program: C. Walton Lillehei and associates became known as "the fathers of open-heart surgery." Lillihei, by the way, spent countless hours in the animal and physiology laboratories developing the techniques that led to the first open-heart surgeries in the country.

CHAPTER 12

SELECTING RESIDENTS SUITABLE TO BE TRANSFORMED INTO SURGEONS

"If you have academic achievement you are admired, if you have great wealth you are envied, if you have great power you are feared, but if you have great character you are respected."

—Lou Holtz

Prospective residents, of course, were medical school graduates, and we required completion of at least two years of a general surgery residency in an accredited program prior to applying for our training program. Each potential resident had to sit for either a personal interview with me or another of our faculty or both before we would consider them.

I learned early on in Minnesota that the surgical residents and interns had a written evaluation of them by every service they rotated through. I spent many long hours reviewing those evaluations, which allowed me to identify the best house officers in the department of surgery residency. I tried to recruit the best of the best of those residents with some success, as time has proven.

During my first several years, I was not aware of any study I could use to help me determine the unique qualities of character, temperament, and intellect that superb surgeons share. At various times during my career, I often thought it would be interesting to collaborate with a psychiatrist or psychologist to design a study that would limn the depths of character and the minds of twenty-five or so leading surgeons to see what unique qualities, if any, they shared. I wanted to know whether renowned surgeons were unique in any way at their core, or whether they simply shared characteristics common to successful, driven people in general. At the very least, that study might have provided me with helpful information to identify the best candidates our department should accept into our training program. Years later, these types of tools did become available in the private business sector, but we had to do without them.

However, lacking such information, here is what I looked for in candidates. I knew that anyone who transited college and medical school had to be reasonably intelligent, but this does not assure they are equal in possessing the qualities of intellect and temperament that would help make them become an accomplished surgeon or surgeon-scientist. Applicants who seemed to have retained an almost childlike curiosity about the world in general and science in particular made excellent residents.

Another area of inquiry was what individual or individuals were most important in candidates' lives. In other words, who were their heroes other than sports figures? I always recommended that they read Roche's book *A World without Heroes: The Modern Tragedy*. What follows is an excerpt from an Amazon.com review of that book:

> The good news, he says, is what *didn't* happen. Materialism says that man must of necessity, and inevitably give up his belief in God, but he has not. Faith, Roche says, is integral to a whole and integrated "heroic" understanding of what man is. Roche pleads for a better-informed, more humble understanding of what science is, and can do,

and a wiser philosophy of man that understands him as a created being capable of free thought, free action, and … heroism! This is an important and challenging book that deserves wide reading by those who care deeply about our culture and the state of man today. It is rich in the history of science and philosophy, and for those who love the ongoing verbal battle of ideas, this book will make you more knowledgeable than you were. It might even change a few minds about where we are, how we got here, and how we go forward.[29]

A side note: Roche appears to have wanted to be a "hero" to his own daughter-in-law, which led to his ruin at Hillsdale College. The details of his salacious fall from grace in fact should not detract from some of the powerful things he wrote. Someone once said about the author Graham Greene, "Listen to the tale and not the teller." Greene was a horrid human being according to many who knew him well, and he was a Communist to boot, while, at the same time being admittedly a great author. One time I sent a book to Greene to be signed, and it was returned with a nasty little note from a secretary stating that Greene only signed books for friends and that, in any event, he was in Moscow to address the Politburo.

I asked candidates about their reading habits, looking for some indication as to just how driven they were "to know." I usually asked, "Which books have you recently read or what book, if any, had the effect of changing your life?" The range of their answers was amazing. Some candidates felt *Time* magazine qualified as a book (I referred them back east to Harvard). Others had read little or nothing outside their required professional reading. Many gave interesting and thoughtful answers. As anyone reading this history can tell, I did not think that *Das Kapital* as a most life-changing book was a

---

[29] Roche, G. (1987) From Amazon review of: *A World without Heroes: The Modern Tragedy*. Hillsdale College Press. Hillsdale, Michigan

good answer (definitely candidates I recommended back to Yale or Harvard).

The candidate's self-image particularly interested me. To get at this, I asked, "What do you see in yourself that sets you apart from the other candidates? In other words, what makes you special?" Of course, that is the same question I was asked in the second interview for an internship at the MGH. I asked them the self-esteem questions rather than having them write their answer since most of them were products of the current educational system in America and I wasn't sure they could spell self-esteem.

After they answered all the first questions, I inquired further: "What are the most important qualities of a resident at the clinical level in the opinion of our faculty?" If they flailed around answering that question, I answered it for them: "The answer is, reliability and honesty," I said. When I answered that question for them, they knew, at least in part, what I expected of them if they came to Minnesota.

I also believed that athletic ability was a desirable quality, especially if they had played a sport requiring hand-eye coordination.

I asked candidates about their families. A great recruiter once told me that the first thing he tried to determine in a job applicant was the applicant's relationship to his or her parents. He adamantly insisted that individuals who had solid relationships with their parents were most likely to be ambitious, stable, and productive employees. Of course, America was a different place in those days since most people had a mother and father. However, I know of two recent presidents of the United States who would have flunked my friend's criterion: Clinton and Reagan. Both Clinton and Reagan had terrible relationships with their fathers and faced tough times in their early family life.

One standard last question was, "Once you complete your residency, do you see yourself as becoming an academic urologist?" If they answered yes, I asked them why. Their answer to the "why" question was very important because it differentiated those giving an answer that they thought I might like from those who had actually thought about becoming an investigator and teacher.

Today there are very sophisticated psychological testing techniques that industrial psychologists employ to evaluate candidates for key positions in the corporate world. (Too bad they do not apply the same in-depth probing for our leaders.) But I did not have such resources, so I did the best I could. I continued to refine the selection process over time, and it worked pretty well for the department's purposes. To be a successful department chair requires developing a sixth sense about people and a jeweler's eye for talent. But above all, you have to be "lucky" in your choices. Our program was fortunate to be lucky over and over again. A hockey coach once said, "It isn't luck if the puck keeps going in the net time after time," but who knows for sure? My system, such as it evolved, helped me choose residents, many of whom became leaders in their own right, and how that happened is subject to debate and further analysis.

A fabled Princeton director of admissions said as I recall, "I never admitted a boy I did not like." So whether I accepted a resident candidate or not depended in part on whether I liked the individual, because I knew if he or she joined us, I would be living closely with the resident for the next few years. Some might denigrate the importance of the "likability factor" in choosing residents, but they would be wrong. Organizations are best served when their people get along with each other, and our people did and still do long after being residents. I recall, painfully, the negative effects resulting from one member of our faculty who tended toward duplicitous and dishonest behavior that did not contribute to harmony in the department.

CHAPTER 13

The Architecture of a Urological
Surgery Training Program

The word *surgery* comes from the Greek *cheirourgen*, made up of *cheir* (hand) and *ergo* (to work). The word means "to work with the hand." Surgery can, therefore, be defined as those manual procedures used in the management of injuries and disease.

Any surgical training program should have a didactic structure or curriculum consisting of regular conferences and teaching rounds on the clinical wards or stations. What follows are the conferences or teaching sessions our department held daily, weekly, or at a minimum once a month. Training residents in a surgical discipline is an awesome responsibility because after the residents graduate and leave, they will have the responsibility for thousands of patients in their practice lifetimes.

1. Grand rounds—case presentations and discussions: weekly
2. Pediatric urology conference: monthly
3. Cancer conference—multidisciplinary discussion of urologic cancers, including urologic surgery, pathology, medical oncology, and radiation oncology: monthly
4. Journal club with staff to review current peer-reviewed papers from other programs: monthly as published in leading journals
5. Laboratory conference—report on research projects: as needed

6. Individual writing conferences with residents preparing papers for publication: as needed
7. Teaching rounds on inpatients and some outpatient teaching during endoscopic procedures: daily
8. We encouraged residents in training to work on preparing scientific papers for presentation at national meetings.
9. Individual meetings with residents to review their operation logs: every few months as needed
10. Death (mortality) and complications conference: monthly. In these conferences the cases of everyone, including the chiefs, were reviewed to define what went wrong and how future problems of that type could be prevented.
11. We encouraged the residents to study the history of surgery dating back to the Hindus, Greeks, and Romans, and up until the more contemporary surgical pioneers.

The second component of a surgical residency is the teaching that goes on in the operating room, which is described in some detail herein.

Training surgical residents is analogous to a construction project. The process is long-lasting, as the resident takes one small step forward at a time. No one can be a nonsurgeon one day and a surgeon the next. As I used to say, "Not even God can make a caterpillar into a butterfly overnight." It goes without saying, minting a surgeon is a complex and demanding process. The training of a surgeon must be comprehensive and well thought out. There is no such thing as minor or trivial surgery, but inadequate training may produce a minor or trivial surgeon.

Laypeople—and some physicians (*'medical types'*)—might be surprised to learn that surgery is as much a proper state of mind (attitude) and having a sound character as it is suture or ligature tying and sharp-dissection scissors or scalpels. We designed resident training by concentrating on three main components: psychological and attitude adjustment (the foundation), learning the scientific underpinnings of the field (the framing, as in framing a house or a constitution), and finally, acquiring the manual skills necessary to become a board-certified surgeon (the finishing details).

At the outset of all residents' training, our faculty attempted to instill in them a certain positive mind-set or attitude about surgery in general and their chosen profession in particular. We warned that some of their medical colleagues had a general disdain for surgeons, seeing themselves as intellectually superior to any surgeon. Well, that is absolute bunk, and today's surgeons should be more than proud of who they are and of what they sacrificed to become what they are. The old attitudes of the superiority of the "fleas" was often dispelled in our program as part of our mentoring.

Being a surgeon is a unique and privileged way of life and extremely fulfilling. The greatest reward comes when, in most instances, the surgeon can proactively treat a patient and restore him or her to health in relatively short order. And that restoration is done primarily by the surgeon's "healing hands," which enhance the surgeon's deep emotional attachment to his or her patients and their well-being. A surgeon often senses that if the patient gets well, it is a direct result of the surgeon's hard-earned skills (with God's help) and not a drug or ancillary treatment devised by others that was primarily restorative for the patient. It is difficult to adequately convey the profound level of satisfaction that restoring a patient to health gives surgeons.

Surgery training is, among other things, a highly and intimate personal experience—for both the mentor and the resident. If a surgeon is confident and secure, he or she will convey a positive image to his or her patients and that helps to instill a positive attitude in the patient prior to surgery. Recent studies have shown what many of us suspected, but were never able to prove, namely: cancer patients who began treatment with a positive attitude had better survival rates irrespective of the type of cancer they had. So patient attitudes are important—very important—at a practical level if those studies are correct. Furthermore, the study that still needs to be done is to examine how the surgeons' attitudes influence the attitudes and outcomes of their patients. It is, of course, our contention that the surgeon should try his or her best to reinforce a positive outlook in the patients at all stages of their treatment. Professor Leadbetter had a wonderful trick: he would say to the patient just prior to discharge, "If your cancer does not come back (or if we have no complications), you will be fine." All most patients heard was, "you will be fine." And that brought a relieved smile to their faces.

It is natural that first-year trainees are apprehensive as they enter the operating room the first few times. In fact, if the truth were known, most beginning surgeons are terrified of the operating room and overwhelmed at first because they are concerned they might harm a patient in some way due to lack of expertise. The new resident must contend with the hustle and bustle of the nurses and ancillary personnel in the operating room and the array of complicated apparatus, some of which they probably have never seen before, all bearing down on them. Trainees struggle initially just to learn how to don a cap, gown, and gloves and how to properly scrub using sterile technique in preparation for the urological operation before they can even think about the surgery itself. Therefore, we set out to disarm them of whatever fears and apprehensions they might have by showing them that a properly trained surgeon with the help of the surgical team can control events during surgery, and that almost always any procedure can be brought to a successful or satisfactory conclusion. Today it is very unusual for a patient to die during surgery of any kind. Professor Leadbetter commented once, "Attitudes are caught, not taught." Our faculty wanted the residents to catch the right attitude about surgery by the examples we set, especially in the operating theater. This early development phase was when, as teachers, we were "pouring cement and driving steel" into the residents in preparation for completing the structure, which was in the last analysis the construction of the best surgeon we could produce.

There is nothing worse for a mentor than the young surgeon who never overcomes his or her initial fear of the operating theater. If surgeons cannot overcome that fear, they will be forever indecisive, vacillating, and timid in their approach to their craft. Knowing this, the faculty made it our first obligation to encourage the residents' confidence that with hard work and proper training and experience, they would be able to handle any problem they might encounter during surgery. That confidence is only built over a long period by constant positive reinforcement and allowing the resident to operate under supervision on cases of increasing difficulty. More than one former resident has told me his or her most important takeaway from residency training was "the confidence that I can handle anything that confronts me in the operating room."

It is important to teach that a surgeon's confidence should never spill over into arrogance or recklessness. Master surgeons approach each undertaking with respect for the patient and what the surgeon is about to do, but not with arrogance that may lead to carelessness; as everyone knows, in surgery the stakes are always very high, and the smallest of errors have lethal potential. Some professionals can afford to be overconfident, careless, or inattentive to detail in their work, but a surgeon does not have that luxury. The results produced by a surgeon are there for all to see, and surgeons are measured by those results. A surgeon in an academic setting has many eyes watching his or her every move—students, residents, other physicians, and quality-control bureaucrats among others. It is easier to evaluate a surgeon based on results, including deaths and complications, than it is a pediatrician or a psychiatrist. A psychiatrist shot back at me one time when I argued it was impossible to evaluate his work; he said, "We are measured by the number of suicides among our patients." Touché. At the MGH we divided good surgeons into those with golden thumbs and those not-so-good surgeons with black thumbs. In addition we had the EITTS surgeons—everything I touch turns to s---. Fortunately, there were not many of those.

We also taught surgeons to attempt the impossible while risking all on behalf of a patient when necessary. We emphasized that courage in surgery needs to be tempered by good judgment, and thus, the surgeon needs to be able to differentiate between courage and foolhardiness. One way to facilitate such an approach is to caucus with your surgeon colleagues to have them evaluate the risk-reward of what you are contemplating surgically. In an academic situation, you usually have several competent and experienced associates who are worth discussing any case with. And today, modern communications can facilitate such consultations by any surgeon, whether private practice- or academic center-based. When I came to Minnesota, Colin Markland was in the department, and he had more experience than I did with certain cases so I frequently asked him to scrub with me early in my chairmanship so as to help me with an operation.

In addition, we taught that a surgeon must also have the courage and character to act postoperatively to address a complication when it arises, as they inevitably will for every surgeon. Addressing surgical complications is one of the most important obligations a surgeon has. The surgery does not end when the incision is closed, the drapes are removed, and the operating room goes dark.

We taught our young surgeons to guard against letting their egos interfere with admitting that one of their postoperative patients developed a complication. The worst decision a surgeon might make for a patient is to let a complication go untreated; doing so may lead to a fatal outcome, as well as a malpractice suit.

From a practical standpoint, we emphasized that failure to deal promptly with a surgical complication is one of the main reasons a surgeon ends up in a malpractice lawsuit. Known complications may not be actionable legally in most cases because neither the law nor any known performance standards hold surgeons to a standard of perfection in outcomes. On the other hand, we clearly explained that if a complication occurs and the surgeon fails to deal with it, this will likely result in a successful lawsuit against the surgeon. Thus, we stressed that all surgical complications are best addressed as early as possible so the patient's condition is not allowed to deteriorate. We taught that the successful surgeon will have the courage and confidence needed to present these facts to the patient. We repeatedly drove home this point during their residency. It has been said that without courage to act or recognize complications, there are no other qualities of consequence surgeons can have. I am reminded in that regard of the Napoleonic maxim:

"l'audace, l'audace,
toujours l'audace!"
(Audacity, audacity, always audacity!)

Applied to surgery, that admonition means to act audaciously and never let disease or complications get ahead of you.

Jack Nicklaus loved golf because, as he said, "No two shots are exactly alike." In the same way, no two operations are exactly alike. This is why it is very important that surgeons must be adaptable or flexible intellectually, and they must be able to think outside the box and confidently take action when the situation demands it. It is debatable if a mentor can teach adaptability and creativity in a young surgeon, but a mentor must try because it is from such thinking that future progress will come. Most great surgeons I have known had that quality of genius and creativity about them, which I often witnessed in my extensive sojourn through medicine. These qualities can be encouraged, and you can attempt to teach some by example, which works in some cases but not in others. It is now clear, whether under the influence of their training at Minnesota or for other innate gifts, many of our trainees did have or developed that quality of inventiveness and creativity in their work, and as a result, many of them helped transform the specialty of urologic surgery.

There is nothing more important than that a surgeon also has the determination to stand resolutely at the operating table until the operation is done carefully and completely. This story illustrates what I mean: In the late 1930s, the German ambassador to Great Britain came to see Winston Churchill, who had just been appointed First Lord of the Admiralty. The ambassador began by unrolling a series of maps and pointed to what Herr Hitler's plans were for those territories represented by the maps: Sudetenland, Poland, and so on. As he rolled up his maps, he asked Churchill what he thought. Churchill looked up and is alleged to have said, "Not much, Mr. Ambassador, but let me ask you a question. Do you know why the English bulldog's nose is slanted backward?" The ambassador, somewhat startled by the nature of the question, responded, "Why no, I do not." Churchill continued, "The English bulldog's nose is slanted backward so he can bite you in the ass, hold on, and at the same time, continue to breathe. Do you get my point?" As he was leaving, the ambassador said, "No, but I will tell Herr Hitler what you said!" Of course, Churchill was trying to convey metaphorically the nature of England's national character of long standing: that is, its dogged determination to resist aggression from any corner and remain free. Hitler should have listened.

We taught our residents to become "surgical bulldogs" so they could bite into a problem (operation), hold on, and stay with any case as long as necessary to obtain a perfect result. I believe to this day that mentors can teach that to young surgeons by example, because that is the way many of us learned that principle.

Robert Linton, MD, one of the world's leading vascular surgeons a half century ago, taught me the importance of persistence. Linton and I, in my days as an MGH resident, would spend almost all day reconstructing a patient's vascular tree only to have Linton step back, feel the distal pulses of the repair, and utter the comment, "That will never, ever do!" I watched with fascination as Linton proceeded to take down as much of his repairs as necessary from those he had just meticulously constructed, and then, he would plunge back into the redo until he was satisfied in the end that the repair was as good as he could make it. The cases in which I assisted Linton, some of the most difficult in the world, often would last ten to eighteen hours. I paid attention to and learned from the fact that Linton even stayed for the wound closure—something his resident could have done for him. He allowed me to do a closure under his supervision one day, and before I started I asked him, "Doctor Linton, do you want the sutures placed too close together or too far apart?" Linton did not think that was funny.

Linton was bald and slightly bent from loss of bone density due to chronic steroid therapy for his asthma. He operated while sitting upon a special contraption he had made. The device had a motorcycle seat joined to the bottom half of a supporting post upon which were mounted multiple wheels. The device allowed him to move around without leaving the seat. Residents fondly referred to Linton as "the Great Bald Eagle." He was an unforgettable character and a legendary surgeon who most saw as a living legend.

There is a Linton interchange I remember vividly. One morning at 2:00 a.m. Linton called me out of bed and requested that I meet him at a certain floor's nurse's station in the Baker Building. He had discovered while rounding late that I had placed a patient of his on SSKI (supersaturated potassium iodide solution), used to liquefy secretions in patients who suffered from a respiratory infection. Linton told me he was most unhappy because he thought the medicine had a terribly unpleasant taste. To cure me of ever ordering it again on one of his patients, he compelled me to take a dose as he watched. Linton was right; I never ordered SSKI again on anyone.

Our staff also emphasized the importance of compulsively checking every detail regarding surgical preparation, as well as every phase of the patient's postoperative course. General MacArthur and Sun Tzu both said, "Most battles are won in planning even before the fighting starts."

Everyone should remember, "Surgery, like aviation, is very unforgiving of incapacity, carelessness, or neglect," as per the image herein. That is why we strove to train every resident to the highest level of competence and compulsion possible. Once again, when surgeons work, lives are at stake.

Figure 16. A similar image hangs in small airports all across Minnesota.
With thanks to Jeanne and Scott Hollington

No great surgical training program will thrive if the staff are not competent surgeons. Most of us did several thousand cases in the course of our time in the program, and a resident worked with us on the majority of cases. There was no ghost surgery in our program. If a resident at the university were allowed to do a case, it was done under close supervision by faculty. At the VA Hospital, the residents had more autonomy, especially after they became chief resident.

By what I have described so far, I do not mean to minimize the importance of the surgeon's skillful "hands that heal." Our entire staff spent hundreds of thousands of hours over a quarter century making sure that each resident acquired the requisite manual skills to carry out most operations in our specialty. Therefore, our entire senior staff, all accomplished surgeons, spent a lot of time in the operating room while directing residents in training to "cut here, cut there, and so on." We worked to marry a proper "state of mind" to great manual skills to produce a well-trained young surgeon who is capable of caring for patients in a competent manner the day he or she leaves the training program.

No training of a surgeon is complete unless the teachers also emphasize the all-important "art of medicine," or what is euphemistically referred to as a good "bedside manner." We taught young surgeons how to be reassuring, gentle, and compassionate in their approach to patients, many of whom are terrified at the prospect of having surgery and naturally fearful of surgeons. We trained residents how to fully inform patients of potential complications of their surgery without scaring the patient unnecessarily. As surgeons ourselves, we knew that what you tell a patient and how you tell him or her depends on the physician's assessment of each patient. Some patients are interested in getting on with their treatment with little discussion, while others want a detailed review of what they are facing. But in all cases, we showed our residents that they needed to be very careful when talking to a patient about his or her surgery. A young surgeon, we reminded them, must learn early not to "talk a patient into surgery." If he or she does and something goes wrong, the surgeon faces a major problem—possibly a lawsuit.

The surgical mentor must prepare a young surgeon to deal with a serious complication or death from surgery. There is nothing as devastating to a surgeon as when surgery goes awry. And as everyone knows, patients sometimes die from a surgical procedure. When either a death or serious complication happens, the emotional pain felt by a surgeon cannot be eased except by the passage of time. It takes time for a surgeon to repair his or her psyche following an operative mortality, but surgeons need to realize that both deaths and complications will occur, no matter how skilled and careful they are, and they need to be able to adjust, pick themselves up, and not dwell on such developments to the extent that it interferes with the care of other patients. So here again, the importance of being confident of your abilities is so important because it sustains you at such times. Conceptually, it is like what the Red Cross lifesaving instructor taught me: never let a drowning, panic-stricken victim grab hold of you when you attempt a rescue because he or she will convert a single drowning into a double drowning that will include you.

Call it what you will; I call it "having an adequate self-protective defense mechanism" that will keep a surgeon functioning under very difficult emotional circumstances, such as after losing a patient. Some might characterize this quality, at least in part, as having strength of character and mastery over one's emotions. In fact, such phrases are mere words and do not begin to quantify the inner strength a surgeon must call on under such a circumstance. It is easier to endure this type of pain if the surgeon is confident that he or she did his or her best for the patient. And that is why we continuously pushed for solid training with high standards and close mentoring.

It is essential that all deaths and complications from surgery be thoroughly reviewed as part of a quality training program. We did this at a regular monthly death and complications conference. These conferences are unpleasant for the one who is responsible for a complication or death, but it is important that a leader ensure that the discussion and finger-pointing ends at the end of the conference and that the emotional interchanges do not linger ad infinitum. The purpose of any review at a death and complications conference is to analyze what went wrong and to develop strategies for preventing whatever happened from happening again. It is not a venue for personal or ad hominem vendettas. I heard rumors that ad hominem was often the byword of such conferences in general surgery, where the personnel from the Lillehei era was pitted against the Najarian-regime recruits. There was a lot of bitterness that did not die easily when C. Walton Lillehei did not become chairman to succeed Wangensteen, and the rancor often expressed itself over the years in one way or the other, including in outbursts in their complications conference.

I usually moderated our death and complications conferences and tried to keep the proceeding instructive rather than destructive, especially for the residents. I believed an individual learned as much or more from mistakes as from triumphs. I felt the mortality conferences at the MGH at the senior level were often too ad hominem. Fortunately, the advances in preoperative preparation, anesthesia, and intensive postoperative care for major surgeries has resulted in an incredible reduction in the number of untoward complications and deaths resulting from surgery. One specific example: radical cystectomy and urinary diversion for bladder cancer had a mortality rate approaching 10 percent when I began my residency in 1963. But today that same operation carries less than 1 percent mortality, which is indeed progress.

To summarize, we set a goal to create a demanding training experience that would produce a surgeon who, at a minimum, was knowledgeable, skillful, courageous, compulsive, and persistent. I do not iterate these qualities lightly and I realize it calls up a reminder to cynics of the Boy Scout pledge, but I know that patients hope these goals are taken seriously by everyone. We also wanted our surgeon house officers to be skilled in the "art of medicine" as well as the science of medicine—there is a big difference. In short, we wanted our residents to possess good character and a passion for their serious work.

We were fortunate as teachers because several of our trainees achieved the added dimension of academic success in our specialty as not only master surgeons but also innovators, scientists, and teachers who transformed our specialty. For me, as it is with all program directors, the ultimate reward came from seeing my residents become leaders in their own right. What is more important to me now is my firsthand knowledge that these young men are passing on the principles and attitudes they learned in Minnesota to their trainees. Together, my colleagues and I can only hope that the passion we helped ignite in our trainees will continue to be passed to others for generations to come.

> If you work with your hands, you are a laborer;
> If you work with your hands and your
> mind, you are a craftsman;
> But if you work with your hands, mind,
> and heart, you are an "artist".
> —Anonymous

Chapter 14

THE SURGICAL RESIDENT IN TRAINING

Do you know what it takes to perform a brain operation or any operation? Do you know the kind of skill it demands, and the years of passionate, merciless, excruciating devotion that go to acquire that skill? That was what I would not place at the disposal of men whose sole qualification to rule me was their capacity to spout the fraudulent generalities that got them elected to the privilege of enforcing their wishes at the point of a gun.[30]

Being a general or surgical specialty resident in training was a unique experience. Possibly no other civilian profession demands the prerequisites or long period of education and training that surgery or most surgical specialties required in times past.

Physicians entering a surgical training program either have sound character from the beginning or the experience should build such qualities in the process. A surgical resident spends long hours, with little financial reward, working under great stress, and he or she endures long separation from loved ones before completing training.

---

[30] Rand, Ayn. (1957) *Atlas Shrugged*. Centennial Edition, Kindle version. New York: Random house. Loc. 178

American surgeons have learned their craft in our country under these conditions since the beginning of formal training programs at the turn of the last century. As a result of the training structure, American surgeons have dominated the past century—the American century of surgery.

The process of training a urological surgeon goes on for more than a decade: college (four years), medical school (four years), internship (one year), and a residency (four to six years). The urologic surgeon who seeks additional specialization in urology beyond his or her formal residency, say in robotic-assisted surgery or urologic oncology or endourology, will complete an additional one- to two-year fellowship. The young man or woman considering whether to invest so much time must realize it is a major commitment that should not be entered into casually.

The old Johns Hopkins surgical residencies established in the early 1900s more or less set the standards for the training of our young surgeons for more than a century. In the Hopkins general surgery program, surgical interns were never off duty during the entire year and were forbidden, of course, to be married. Some argued that the Hopkins surgical internship mirrored the plebe year at West Point or worse.

William Halstead, the first academic general surgical chief at Hopkins, established the tradition of total immersion in learning the profession in 1899, and his model lasted to one degree or another for over a century. Apparently Halstead drew from the German system as a model for his own program. It was about this time that dominance in surgery passed from Europe to America. The Hopkins training required six or eight years after the internship. I know of no other profession in American history that made or makes the demands that Hopkins did on nascent surgeons, or that are still being made on the aspiring surgeon to this day in the first-rate training programs.

By the time I was a resident at the MGH, the training programs had "relaxed" the on-duty standards slightly. We were only required to be on duty every other night and every other weekend. Thus, we could see our families for a short time every few days. That may sound more reasonable, but we were so tired most of the time that any time off was not quality time, since we slept most of it away. On weekends our families would come to the hospital when we were on duty to share the noon meal because it was free.

Recently, many physician-training programs have been forced to reexamine the working conditions for young physicians, especially putative surgeons. Various regulators and oversight types have pushed to reduce the hours a resident in training will be *allowed* to be on duty. I wrote the following editorial on the subject of duty hours in response to such suggested changes in the structure of surgical training in particular:

THE TRAINING OF A SURGEON: WHEN IS ENOUGH, ENOUGH?

I was surprised to learn that resident trainees in a surgical specialty (urology) in some European countries are now only allowed to work thirty-some hours a week. That suggests to me such residents will not be properly trained at the end of their residencies, especially when compared to their American colleagues who spend many more hours in surgical training programs of all stripes.

William Halsted established the first formal American residency programs for general surgery in the early part of the last century at Johns Hopkins. The Hopkins residency demanded a level of commitment and dedication among the allegedly celibate trainees that is difficult to comprehend in today's world of declining standards. For example, interns who also were paid poorly were on call twenty-four hours, seven days a week, which left no time for marriage. Becoming a Hopkins surgical resident back then was akin to entering the seminary to become a priest. It was not unusual in those days for a Hopkins resident, after completing the internship, to work at least forty-eight hours without rest several times per month for the remaining five years or more of his training. These trainees often worked well over one hundred hours per week.

The Hopkins surgery program changed very little for more than half a century or until the early 1960s, just before I applied for a surgical internship at Hopkins. By that time Hopkins had only shortly before changed the on-call schedule for interns in surgery from every day and night 24/7 to an every other day and night, which was similar to the on-call schedule for interns and junior residents at the Massachusetts General Hospital (MGH), where I had my surgical internship and residency. During my Hopkins interviews, both staff interviewers gave me the impression that they were "old school" and had opposed the change in the work requirements for interns.

Rigorous university-affiliated surgical training programs like those of Hopkins and the MGH produced almost all the great surgeons of the last century, who in turn developed, among other fields, those of cardiovascular surgery and organ transplantation and, in urology, the field of endourology. The last century was truly the "American Century" in surgery.

Eventually I was appointed chairman of urologic surgery at the University of Minnesota, where I established an

MGH-like training program, with a demanding workload and similar type of on-call schedules. However, after the first few years, there was increasing agitation among the residents and their spouses for less in the hospital night call. Gradually we eased up on the work requirements, especially night calls, with the cooperation of residents, and we thus established more humane work requirements.

Then, after having been chairman for several years, the dean informed me that our residents were working too many hours—actually, according to the dean's records, our residents were clocked at 111 hours per week. Frankly, I was quite pleased because it suggested that the residents were still, even with less night calls, at least putting in enough hours to become well trained. And I found out that the only residents working more hours were neurosurgeons, at 112 hours per week. I told the dean, much to his consternation; we would never finish second again! My thought at the time was he was having enough problems being dean and therefore he should leave the training of urologic surgeons to me. I did not foresee the clouds gathering on the horizon regarding our being forced to circumscribe the work hours of their training programs.

Around the same time of my dean's meeting, the press in the East began to run stories about "overworked" house officers and the errors they made because of sleep deprivation, and so the bureaucrats were off to the races with, like Lancelot, new wrongs to right. Actually I think the precipitating incident that may have led to a reexamination of hours worked by residents occurred in New York City, where a famous person died following uncomplicated gall bladder surgery allegedly due to a house officer's medication error or lack of attention by a nurse. Soon thereafter, individuals at various levels began to enter the debate about house officer working conditions. For example, Dr. Richard Corlin, president of the American Medical Association, called for reevaluation of the training process, declaring, "We need to take a look again at the issue of why is the resident there." Also, the Accreditation Council for Graduate Medical Education (ACGME) got into the act and recommended limiting the number of work hours to eighty hours weekly, overnight call frequency to no more than one overnight every third day, thirty-hour maximum straight shift, and ten hours off between shifts. While these limits were voluntary initially, now adherence has been mandated for the purposes of accreditation. The bureaucrats strike again. In my opinion, once this process has started it will, if we are not careful, lead to progressively more interference and lowering of standards, especially in the training of surgeons, and there appears to be in some of these recommendations an underlying assumption of a "one size fits all" approach to training residents in disciplines that are far different one from the other.

The training of a surgeon or surgical specialist is a complex and time-consuming process, and the training requirements are far different than those for training a radiologist, pathologist, or pediatrician among others. First, most laypersons would be surprised to learn that training a surgeon involves their mentors teaching them a proper "surgical mind-set" by building up their confidence that surgery can usually be successful and by nurturing those qualities of character found in great surgeons—such as dedication, persistence, attention to detail, and last but not least, courage. Not even God makes caterpillars into butterflies overnight, and developing all the skills of both mind and hands that a surgeon needs to acquire indeed takes time. I have always contended therefore that "surgery" is as much a "state of mind" as it is having the requisite manual skills to perform the hands on cutting and sewing.

In his classic book *Outliers*, Malcolm Gladwell reported on the studies on genius that showed for an individual to attain world-class proficiency in a given field requires consistently approximately ten thousand hours of practice; that practice requirement seems to hold across many fields, from music to athletics. Accordingly, I made a best-effort estimate as to how many hours a surgical resident or surgical specialty resident would have "practiced" in six years of internship and residency working in a program requiring at least one-hundred-hour workweeks, and I came up with a figure of between 9,600 hours and 12,000 hours a trainee would have "practiced" during that six years of training. This suggests that the ten-thousand-hour practice requirement may also even apply to minting a new surgeon.

There is no shortcut to excellence in surgery or any other field of medicine; greatness under most circumstances is characterized by one word, and that is, as Lou Holtz preached, sacrifice. That sentiment is nicely summarized in a passage in Colleen McCullough's novel *The Thorn Birds*:

> There's a story ... a legend, about a bird that sings just once in its life. From the moment it leaves its nest, it searches for a thorn tree ... and never rests until it's found one. And then it sings ... more sweetly than any other creature

on the face of the earth. And singing, it impales
itself on the longest, sharpest thorn. But, as it
dies, it rises above its own agony, to out sing the
lark and the nightingale. The thorn bird pays
its life for just one song, but the whole world
stills to listen, and God in his heaven smiles.[31]

I do not know precisely how many hours an average surgical resident
should work during his or her training, but if I were that resident's
future patient, I would prefer he or she had "practiced" a few too many
hours rather than too few. We must be very cautious about "dumbing
down" our training methods that have served us so well in this
country for so long, lest we risk the chance that we will be producing
surgeons not properly qualified to care for patients. America is an
exceptional country in part because of its exceptional medicine. The
standards for American medicine will continue to be set in the great
academic training centers and by principled program directors who
insist on doing it right. The proper training of a surgeon takes time.
I doubt we will ever know with certainty when enough is enough.

In summary, then, becoming a surgeon involves ten to fifteen years of
education and demanding training. But more to the point, it is a life
that requires the surgeon to always keep on becoming more educated
just to stay current for the rest of his or her practice life. Today's
surgeons will not only have to pass their initial board-certification
exam, but will be required to be recertified by taking professional
reassessment exams periodically as long as they continue to practice.
Therefore, it is the task of every quality surgical training program to
train residents (or house officers, as they were called at the MGH) to
become not only technically competent and educated in the present,
but also to be scholars with a commitment to learning and relearning
during their practicing lifetime.

---

[31] McCullough, Colleen, *The Thorn Birds, Harper & Row New York, 1977*

Modern medicine changes rapidly, and physicians must keep abreast to serve their patients competently and ethically. For example, urology has changed greatly just in the last twenty-five years in that, among other developments, we have seen progress in significantly reducing the morbidity and mortality of urological surgery because of advances in minimally invasive surgery. This occurred in great part as we incorporated the new minimally invasive techniques of endourology and robotics, and meticulous preoperative preparation in the treatments we devised for patients. Thus, we have evolved to the near-ideal state of being able to do minimally invasive or keyhole surgery in many patients for a variety of diseases treated previously only by open, invasive surgery. This progress has not only improved patient care and comfort, but also reduced the cost of medical care because of the shortened hospital stays.

Finally, the methods of training a surgeon are changing rapidly. Professor Rob Sweet at the department of urology at the University of Minnesota, and others, have developed models of human anatomy that allow a resident to practice certain simulated surgeries in the models developed by Sweet and his colleagues. These models help train surgeons in the techniques of the new approaches to minimally invasive surgery. Consequently, the department at Minnesota has developed a large simulation center for training urologic surgeons. How effective this approach to teaching some types of surgery will be is yet to be determined, but my guess is that it will be quite effective. It also may be of use for retraining older surgeons or surgeons from less-developed countries.

(By the way, I know of only one book on the subject of how one becomes a surgeon: *The Making of a Surgeon* by William Nolan, MD, who, incidentally, was a general surgeon from Litchfield, Minnesota, and a gifted writer and physician.)[32]

---

[32] Nolan, William A. MD, *The Making of a Surgeon*: Random House, New York, 1970

Chapter 15

ADVICE TO PATIENTS FACING SURGERY

Figure 17. "You are lucky if they can operate." —Francis D. Moore, MD, Former Chief of Surgery, Brigham and Harvard.
With thanks to Francis D. Moore, Jr., MD

I hope this section contains information that is useful to all potential patients. It is better to know what surgery is all about before one finds oneself sedated on a gurney half-naked in only a surgical gown awaiting surgery.

There was a cover story in *Time* magazine (May 3, 1963) with a photograph of Francis D. Moore, MD, the famous Harvard Medical School surgeon, which had a subtitle of the important message— *"you are lucky if they can operate."* I had such fond memories of Professor Moore, and also, the magazine with that cover was issued on my birthday back when.

I was a fourth-year medical student when I was summoned to Professor Moore's office because he wanted to know why I had not applied for a surgical internship to the Peter Bent Brigham, where he was chief of surgery. I sat on a couch, with a coffee table in front, in his office. A formal tea service and some cucumber tea sandwiches were on the table, but I was not interested in high tea. He gave me a pitch for the Brigham by comparing it with the MGH where he trained; he said the MGH was like a big battleship lumbering slowly through the water, while the Brigham was more like a destroyer knifing through the water at high speed, and he as much as told me an internship with him at the Brigham was mine for the asking. Of course I was more than flattered that he even knew who I was. However, my goal for my training was the MGH, which he apparently already knew, and he failed to convince me otherwise.

This little story illustrates that all the Harvard hospitals were interested in getting the potentially best residents, as they perceived it, in each HMS class, so some students were competed for by the service chiefs of each institution. For one thing, after four years, they had a good idea of who we were and what our abilities and shortcomings were. Someone from another medical school was more of an unknown, even though most of them had outstanding records if they were candidates for a Boston internship in any of the Harvard teaching hospitals.

In the end, I demurred to apply to the Brigham as politely as possible, but the pleasant memory of the meeting with Professor

Moore lingers. As students, most of us were in awe of Professor Moore, and of course few of us ever had a one-on-one with the great man. Professor Moore became famous early in his career as a result of the treatments he devised for burns while still a resident in surgery at the MGH. One of the great tragedies of that time was the 1942 Coconut Grove Nightclub Fire in Boston, which killed over four hundred people; many more were severely burned, most of whom ended up as patients at the MGH. Hospitals had geared up to meet large-scale disasters during World War II. Not much was known in those days about how to treat severe burns, but Moore and his colleagues developed strategies, especially with regard to the burn patient's fluid and electrolyte balances, that saved many lives. Moore parlayed that experience into several articles and textbooks and the professorship at the Brigham. Also, I liked his statement in the *Time* article, "You are lucky if they can operate." Patients should keep that in mind.

First of all, if this book accomplishes anything, patients facing surgery should be comforted in knowing the stringency and care with which surgeons are trained. But if a patient wants to do further due diligence regarding his or her choice of a surgeon, here are some suggestions.

To begin with, patients should not be intimidated by any medical practitioner. If a surgeon is haughty, condescending, or dismissive in answering your reasonable questions, find another surgeon or physician. Your life is on the line, not the surgeon's. That type of behavior by physicians may have been acceptable in the past, but not today. I remember the days when it was not unusual for overwrought surgeons to throw instruments against the wall and curse out everyone in the OR when something went wrong in a difficult case. The only thing such behavior accomplished was to turn the entire OR personnel against the surgeon, and thus it potentially harmed the patient.

Next, if the surgeon practices in an academic center, one of the best evaluation methods comes from talking with the residents in training and the operating room nurses. In an academic center, the eyes of medical students and residents are always watching the surgeon to determine how he deals with patients and the level of his surgical skills. There is usually some way for a patient, with effort, to get to these ancillary people for an opinion. Probably the second-best evaluation will come from other practicing physicians familiar with a given surgeon's work and his reputation.

Third, you can check with local and state medical (surgical) societies to determine the surgeon's history of complaints or lawsuits against him or her—if any. Your local medical society can point you to the national physicians' data bank, which retains similar information. Furthermore, you have a perfect right to ask a surgeon if he or she has ever been sued or is facing any pending lawsuits.

Ask the surgeon for a copy of his or her curriculum vitae and bibliography (sometimes available on the Internet). With this, you can judge the quality of his or her training and the extent of his or her contributions to medicine.

Perhaps the most important question you can ask the surgeon is exactly how many of the particular surgeries you need has the surgeon performed. This is particularly important if the surgery is truly a difficult or unusual procedure, with which most surgeons may have limited experience. In advanced or difficult cases, you need a world-recognized expert with good experience. Usually a true expert with experience can be found with enough digging. Many such surgeons will have published research on the rare cases they have treated that can be obtained through a medical library.

Finally, it sometimes useful to have at least two opinions about your case, especially if the case is something outside the ordinary. If you ask a surgeon for a recommendation for a second opinion and that surgeon gets upset, thereby suggesting you are being contumacious rather than just careful, leave skid marks on the floor getting to a new surgeon. Accomplished, secure surgeons have no problem with patients obtaining a second opinion, especially in unusual or difficult cases. I kept a list readily available of surgeons I recommended to patients who asked for second opinions. If you seek a second opinion, be wary of the surgeon who makes you feel as if he or she is recruiting you away from the first surgeon; doing so is against the ethical cannons of surgery.

Chapter 16

CREATING AN INCUBATOR FOR YOUNG ACADEMIC SURGEONS

It is important to plan carefully before you set off toward any goal. In that regard, there is the story from World War II when a pilot radioed back to his home base: "I am lost, but I am making record time." As mentioned previously, I had been formulating my plans to build a high-quality academic urology department for several years prior to going to Minnesota, especially during my training and post-training period. The "incubator for academic surgeons" was an extra dimension of our program. It is essential to train young surgeons clinically first and then provide those who are interested in an academic career a sheltered environment in which to develop a research program and publish, from which they could build their academic reputation as a surgeon-scientist.

Producing a professor was a four-step process: start with good men or women, motivate them, train them surgically, and then provide a nourishing protected junior faculty slot for their academic development. The care and feeding of a surgical academician is a demanding and expensive undertaking. I believed this should be done in the clinics or in the laboratory, or in rare instances, in an equivalent environment outside our department. I always knew if the young academicians had grants awaiting at the end of their academic development, other teaching centers would see them as more attractive candidates; they would bring with them their own money or the potential of having the same. But I also knew that when they arrived at their new department, they would need to be superb surgeons who could attract patients and, thus, have financial resources for their departments. We were particularly blessed with having quality staff surgeons, and as time went on and many of our well-trained residents joined our staff as a first step in their pursuit of an academic career, these staff surgeons served as mentors to the residents. All the faculty, including myself, spent thousands of hours in the operating room with the residents teaching them the manual skills required of a urological surgeon. There are few pleasures in life greater than watching the development and professional growth of a young surgeon; in a sense, that was our immortality.

I employed that binary type of training and development in our department, and it helped make many of our trainees the best, and they were that—a fact not now in dispute. These brilliant young men and women in many instances became prototypical young surgeons—scientists and innovators, as well as trainers of young men and women in our specialty. I still feel it was such a privilege to play some small role in their lives.

A funny thing happened when the program was in its full bloom and these young people were becoming recognized for what they were. A cynic from another program harrumphed, "Those guys were so good they could have done what they did anywhere. The Minnesota program is nothing special." When I heard that comment, it greatly upset me. In fact, I was mad as hell—like Krakatau erupting— because I knew the individual who had made that crack and I can assure the reader his main concern was never leaving footprints in the sands of time. Put another way, his bandwidth was quite narrow. But upon reflection, his comment, for once, was spot-on. Our young people were, in fact, so good they probably would have done what they did anywhere. But the fact is they did what they did as products of Minnesota—over and over and over again. There is nothing as pointless as what-if history. What might have happened elsewhere was not even sufficient justification for a history term paper, any more than projecting jobs saved is a legitimate economics thesis.

We needed to find a predictable and satisfactory funding source so the future academicians could be supported financially during their development. Many of them had families and sacrificed income by eschewing the rewards of private practice after finishing their residencies. I had enjoyed that type of developmental environment at the NIH, but not everyone could go to the NIH.

By the way, at the time I went to the NIH, I was afforded a barely livable annual salary of $12,000, but there was no similar opportunity in any urology department in the entire United States at the time (mid-1960s). To prove that point, as I approached the end of my second year at the NIH and was thinking of leaving, I wrote to approximately one hundred different urology departments or divisions seeking a position in which I could develop academically. I had no intention of seeking a chairmanship at thirty-two years of age, but rather thought a junior faculty slot would be a good starting point in academic urology/medicine. Much to my dismay, only three chairmen even bothered answering my letters: Hartwell Harrison at Harvard and the Brigham, Jim Glenn at Duke, and Willard Goodwin, chairman at UCLA (all of these men are gone now). In essence, they all allowed that they had no such position and did not know even where I should look. Think about it: only three out of one hundred or so urology chairmen even answered my letter, even though it gave them a chance to recruit someone with Leadbetter clinical training and an NIH laboratory experience and a fairly extensive bibliography. Such was the primitive state of academic urology in the mid-1960s.

As a result of experience and planning, we created a program with proper developmental positions for academically oriented urologic surgeons as a way of strengthening the specialty through the minting of future leaders. I also knew I needed to find sustainable financial support for the developing academician so that such aspirants would be in a position to become candidates for departmental chairmanships at the end of their development. Departments that did not create similar opportunities and environments and were unwilling to "pay the tab" never produced anyone, despite the fact that they had far more in the way of resources than Minnesota did. By my calculations, rough as they may be, each professor we produced in those days cost the department a net six-figure amount; that money in large part came from our clinical practices. Of course, some academic trainees also contributed mightily to their own support by virtue of the limited clinical work they did as faculty. Again, this testifies to the importance of patients. I cannot overemphasize this point: without the clinical patient-care monies we all earned, we would not have been able to support the development of the young staff to the extent we did.

There was no source of money in urology or surgery designated to provide financial support for young surgeons who wanted to spend time postresidency developing a laboratory program.

Because of my interest in nurturing young academic surgeon-scientists, I conceived of an American Urological Association (AUA) scholarship to be used to fund budding young academicians postresidency. I sent that idea with a suggested structure for such a program to Walter Kerr (MGH staff urologist and later president of the AUA), whom I had known in a staff-resident relationship when in training. Incidentally, during my MGH residency, Walter would show up at our house periodically with a station wagon full of food for our family. Those were, in fact, the days in every sense. Walter and others in Boston got behind the AUA scholarship program, as did

Professor Ruben Flocks in Iowa. All of the supporters, known and unknown, deserve credit for starting the AUA scholarship program.

The AUA scholarship eventually came to be, but not without a lot of *sturm and drang* and lobbying and arm-twisting. At the time, the only previous financial contributions from the AUA back to academic urology were a few onetime research grants of $5,000 or less. People with little or no laboratory training were deciding who should receive these grants. Actually, in all fairness, the AUA eventually helped us buy our first tissue culture laminar flow hood for our new Stone Building laboratory with one such grant, so they had my gratitude for that.

As it turned out, many of our trainees benefited from an AUA scholarship as they began their academic careers—usually when they were developing a laboratory program. Our department had at least seven AUA scholarships that helped jump-start the careers of our aspiring academicians. Many of these trainees remained in our department while being supported by the AUA scholarship, while others went elsewhere. Irrespective of where they were working, our department supplemented their scholarships from our departmental clinical funds.

The AUA scholarship concept has been expanded by the AUA, and additional scholarship funds are now available, essentially for the same purpose but under different named grants, such as the Leadbetter Scholarship. But what we did broke the logjam for getting organized urology into raising money to foster academic development of young people in the specialty. Convincing organized urology to agree that its members needed to give something back was an important contribution that received its impetus from Minnesota.

The American Urological Association was an interesting organization in 1969. The hierarchy was made up primarily of private practitioners, and it is not an exaggeration to state that their primary focus was to communicate information at the national meeting that practitioners could use to increase their incomes. The meetings were, among other things, fun to attend because they were a tax write-off and they were always held in a nice or exciting place. One of the most important events was the afternoon golf tournament. When Wyland and Ruben Flocks introduced the idea of having an afternoon devoted to research—an official Research Forum—it took several years to get accepted, but it was allowed initially only if it were held on the afternoon of the golf tournament. The AUA oligarchs reasoned that the forum would be harmless if it were held on the golf day because they believed that no one would attend if it were in competition with golf. Such was the state of Denmark in those days.

Incidentally, I started the same trend of giving back to the specialty with American Cystoscope Makers, Inc. (ACMI) and the Wappners, who owned the company. In the early 1970s, ACMI had a monopoly on the manufacture and sale of urological instrumentation in this country for many years. I met with Reinhold Wappner in Minnesota early in my chairmanship and gently excoriated him about the fact that his family had a virtual monopoly in our specialty but they were investing very little into R & D. I told him directly they also weren't doing anything to strengthen the specialty that served as the very wellspring of their success and wealth. I warned Wappner that real competition would arise someday soon and that it would succeed because of their lack of R & D. I may not be Nostradamus or Jeanne Dixon, but I saw that coming, and did it ever come, particularly from the German and Japanese instrument makers.

So the plan for the department was to recruit good people, marshal resources of all types, and create an academic environment that included basic science laboratories in which young academicians could flourish. Having our own medical editor was an important adjunct to the plan. I went into the ranks of the interns or residents in surgery and plucked out a few good men, like Ralph Clayman, Dick Williams, Ricardo Gonzalez, and Curt Sheldon. I recruited other winners, like Bill DeWolf and Paul Lange, from outside surgical programs. Arthur Smith and Keith Kaye came from South Africa, and Ami Sidi came from Israel.

Arthur Smith was an interesting story. One late fall afternoon I was in my office when Arthur showed up unannounced seeking a position so he could emigrate from South Africa. The race problems in South Africa were reaching a critical point, and whites were fleeing the turmoil the best way they could. Many countries, including feckless, Labour-government Great Britain, said they would not allow white South Africans to emigrate under any circumstances. Because Arthur showed up unannounced, had a certain look of desperation about him, and was not exactly dressed for Minnesota's cold, I had the sense he was an anachronistic figure. He had been to almost every training program in the country trying to find a job. His last stop had been in a program south of us—not Mayo. I asked him to excuse himself while I talked with the program director he had just visited. The conversation was short because I was told, "Christ almighty, that guy has been to every program in the country trying to get a job; I am not interested." I thought about it for a minute after I hung up and concluded that Art must be extremely motivated to go to such an effort, so I offered him a post, the details to be worked out when he arrived. I had no idea at the time how I was going to provide for the Smiths, but I was determined to help anyone who I thought at the time might be massacred if they stayed in their own country. I therefore was determined to help relocate as many physicians as possible from south of the equator in Africa. Art turned out to be a major find, and he subsequently played a major role in the development of endourology, for which he recently received one of the highest awards in urology from the AUA. In addition, his family—now Americans—all adjusted well and have become major contributors to our country.

I also talked the medical school into letting me use the training grant faculty salary to recruit Tom Hakala, whom I subsequently sent to the NIH for two years to train in the laboratory with Don Morton. That move is an interesting story in itself.

The dean thought Tom was in Minnesota because I never told him otherwise, but for the better part of two years, Tom was actually at the NIH. Occasionally the dean would ask to meet him. I kept the dodge-and-weave up until Tom arrived back in town; by that time the dean had moved on to other problems. I always operated on the basis that it was easier to get forgiveness than permission. At one point, while Tom was at the NIH, I had to go to the student health service to have a required annual chest X-ray and physical as Tom Hakala. The people in the health service seemed to have forgotten I was there a week or so before as Hakala when I went for my own staff physical. Fortunately I did not encounter the same examining physician.

I wanted Tom Hakala because I knew, if given a chance, he would become a major asset to the specialty and our department, and here is how it came to be. Tom is an immensely talented surgeon and one of the brightest people I ever met. I knew Tom from our days at Harvard Medical School, and we were fellow interns in surgery at the MGH. Tom practiced in Sacramento at the University of California at the time I came to Minnesota, and he was in a semi-academic position, where he did a variety of things, including kidney transplants. I flew to Sacramento to see Tom and told him I had a written plan to present to him that would be a blueprint for his academic development. When I first arrived, Tom, ever the shrewd character, having already figured out what was up, went to great lengths at the outset to state why he would never leave Sacramento. He said clearly, "You are wasting your time." Tom loved the Sierra Madre Mountains and that area of California, as did his wife. I let him finish, and sitting in the front seat of his car with the mountains in the distance, I presented the argument as to why he should come to Minnesota, where I would help him become a chairman. "How long would that take?" Tom asked. "Five years," I said. We finally came to an agreement later over a handshake, as Tom indicated in his contribution to *The History of Urology at the University of Minnesota* by Robert W. Geist, MD.

As it turned out, Tom received his job offer as chairman from Pittsburgh University Medical Center almost precisely five years after coming to Minnesota. Nostradamus I am not, but that estimate that it would take five years for him to become a chairman was not a bad estimate. Tom spent two productive years studying and practicing at the NIH, and he received that all-important protected laboratory experience learning tumor immunology under Don Morton. While he was at the NIH, we worked to get a tumor immunology lab set up at Minnesota with the help of the Minneapolis VA Hospital. When Tom returned to Minnesota, he had a nearly functioning tumor immunology lab waiting for him.

In addition to people, we needed financial resources, and I knew early on the university would not help us to the extent we needed. The university's major financial contribution came as initial seed money of approximately $200,000, which I used to remodel and partially equip the laboratories in Diehl Hall. Most of that money for our department had come directly out of funds other departments generated from their clinical practice. This was part of the tradition of how monies generated from private practice were used to develop and sustain the medical school at the university. A mistake I made was that I did not exert much effort trying to ask donors for money. My upbringing placed emphasis on being independent and never asking for or taking money from strangers—and that advice included government.

To recruit patients, I developed what became known as "outreach." This involved flying all over Minnesota and neighboring states to give talks to groups, sometimes as small as two or three physicians, and over time, referrals began to come. I could write a novella about those trips, often made at night and in bad weather. Not only did we have some near-catastrophes in the plane, but the reception we received was, on occasion, less than friendly. The arrogance of much of the university staff over the years had taken its toll with referring physicians in the five-state area. I remember one such talk where I discovered that the group wanted to have a business meeting before I talked, and in addition, they had no slide projector. I insisted on giving my talk then and there so we could get back to Minneapolis— several hundred miles away. While I was talking, they just passed the slides around and held them up to a light—that is when they were not coughing from cigar smoke. Some of the other departments, like pediatrics (Al Michael) and pediatric surgery (Arnie Leonard), came with me on some of those trips, and that helped to promote the entire university clinical effort. Taking the university out to the practicing physician was a novel concept among most of the university medical faculty in those days.

Over 60 percent of the monies earned clinically during the first few years were poured back into the laboratory and the department. To give the reader an idea of academic costs, we had seven or eight typewritten pages of our contributions to an AUA meeting in Boston. The total cost of that effort to the department for per diems, rooms, airfare, and slide and exhibit preparation costs was over thirty thousand dollars—that is a lot of prostates. And that is why university administration established the practice plan inside the medical school in the first place—to make that possible.

We finished the remodeling of our 1,200-square-foot lab in Diehl F-130 with the seed money provided by the university, and I began to recruit scientists for the labs; these scientists initially were salaried, as usual, with clinical monies. At one time, we had six PhDs working for us in the laboratory, not the least of whom was Art Elliott, a remarkable young scientist at the time who went on from Minnesota to head up the Merck & Co. vaccine production effort.

Some grants followed, but we built the lab in the early days with patient-generated funds, as well as some funding from the VA and the AUA. We worked with the Minneapolis VA Hospital to establish the tumor immunology laboratory, where the likes of Tom Hakala and Paul Lange developed their academic careers and honed their clinical skills prior to becoming chairmen. The VA turned out to be exactly what I predicted, an NIH-like resource for the university urology department.

After completing the Diehl Hall laboratory expansion, we renovated the abandoned Stone Building, which sat a few miles down University Avenue from university hospitals, but close enough to be functional. We added over two thousand square feet to our laboratories with the rehabilitation of the Stone Building as that space came on line. We did most of the tissue culture work in the Stone lab and also had a mouse farm in that facility. Bringing that old building on line as a laboratory was a major undertaking.

I came to Minnesota as head of the division of urology, which was part of the department of general surgery. All the other surgical specialties had become departments after Najarian succeeded Wangensteen as chief of general surgery or before. The medical school kept urology as a division so Najarian could control the appointment of the new division head. Of course, Najarian had more than one motive to hand pick a new chief of urology. For example, he probably wanted, among other priorities, to have someone in urology that would support his transplant program while sticking to transurethral resections (TURP) or partial removals of the prostate. I doubt he was interested in hiring a surgical competitor.

Nonetheless, I negotiated my appointment agreement so that departmental status was to follow thereafter, which meant Najarian, and not the dean, would make or at least recommend the appointment as head of the division of urology. Najarian losing control over urology was no great loss for him at that time based on the condition of the division documented herein. In fact, it was a plus, given the problems urology had. I did not find it surprising that John made good on his promise to let urology become a department as soon as I requested departmental status. As a man of his word, Najarian allowed the change in status of urology from division to department irrespective of what his early motives may have been. With departmental status I could negotiate my budget and other issues directly with the dean.

I requested that the division of urology become a department within a year after taking the job, and also that it be renamed the department of urologic surgery. What I failed to realize was that, although departmental status was guaranteed before I came, there was no guarantee that I would be appointed as chairman after the university changed the status of the division to a department. That change in status introduced a whole new set of potential administrative steps that could have led to a search for a new chairman. My appointment required a separate action by the medical school's administrative board to make me the chairman of a new department. Another mistake: I never should have left myself vulnerable on that issue. I should have insisted that such a move be made prior to accepting the position in the first place. But in all fairness I was not aware of such bureaucracies within a medical enterprise; my focus was patients and resident training.

Jack Shirra took care of the administrative minutiae of my appointment as chairman. At the time, Shirra served as chief of obstetrics and gynecology. He had the administrative board rigged so that once we were officially a department, he immediately moved to make me chairman, and he had the votes committed to get the resolution adopted. It was over in less than a minute. He was masterful.

The OB-GYN department had other strengths. I have only known two gynecologists who could operate well: one was John "Red" Lewis, chief of gynecologic surgery at Sloan Kettering, and the other was Konald "Konnie" Prem at Minnesota (I called Konnie "the general" because he served as a brigadier general in the US Army reserves). Konnie was a superb surgeon in the female pelvis. Prem succeeded Jack Shirra as chairman after Jack left. Konnie Prem became a great colleague throughout the years, mainly because he was an honest man, as well as a competent surgeon.

The new urologic surgery department (my choice for a name) needed to establish a laboratory program with scientific credibility as part of the environment in which to attract and develop academicians. As it turned out, many future chairmen and leaders passed through our laboratories. The actual program for developing young academicians began at the NIH, where Dave Paulson worked with me for three years, and then in the Minnesota labs, where Paul Lange, Tom Hakala, and several others spent considerable time. Some putative professors from our department found homes, with or without our support, in labs as disparate as Boston (DeWolf and Narayan), Dallas (Clayman), and San Francisco (Dick Williams). Williams worked independently of us from the time he went on the academic staff of the University of California in San Francisco.

We established the labs to provide a developmental environment for academicians, to create and build our extensive human tumor and serum banks, and to establish cell lines in tissue culture derived from urological cancers that were used for research all over the country. The cell lines derived from our urological neoplasms, except for renal cancer, were not otherwise available. Our human tumor and serum bank became very important when tumor markers came into clinical use, and our culture bank helped to foster cooperative research with the NIH and others; it also facilitated proving the clinical utility of the markers, especially of the testis cancer tumor markers and, later, PSA (prostate-specific antigen).

The academic program we built was like a stool with four legs: people, space and equipment, funding, and a highly competent medical editor to help with publications. I tried several people as editors until I found the magnificent Judy Bronson. My memory is a little hazy as to precisely how Judy came to us, but she did and Judy was incredible.

With Judy's help, at one point we produced more than one hundred peer-reviewed publications of various stripes per year. I believe we had one of the three or four most published departments in the country for over twenty years. In addition, Judy helped with grant submissions, newsletters, or anything else that required writing and editing. We were very fortunate to have Judy's assistance. She helped many young men and women to achieve their academic positions in urologic surgery. Ours was one of the few surgical specialty departments, or even general surgery departments, in the world to have our own medical editor.

Figure 18. Our fabulous medical editor, Judith Gunn Bronson, MS, FSTC.
With thanks to Judith Gunn Bronson

CHAPTER 17

Evolution of the Department

"He set another parable before them, saying, 'The Kingdom of Heaven is like a grain of mustard seed, which a man took, and sowed in his field; which indeed is smaller than all seeds. But when it is grown, it is greater than the herbs, and becomes a tree, so that the birds of the air come and lodge in its branches.'"

—Matthew 13:31–32, *World English Bible*

One of the first major problems that had to be dealt with was the program on surgical sex reassignment that existed in the division. I knew nothing about this so-called "sex change" surgery, but I did not like the concept. The Minnesota program was a joint effort between psychiatry and Colin Markland in urology. Rather than stopping the surgery by decree, I asked the essential question that should be asked about any surgical procedure: "Does this surgery benefit the patient?"

To make a long story short, our group and the other main university program, at Johns Hopkins, could not demonstrate to my satisfaction that there was any long-term benefit from sex or gender reassignment surgery in these epicene patients. We went through an extensive review of all the operated patient follow-up records before we reached this conclusion. In summary, there was little evidence that the surgery led to a more stable, well-adjusted life for the bulk of these patients. In addition, the follow-up records of the transsexual patients showed that they caused an unusual amount of management problems related to proper follow-up protocols and requests for pain medicine prescriptions. In short, many of them had their surgery and then simply disappeared and never contacted us again, so the results of surgery could not be evaluated. This was a time when physicians were becoming even more aware of malpractice actions, and frankly, I feared that caring for such patients carried an increased liability risk, but that was not the principal reason for stopping the program.

Eventually after all the facts were considered, I stopped the surgery, and not long thereafter, Johns Hopkins also stopped their similar program. Hopkins had conducted an independent review and also failed to show that the surgery was beneficial. The last time I checked, many health insurance plans have been mandated that they must cover the cost of gender reassignment.

I do not want to get too deep in these weeds in this area, but I learned recently that there are centers that have gender reassignment programs for children. Interested readers should research the subject and come to their own conclusions.

So, we set out to build a world-class urology residency program. Our program matured in roughly five-year increments. The first five years or so saw the laboratories established and expanded, and the residents recruited who, after they were trained, would be candidates to join our faculty. Some of our residents whom we saw as headed for academic stardom were primarily in developmental positions for the first few years, and thus were active clinically only part-time.

Anyone who thinks he or she can have a first-rate surgical training program without a sufficient number of patients is mistaken. The core of the greatness of the MGH surgical and urology training programs was the variety and number of patients that benefited the training of residents. Having enough patients in Minnesota sixty-six miles up the road from Mayo and sixty-six feet down the hall from big John Najarian, who had a fondness for kidneys, was always one of my concerns, but we managed, in large measure because of the patients we attracted, the quality of our staff, and the innovative new treatment programs our faculty devised. Najarian was a powerful force in the school, so I had sense enough not to confront him on issues concerning which I knew in advance I could not win. In a word, in the beginning I chose carefully the hills on which I wanted to die.

Although we had an active laboratory program, we were also productive clinically. For example, the department pioneered the development of the field of endourology, and I gave the name endourology (the first iteration was endo-urology) to the field. The term *endourology* was invented to describe the various closed, controlled procedures we developed for treating diseases of the kidneys, ureters, and bladder using minimally invasive techniques. In order to evolve treatments for various urological diseases without open surgery, as had been the custom in the past, we also contributed to the design of a vast array of new instruments and devices for use by the endourologist that, in principle, had applications in other surgical fields. That name, endourology, was an important contribution because it meant the field would forever be identified with its origin; that is, the specialty of urologic surgery. The techniques introduced by us in endourology transformed our specialty.

In the late seventies, work began in the department of urologic surgery at the University of Minnesota that changed the paradigm of urology. Prior to 1979, a few mustard seeds were being sewn elsewhere as, for example, when in 1912, Hugh Hampton Young passed a pediatric cystoscope percutaneously into a massively hydronephrotic kidney without open surgery. In 1955 the late Willard Godwin at UCLA published a report that demonstrated access to the kidney was possible percutaneously using radiological guidance and without open surgery—another mustard seed. In 1976, Fernström and Johansson even performed a percutaneous nephrostomy (PCN) specifically to remove a kidney stone—another mustard seed. Such a less-invasive, percutaneous approach allowed for, among other things, a nephrostomy tube to be placed in the renal pelvis to drain an obstructed kidney or as a new approach to kidney stones. But none of this work was exploited, and up until the late seventies nephrostomies were still done open with an incision and, in addition, urinary stones that would not pass spontaneously also continued to be treated by open surgery.

The above beginnings of using minimally invasive surgical techniques (MISTs) in urology were little noted until Paul Lange of the department of urologic surgery at Minnesota called Godwin's paper to my attention and proposed that nephrostomies at Minnesota should thereafter be done percutaneously, in almost all cases without open surgery and with the collaboration of our radiological colleagues. This was truly an inflection point in urology. That first step to broadly apply a less-invasive approach to the urinary tract was not unlike a big bang in the universe of urology, and treatments of urological diseases by MISTs have continued to expand in number and complexity since that time. Many new innovations in medicine are met with scorn or derision like the reaction Bill Herbst experienced and progress is thwarted; but not in Minnesota.

The Minnesota University environment had a long tradition of encouraging innovation in medicine, which began with the heart surgeons who carried out the first open-heart surgery in the world. But the key to the progress that followed was devising the various approaches for gaining access to the upper urinary tract by minimally invasive techniques. The other two early movers in this field in Minnesota besides Paul Lange were Arthur Smith, and Bob Miller at the VA; they, along with Paul, were primarily responsible for developing the new field of endourology. These three outstanding young men at the time cross-fertilized ideas with each other and rapidly expanded the scope of what they were doing. It was the beginning of open surgeons thinking about employing less-invasive approaches to surgery. When Smith left, Ralph Clayman picked up the flag and did much to expand the field.

Minnesota's work in urologic surgery stimulated the growth of MISTs in other surgical fields. The application of minimally invasive techniques across the surgical disciplines led to significant decreases in both costs and morbidity for patients with a wide universe of diseases.

As activities using MISTs continued to expand, it was important to create an all-encompassing term that would describe and codify this new field as a subspecialty within urology. It was important that this new field be forever recognized as a branch of urology and not just one more activity of, for example, interventional radiology. The first iteration of the term devised to define the new field was endo-urology, which evolved into endourology, and the unhyphenated term stuck as a new word for *Dorland's Medical Dictionary*. Thus, not only did the Minnesotans invent a new field; Minnesota University urology also invented the *word* by which it would forever be named. Today there are almost no major scientific meetings in urology worldwide that do not include a major part of the program devoted to endourology, so the appellation for the field has been accepted universally. In fact, several new freestanding meetings and publications are now devoted to the field.

As the work expanded, the Minnesotans' first treatments were evolved primarily to treat kidney, ureteral, and bladder stones. New instruments and technologies were developed or improved to remove or shatter the stones in situ. Stones were broken by the endourologists into small-enough fragments within the urinary tract so that usually the fragments could pass out of the body with minimal difficulty or the fragments became removable with forcepslike devices. When the lithotripter came along, the skills of the endourologist were often required to definitively rid the patient of the stone fragments irrespective of how they were created. As endourology pushed forward, treatments for other diseases or disorders ranging from congenital obstructions to certain other lesions such as iatrogenically damaged ureters were evolved.

Recently I had the privilege of attending a lecture by Ralph Clayman, during which Ralph demonstrated new treatments for small polar kidney cancers using endourological techniques. Even though Ralph had already done the first laparoscopic nephrectomy using minimally invasive techniques, it was only possible to enlarge the field of endourology by developing new instruments, catheters, and other devices that could be placed inside the urinary tract as means for effecting treatments for one condition or another. Several companies and the Minnesota radiologists, especially Kurt Amplatz, Bob Miller, and Willie Castaneda, all cooperated with our urologists to further progress in the field. The training and techniques that were developed by the Minnesota endourologists facilitated the rapid expansion of the use of both the lithotripter and robotic-assisted surgery. The ideal individual to apply robots and the lithotripter as adjuncts to surgery was the well-trained endourologist. The application of all three methodologies has facilitated the advance of MISTs in urologic surgery.

Finally, Minnesota played a seminal role in teaching the craft of endourology to thousands of urologists around the world because the work in Minnesota also gave birth to many instructional hands-on courses, scientific papers, and textbooks far too numerous to count, which have served to keep practicing urologists current in the field wherever urology is practiced. The work in Minnesota led to the founding of the *Journal of Endourology*; the annual World Congress of Endourology (now in its thirtieth year to be held in Istanbul), which draws upwards of 1,500 urologists from over sixty countries;

and the founding in 1984 of the Endourology Society. These facts alone demonstrate the profound extent to which endourology has bent the arc of progress of the specialty of one of medicine's oldest disciplines—urology.

Having outlined what we did in developing the field of endourology, let me back up a little. One day, the potential that Paul, Arthur and Ralph, had already envisioned, of an entirely new approach to stone disease dawned on me, after having just seen a stone removed in the cystoscopy room by instruments passed into the kidney through a percutaneous nephrostomy (PCN) tract. This potential was further enhanced about the same time when Arthur used a PCN to place a stent in a leaking ureter. He was off to the races in using endourological techniques for treating problems other than stones by closed technique.

Around this time I called the department of radiology to locate Kurt Amplatz, the famous interventional radiologist, who I eventually found sitting at a small table with John Najarian, having coffee in the little coffee shop across from the main OR desk, a shabby little loitering spot in those days. I interrupted them in my enthusiasm and laid out all the potential for what we were doing, and asked Kurt if he were interested in helping with the interventional radiological component of what we might be able to do. He stuck his nose in the air, and with a haughty sniff proclaimed, as if issuing a papal bull (bull was the appropriate description for the quality of his comments), "Such an approach will come to nothing." He made me feel about two millimeters high, and in front of John. I stormed out thinking, *we will do it ourselves.*

Next, I called Paul Lange, who told me he was already working the problem with the radiologist Bob Miller and his chief at the Minneapolis Veteran's Hospital, and Miller turned out to be a true magician with his closed interventional radiological techniques. As usual, Paul was a few steps ahead of me. Consequently, I let it rest for a time with Amplatz until several weeks later when Bob Miller came to radiology grand rounds at the university and presented a series of fifty or more cases of percutaneous stone removal or urinary tract manipulations that had been done at the Minneapolis VA in collaboration with our VA staff. Well, Amplatz left skid marks on the floor getting up to my office. Of course, he wanted to get on board. So I listened to him and then said I'd have to get approval from the guys at the VA to allow him to participate in the program we were developing since he had turned me down before. I left it that I would get back to him.

I talked it over with "the comets," who, of course, were happy to have Kurt and his colleague, Willie Castaneda, involved with a combined minimally invasive university stone program, as I knew they would be. I called Kurt to the office and gave him the good news, but also said something like, "Kurt, there is just one thing you have to know. I respect you, but I know you and your giant ego—which I admire— might attempt to take over this program, and you may, of course, attempt to get all the credit for it, but that is not going to happen. Let me be clear: our guys started this and they are going to get at least part of the credit. You are already famous, but they are not." What I said to Kurt was said with a smile even though I was dead serious, but if we had given stones and other closed urological procedures over to the radiologists, it might have been the end of urology, and not the birth of endourology.

In summary, it is Bob Miller and his chief, Don Reinke, who really should get credit for being the original radiologist to help start the endourology program; Amplatz and Willie Castaneda from the university department of radiology came somewhat later to the project Nonetheless, Kurt and Willie turned out to be a tremendous help and fine collaborators; I doubt we could have pushed the development of the field as far as we did without their help.

History shows clearly that Kurt Amplatz, in particular, was a giant in his field, so we were lucky to have him at Minnesota. Kurt and Paul Lange eventually even wrote an excellent endourology textbook, one of at least three different major urology textbooks that had their genesis from that time.

One thing most people, and even some scientists, do not realize is that collaborations in science and medicine seldom work. I am not sure why that is, but it is a fact of life. Maybe human nature is at the root of most failed collaborations? One wag once said, "It is too bad science is done by men." But we made the collaboration with radiology work to the betterment of both specialties and patients. We also had good clinical collaborations with medical oncology thanks to B. J. Kennedy I know of no other collaborations between departments at the university that were as productive as ours with radiology and medical oncology.

There is one other aspect to endourology that has not been documented as far as I know. In order to develop the techniques of performing the equivalent of surgical procedures that did not require an incision, urological surgeons (endourologists) were forced to work in a closed, as opposed to an open, surgical environment and to perform their magic while peering through instruments that provided limited fields of vision. Although the facts may have been lost to history, members of our staff soon extended the scope of endourology to the point where certain of what formerly were procedures only done by open surgery were being done by closed techniques and instrumentation they had developed, and this was long before robots.

In a very great sense, then, the endourologists, and especially those who also had quality open-surgery training like our people did, were well prepared to adjust to the advent of the robots, which allowed them to further hone the minimally invasive surgical skills they developed, both as open surgeons and as endourologists. These skills made it possible for them to carry out more and more elaborate closed procedures as treatments for urological diseases other than stones without incisions or open surgery. Endourology established the idea or principle that even certain operations for cancer could be accomplished by closed techniques, although the long-term results from such procedures are not yet known.

In summary, there is little doubt that robot-assisted surgery was accepted more rapidly in urology because of the preexistence of endourology. My concern is that the time may be coming when residents will be trained mainly in minimally invasive or robot-assisted surgery or other closed techniques and they will not have the requisite open-surgery training to handle the cases that require it. My bet is that even the most skilled surgeon will always be the surgeon who brings the best of open and closed techniques to his or her operations, whether open or robot-assisted.

When we were developing the field of endourology, you would have had to be Helen Keller not to foresee that the future of surgery in general was moving toward less-invasive procedures. Our work gave impetus to that trend. In that regard, I wrote to several of the general surgeons at the university early on and invited them to assign a young staff member to our team to explore the development of new closed or minimally invasive general surgical operations. In that letter, I predicted that appendectomies, cholecystectomies, and hernia repairs would be done in the near future by minimally invasive techniques. Najarian and his associates were so tied up in his transplant program that they appeared to have little interest, which is understandable given the demands of running a big transplant program. So I was not surprised the general surgeons never even acknowledged receipt of the letters. In any event, no one is right all the time, and I should have pushed the issue more with the general surgeons.

In fairness, maybe John himself never saw the letter. He had a big staff, and I was on the outs with his principal administrative assistant: I had fired a secretary she liked while we were still a division without consulting her, and believe me, she thought she should be consulted about everything. Later our relationship improved because I took care of one of her family members who was a delightful person as was she. Incidentally, I fired that girl when I noticed my dictations were not coming back, among other deficiencies. We found a pile of un-transcribed disks in her desk after she was let go, so at least the mystery of the missing dictation was solved.

John Najarian did a superb job with the transplant program that did not exist at the university before he came, and thus he established Minnesota as one of the premier transplant centers in the world. In that sense, he followed in the footfalls of the heart surgeons and Wangensteen and made them proud. His treatment by the university and the federal government toward the end of his career is one of the sorriest stories in the history of American medicine and surgery. By their assault on John, the "looters" managed to destroy one hundred years of surgical history at Minnesota, but that's a story for another day.

One final thing about John: he was one tough hombre to deal with on occasion, but he was very fair with me most of the time. I had a much better situation relative to general surgery than did many of my urological colleagues around the country. John certainly helped our department to grow and thrive by just leaving us alone, another one of his many contributions to the medical school. One of the biggest inhibitors to progress in medicine is the micromanaging departmental chairman or dean.

Anyone trained by Wyland Leadbetter owed it to him to emulate him at least in the sense of training people who became leaders in their field. Wyland traced his lineage back to Hugh Hampton Young, MD, the "father of urology" at Johns Hopkins, where he was one of the last residents to be trained by Young. Wyland's great contribution to urology, besides the people he trained, was to establish that urologists were surgeons and not just venereal disease or clap doctors. The first urologists, of course, were venereologists, not surgeons. It was Wyland, Victor Marshall, Joe Kaufman, and Lester Persky, among others, who established urology as a surgical specialty in the years immediately following World War II. Many of these men, including Wyland, developed some of their open surgical skills because they were forced to do so as a result of working in World War II surgical triage units (the so-called MASH units of their time). It is unfortunate that much surgical progress came about historically as a result of having to do desperate lifesaving battlefield surgery. So war was, in fact, the origin of progress in much of modern surgery, beginning especially with the War Between the States. Another Minnesota surgical giant, C. Walton Lillehei, also received his surgical baptism under fire in World War II. The sense of obligation all his trainees have to Wyland and his cause was well summed up by a Senator Ted Kennedy quote as follows:

> "The work goes on, the cause endures, the hope
> still lives, and the dream shall never die."
> —Senator Edward Kennedy

Although we did not train quite as many chairmen as Wyland did, we came closer to doing so in numbers and quality than any of Wyland's other trainees—at least as far as I know. Also, producing a professor was much more complex and more expensive during my era because excellent clinical training alone, in most cases, was not a sufficient platform for launching an academic career, as it was for many of Wyland's trainees. Since the MGH program had no urological laboratory, those of us who wanted a laboratory experience had to find it elsewhere, like the NIH.

Tom Hakala, and possibly Ben Gittes and I, were the only Leadbetter trainees who ever spent time in the laboratory before or after residency. My laboratory stint helped me to understand what was required in my era to train future professors since I believed they would have to have laboratory experience in basic science as credentials to be competitive. I wanted the laboratory experience for our trainees to occur in Minnesota rather than having them travel elsewhere, but that was not always possible. Also, our program at Minnesota did not have access to a pool of Harvard AOAs[33] as Wyland did, so history must judge whether our relative achievements in producing good people matched Wyland's or at least came close. What is more important to me is whether Wyland would think we did a credible job. Maybe, just maybe, I'll have that answer someday soon since we are getting closer every day.

There were also several external forces that had to be dealt with early in my chairmanship because the field of urologic surgery, more than any other surgical specialty, was under "assault" from all sides. For example, the radiologists kept trying to maneuver themselves into a primary position in the stone business, which we thwarted; the pediatric surgeons were meddling in pediatric urology without any urological training; some of the gynecologists actually had the effrontery to call themselves *gynecological urologists*, whatever that meant coming from a group with no urological, or I might add, little general surgical training; and the radiotherapists, with the complicity of the nonoperating urologists, who, at MD Anderson and Stanford, were making inroads in the field of urologic oncology in general and in the treatment of cancer of the prostate in particular.

Our department was either the first or one of the first to develop subspecialists within urology, and it was done primarily to counter those who were attempting to poach on and thus diminish our

---

[33] Alpha Omega Alpha, the honorary society for medical students with high academic achievement—a rough equivalent of Phi Beta Kappa for undergraduates

specialty, as well as to attract patients for training purposes. I am proud of what our entire staff did to defend *fortress urologica*. It was one of our best contributions. Our vigorous defense of the specialty, of course, produced another barnacle on me because I took no prisoners and also shot the wounded when up against anyone trying to diminish our specialty. I decided that to strengthen urologic surgery, we would hyper-train our staff and develop subspecialists within urologic surgery to further protect and expand urology to the greatest extent possible. I sent Ricardo Gonzalez off to Boston to train with the remarkable pediatric surgeon, Hardy Hendren at the MGH in pediatric urology. We had a staff that invented the field of endourology, and we pushed on the development of that new field extensively. We convinced the hospital to purchase one of the early lithotripters (stone machine) from Dornier Corp. in Germany, and the always-conniving former head of radiology tried, in behind-the-scenes maneuvering, to get the lithotripter sited in the department of radiology, which I also stopped through friends and patients of mine on the university's Board of Regents. We also hired a staff man with in-depth expertise in male fertility, and also developed a person with a special interest in urodynamics and incontinence. Not all of those hires turned out well for the department, and those who were there at the time know my meaning.

The European radiotherapists were even claiming good results treating testis cancer with radiation until I blew the cover on their claims. In essence, they used a tumor tissue classification system that obscured the real results and made comparison with the American results impossible. For example, they were mixing the seminomas in with the non-seminomatous cancers, which is fundamentally dishonest since the survival for most seminoma patients approaches 100 percent no matter how you treat them. I went to London to review a series of British cases including the slides, and that is how I discovered they were including seminomas along with non-seminoma germ cell cancers in their series. That meant the British were comparing treatment results of both seminomas and non-seminomatous testicular cancers with treatment results of just non-seminomatous cancers as were being reported in the United States. By the way, that episode shows the value of our MGH training. When I was a resident, we reviewed almost all of the pathology slides on our patients, often with Leadbetter or a pathologist or both, late in the day just before going off duty. We, therefore, trained ourselves to become pretty fair urologic pathologists, and that knowledge saved many of my patients immense grief at various stages in my career.

In Minnesota there were some cases in which I overrode, at great legal risk, the opinion of the pathologist, who, frankly, I thought was borderline incompetent. This was never necessary after Juan Rosai, a world-class pathologist, and his associates came to Minnesota as head of anatomic pathology in the 1970s. Professor Rosai and his associates solved the pathology problem to the extent there was one.

As we went out to speak to frontline physicians in the state, we received increasing numbers of requests to provide consulting services on-site in their hospitals and clinics. The small outstate hospitals were beginning to suffer because of shorter hospital stays and diminishing numbers of patients; thus, the Outreach Program was born. The first outreach clinic was established in Onamia, Minnesota, but the program grew rapidly as word spread among family physicians in the state, until we were providing outreach services from one end of the state to the other within a year of starting the service. I came to the conclusion it was about time that specialists at the university should reach out to the state, rather than waiting for the patients to come to them. This program turned out to enhance the number of patients coming to the university and provided teaching material for the residents and students. Of course, the forces of darkness (including some at Mayo) used just about any political trick they could conjure up to stop outreach.

But that is par for the course; as has been said many times, politics of any kind is a contact sport and not a beanbag, especially when money is at stake. I understood their concerns and did not overreact to their antics.

The fury over outreach reached a crescendo when twenty or thirty of the private practitioners stormed into the dean's office demanding I be fired. Of course, they saw outreach as a real economic threat to their practices. But Dean Neal Gault held fast, and as he told me later, "I told them, 'Fraley is my captain and that will not change.'" Several weeks after their meeting with the dean, the downtowners were all probably singing that old Gracie Field's 1939 music hall song "He Is Dead, But He Won't Lie Down." If the local practitioners had supported the department from the beginning to any degree whatsoever, outreach would not have been necessary. As I told the downtowners on several occasions, "I am sorry, but I did not go to Minnesota to preside over the demise of urology or anything else at the university." And after all their complaining, many, if not most, private practice groups eventually started their own outreach programs. As Samuel Butler said, "Morals depend in large measure on the customs of a country—to whit, cannibalism."

Our outreach program compiled a sterling record for safety and service, and I would do it all over again under similar circumstances. It in fact started a national movement of universities and other centers of excellence taking excellence to the people they were supposed to serve. We endeared ourselves to the outstate physicians and patients, and brought untold resources of the entire university clinical center to rural Minnesota. A corollary benefit was that we were able to provide superior clinical resources for training residents. I should have trademarked the term *outreach*.

The downtowners tried to recruit literally every resident we produced because they knew our residents were superbly trained. Of course, many of our best trainees were not interested in the blandishments of private practice because they were motivated to achieve great things in academic urologic surgery, and we helped keep many rural hospitals viable.

So, in summary, the specific contributions we made are listed below.

CLINICAL ACCOMPLISHMENTS

In the field of endourology, one of the first percutaneous stone removals was performed in Minnesota, and the development of closed treatments within the urinary tract based on the percutaneous nephrostomy portended the development of an entirely new field that survives and thrives today. The invention of endourology changed the paradigm in urology, and it was the equivalent of the big bang in the urology universe. Just as the universe continues to expand outward, so do new techniques and instruments that are still evolving not only in urology but also in other fields of surgery that had their origin conceptually in Minnesota urologic surgery. Today the word *endourology* is found repeatedly in the program of almost every major urology meeting in the world.

There were several important developments in urology during my time: the treatment of advanced testis cancer with chemotherapy, the development of cancer markers for prostate (the PSA test) and testicular cancers, nerve sparing to preserve sexual function after radical prostatectomy, and the invention of endourology. Endourology was one of the first new areas for subspecializations in urologic surgery. In terms of a lasting breadth of influence, endourology would have to rank near the top in terms of significance in the progress that was made in our field between 1970 and 1990. It started a trend of surgeons in general trying to formulate treatments that did not involve open surgery—imagine that. Of course, we were also involved in developing applications for the tumor markers, especially in testis cancer.

Our outreach started a national trend in medicine of taking the excellence of the university into the rural towns of any state. This model has been recapitulated elsewhere in the country.

We helped beat back the claims of the radiotherapists that radiotherapy was an effective treatment for cancer of the prostate. It was hard to argue that they were killing cancer when the PSA continued to rise and biopsies showed viable cancers persisting after treatment, although that did not stop them from trying. As I understand it, they are back at it today with all their new techniques, but my bet is the results will be the same. Cancer of the prostate is a resistant cancer, and the most effective treatment in my opinion is total removal. A radical prostatectomy is associated with less morbidity thanks to the robot-assisted prostatectomy that is done as a closed, minimally invasive technique.

Thanks to Lange and Dr Pratap Reddy, another of our trainees, we were among the first to create neo-bladders from sigmoid colon following radical cystectomy.

We made some original contributions to the management of cancer of the penis. First, I showed that a penile cancer that was either in situ or well differentiated did not require a primary radical groin dissection. Second, I showed that once the cancer metastasized to nodes, it became inoperable in short order, so that is why "watching and waiting," as practiced at MD Anderson, was such a poor idea because unless the patients were followed at least every month, many patients were inoperable when they returned for follow-up. We also taught cancer-of-the-penis patients rigorous daily self-examination as a part of any follow-up if the patient refused immediate surgery. Our biggest contribution was development of the "skin bridge technique," which kept the inguinal vessels from breaking down post-surgery because they were covered by skin.

We also developed a technique for treating cancer of the urachus, an orphan cancer because of its rarity, that involved removing the umbilicus and a tube of skin and underlying tissue from the umbilicus combined with a radical cystectomy. Dick Williams was the senior author on the report of the technique I advocated for treatment of cancer of the urachus, mainly because it was a means of promoting him up the academic ladder. Once he got there, he was a chairman of first rank.

I laid out a template for a retroperitoneal dissection in testis cancer that preserved, in most cases, fertility and antegrade ejaculation postoperatively. That nerve-sparing operation eliminated one argument of those who advocated against retroperitoneal dissection because of the morbidity it caused.

The idea of the AUA scholarship program to support putative academicians was a Minnesota concept. This effort was part of introducing to organized urology the concept that private practitioners had an obligation to support the advancement of the specialty by supporting the minting of well-trained academicians.

We developed unique diagnostic studies and surgical techniques for treating renal pain and described the syndrome of renal pain caused by intrarenal vascular obstruction—Fraley's syndrome.

We published the first comprehensive manpower study in the specialty.

Laboratory Accomplishments

We established tissue culture cell lines derived from urological cancers used in many labs around the world.

Our tumor and serum bank was useful in accelerating the clinical use of serum tumor markers in testis cancer and in prostate cancer (PSA). This was one of, if not *the,* first human tumor and serum banks in the world. It was the foundation for an early collaboration on serum tumor markers with Waldman and Macintyre at the NIH. We developed an in-vitro model using cells derived from germ cell tumors of the testis that were probably one of the first cell lines that showed differentiation in vitro. That work was the forerunner of today's efforts on stem cells. These cells contained oncornovirus particles, an observation confirmed in two other labs, at Wistar and in Germany. This observation is yet to be exploited. It was a real crime that this work was never carried to its conclusion. Furthermore, no other group has exploited the human germ cell in-vitro model. We were working with cells that were the analog of primitive embryonic stem cells.

Drs. Hakala and Lange published many basic research papers in the field of tumor immunology, a field that has not yet fulfilled its promise in terms of developing effective new treatment for urological cancers, with the exception of BCG treatment of superficial bladder cancers.

Many of the trainees that passed through our laboratories went on to be heads of investigative programs in other laboratories.

We were responsible for establishing grants to support postresidency academicians by introducing the idea for the establishment of the first AUA scholarship, as mentioned previously.

Further details regarding our laboratory achievements are found in Dr. Robert W. Geist's recent book *The History of Urology at the University of Minnesota.*[34]

---

[34] Geist, Robert W, *The History of Urology at the University of Minnesota* 1932-2012: Geist, University of Minnesota, 2012

CHAPTER 18

CONTRIBUTIONS TO
ACADEMIC UROLOGY

"A professor can never better distinguish himself
or herself in their work than by encouraging
a clever pupil, for the true discoverers are
among them, as comets amongst the stars."
—Henry Brooks Adams

Yes. Spotting talent is one of the essential elements of
great leadership. Washington had it to a remarkable
degree. Washington was not an intellectual. He wasn't a
spellbinding speaker. He wasn't a military genius. He was
a natural born leader and a man of absolute integrity. And
he could spot ability when it wasn't necessarily obvious.
Washington didn't much like New Englanders, but his two
best men were bred-in-the-bone New Englanders. Henry
Knox was a big, fat, young, and totally inexperienced
Boston bookseller who had a brilliant, brave idea—to go
to Ticonderoga, get the big guns there, haul them back to
Boston, and thereby drive the British out of the city. And
all this was done in the dead of winter. There were all
kinds of reasons why it wouldn't work, but Washington

not only saw at once that it was a very good idea; he saw
that Knox was the man to do it.

—David McCullough[35]

Figure 19. Academic staff of the department of urologic surgery, 1969–2003
Back Row L to R: **Marcos Pinto, Dan Merrill, Thomas Hakala, Rei Chiou,
Perinchery Narayan, Keith Kaye, Curt Sheldon, Ralph Clayman, Paul
Lange, Clyde Blackard, Arthur Smith, Tim Moon, and Pratap Reddy**
Front Row L to R: **Kalish Kaedia, Bill DeWolf, Ricardo Gonzales,
Professor Fraley, Colin Markland, and Dick Williams**
Drawn by Mary A. Albury-Noyes

In the final analysis, it is the obligation of any academic surgical
department to train some academicians who will become leaders
in their field. In that regard, the department produced a number
of trainees (10 percent of all our resident trainees) who went on to

---

[35] McCullough, David, *Harvard Business Review. March 2008*

become leaders and innovators in urologic surgery. Thus they became, as per the Adams quote, *Minnesota's comets amongst the stars*.

The following is a list of our academic trainees at Minnesota or individuals who spent significant time in my laboratories at the NIH before I came to Minnesota. Some developed their academic credentials primarily as clinicians, while others had academic credentials that related to both clinical achievements and laboratory research that, in part, came in an institution other than the University of Minnesota after they finished their residencies with us.

ACADEMIC TRAINEES, FACULTY, OR FELLOWS

David Paulson—three years working together in the lab at the NIH, became professor and chairman at Duke University.

Jean deKernion—one year in the lab at Minnesota and professor and chairman at UCLA.

Ralph Clayman—resident trainee, faculty, and now professor and head of urology and dean at the University of California at Irvine. Ralph is a delightful man, a gifted technician, and a great surgeon. A legion of endourologists are indebted to Ralph for developing their skills.

William DeWolf—professor of surgery at Harvard Medical School and urologist-in-chief at the Beth Israel Deaconess medical center in Boston. He is also director of the urologic research laboratories in the Harvard program.

Arthur Smith—resident trainee, faculty, and head of the service and professor of urology at Long Island University and Jewish Hospital, winner of various clinical awards.

Paul Lange—resident trainee, faculty member, and finally, professor and chairman at the University of Washington. Paul is a superb person and an excellent creative surgeon, who did a superb job as chairman at the University of Washington.

Richard Williams—resident trainee, faculty, and later, professor and chairman of urology at the University of Iowa.

Curt Sheldon—professor of surgery, University of Cincinnati School of Medicine, and director of urology at Cincinnati Children's Hospital Urology.

Pratap Reddy—resident trainee, faculty, interim chairman at Minnesota, and now a distinguished surgeon in private practice in Minneapolis. Pratap should have been made permanent chairman at Minnesota. There are very few individuals in this country with Dr. Reddy's surgical abilities.

Perinchery Narayan—resident trainee and pursued a career in academic urology before going into private practice in Gainesville, Florida.

Tom Hakala—Tom spent five years being supported in the lab at the NIH and on the staff at the VA Hospital, where he developed the tumor immunology laboratory before leaving for Pittsburgh. Tom is a superb human being—very smart and a great surgeon. He went from Minnesota to the University of Pittsburgh, where he served as chairman of urology and initially started the kidney transplantation in that institution. His scientific contributions are many and varied.

Ami Sidi—fellow, trainee, and faculty, and now department of urology, Wolfson Medical Center, Sackler faculty of medicine, Tel Aviv University, Israel.

Keith Kaye—Keith came to us from South Africa and was on our faculty until he moved to Australia to become professor of urology at the University of Western Australia, the first full professorship of urology in Australia.

Eduardo Fernandez—now an important member of the university faculty and head of the service at the Minnesota VA Hospital.

The above men have won just about every national award possible in recognition for their contributions to their specialty.

We also had a number of fellows, some of whom went on to academic careers, many of whom are still having a positive impact teaching and advancing the science and practice of urology.

Figure 20. Reunion of academic stars, 2008
L to R: Richard Williams (deceased), Paul Lange, William DeWolf,
Elwin Fraley, Ralph Clayman, Arthur Smith, and Pratap Reddy
With thanks to Manoj Monga, MD

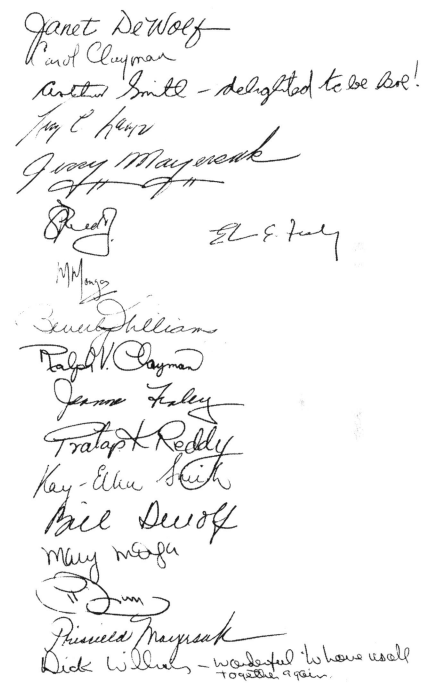

Figure 21. Autographs from reunion at Interlachen Country Club

Chapter 19

THE LOCUST YEARS

"And I will repay you for the years that the
swarming locust hath eaten, the creeping locust,
the stripping locust and the gnawing locust."
—Joel 2:25

At a meeting of Ivy League presidents, Dwight Eisenhower, who was at the time president of Columbia University, leaned over and whispered to Harold Dodd, president of Princeton, "Harold, be damned glad you do not have a medical school to deal with."

"Cry havoc and let slip the dogs of war."
—Shakespeare

"They sow the wind and reap the whirlwind."
—Hosea 8:7

"When half of the people get the idea that they do
not have to work because the other half is going
to take care of them, and when the other half gets
the idea that it does no good to work because
somebody else is going to get what they work for,
that is the beginning of the end of any nation."
—Anonymous

The University of Minnesota School of Medicine, prior to 1970, earned distinction as a result of the economic freedom and the rich tradition of innovation fostered by the department chairmen and their faculties. But as detailed herein, this all changed, creating serious negative consequences for the medical school that reverberate to this day.

Even though the division of urology was in disarray in 1969, it was possible to rebuild it into one of the finest departments of its kind in the world. The key elements that contributed to our success included an entire staff who had both economic and personal freedom and the academic and financial incentives to accomplish what we did. It is easy to believe you are part of something greater than self when you are being well paid.

One of the macro (or locust) forces that worked against the medical school and medicine in general, beginning roughly in the early to mid-seventies and still continuing, was the rapid growth of both health maintenance organizations (HMOs) and Medicare/Medicaid with their meager physician reimbursements. Remember, Minnesota gave birth to the HMO, and it took root there. Congress passed the HMO Act in 1973, and from the start, the federal government increased its influence over medical care and used taxpayer subsidies to entice employers to sign up. Federal law also required insurance agents to present the HMO as an option to employers if an HMO existed in the area.

Once the law passed, HMO enrollments started growing locally. This provided other third-party payers a convenient excuse to slash their reimbursements to both university hospitals and their physicians. Thus, the term "usual and customary fees" became an inside joke. The decrease in patient revenues proved especially critical at the university in general, and to us in particular, because all the clinical departments primarily relied on patient revenues to indirectly fund the entire medical school; this included the basic sciences through a "dean's tax," money used to pay salaries, academic travel, benefits, and so on in departments that needed to be subsidized. The university medical enterprise sat like a house built on the edge of a financial San Andreas Fault because neither the state nor private endowment monies were sufficient to support or supplement the clinical revenues upon which the clinical departments of the medical school depended for their continued viability.

Teaching and training institutions are expensive because of the additional cost of educating medical trainees (nurses, medical students, technicians, physicians, etc.). The state of Minnesota never did step up to cover those costs (which were, in fact, state obligations as judged by the financial structure of similar public institutions elsewhere in the country). Rather, in order to meet the financial needs of the medical school, university bureaucrats attempted to loot the physicians as if they were the school's enemies, despite the fact it was the physicians' hard work and talents that had brought so much fame and resources to the University of Minnesota Hospitals and Medical School over many years. Minnesotans thought, for example, that in the days prior to Nils Hasselmo becoming president of the University of Minnesota, the medical school was actually one of the "crown jewels'" of the entire university; their conception was right, and the world of medicine recognized it as well.

In any institution or enterprise, things are great and most people are happy when there is plenty of money. Despite what others may say, it is, in fact, money that is the basis of many, if not most, human and organizational conflicts.

As the flow of practice money began to decrease, things started to get ugly for all the clinical departments. Added to this volatile mix were an increasing number of medical school and university administrators that embraced an extreme-leftist political ideology— what is yours is not yours, it is mine. These administrators, at the very time of declining resources, began to increase the demands on the individual departments (chairmen) for money from their practices to "run" the medical school. As far as I know, none of these bureaucrat "looters" met with the department heads to lay out a strategy for helping the departments cope with their financial problems—not once, at least in my case. Their modus operandi was to attempt to take, not give or help. This pitted the makers—our academic medical teams—against the takers, the bureaucrats. Frankly, the bureaucrats had lived off the generosity and productivity of the clinicians for so long their survival skills were severely atrophied.

The various administrations became like the listless cows at the salt lick on my grandfather's farm, rather than the alert, wild deer with keen survival instincts, who lived by their wits, unprotected but free in the woods well beyond any fences. Also by this time. Lyle French, our main liaison with the state legislature and an iconic Minnesotan, was retiring. Without Lyle, the medical school administration became increasingly ineffective in obtaining financial resources for the medical school from either the legislature or the private sector.

Most of the administrators could not seem to relate to successful laypeople in general because they apparently did not have the savoir faire or social graces to woo donations from wealthy Minnesotans. Thus, the medical school administrators made minimal efforts to obtain private funds for a medical school endowment. For example, I gave them a list of names from the "Minnesota A List," many of whom we knew and who might have become donors to the medical school if approached properly; as far as I know, none of them were even contacted. As a consequence, much of the private charitable donation money in town went elsewhere—primarily to Abbott Northwestern Hospital in Minneapolis, or Mayo.

Furthermore, as time passed, some of the money requests (demands) the dean made on the clinical departments were either for ill-conceived special projects that did not deserve funding, or the dean used them to support the burgeoning number of bureaucrats in the university health-care enterprise (Buchwald called this the growth of "administrationacracy"). Remarkably, the administration seldom consulted with the clinicians about how the clinicians' money was being spent. What I witnessed is the fact that moochers and looters are unable to resist their impulse to do good with other people's money. Or as the often-quoted Margaret Thatcher said, "Socialists do well until they run out of other people's money."

The administration squeezed funds out of the clinical arm of the medical school, reducing much-needed revenue for the individual departments, and at the same time, the medical school administration, with the tacit support of the university's central administration, kept increasing its demands for money on all of the clinical departments. This was all occurring as fee-for-service revenues began to diminish. The department chairmen and clinicians found that life had become intolerable, and as a result, something had to give—and it did. Going to work in those days was like crawling through the steaming and hissing radioactive ruins of post-explosion Chernobyl to get to your office.

The forces arrayed against private practice of medicine at the university really came together in 1988 under the leadership of the new university president, Nils Hasselmo. The first contact the department chairmen had with Hasselmo was at a meeting he called at the University Campus Club in the early evening about two weeks after he became president.[36] At that meeting Hasselmo made a series of pronouncements about "our money" (the practice monies) and how it should be used. Among other things, he said something akin to this: "We all know that the practice monies can be better utilized if they are under some measure of central control." The thought flew through my mind: *Yes, Karl [Marx], central economic planning has been such a great success.* The money from the practices at that point legally belonged to the physicians and not to the university, but never minding the facts, Hasselmo made it clear that at long last, the central administration would be coming after that money. As Ayn Rand suggested, in rough summary, the moochers and looters should have the bell of a leper attached to them to warn of their approach. Or as Jefferson said, the meeting with Hasselmo should have been "a fire bell in the night" to the successful medical faculty practitioners.

In that evening meeting, Hasselmo did most of the talking. He kept referring to the clinical monies as "our money" (the university's money, that is). *Au contraire*, at that point the money belonged to the clinicians legally, as did their liabilities from their practices, a fact to which all parties had previously agreed under the existing Regents' Rules of Practice. Hasselmo focused on money and only money, and did not discuss how to maintain a first-rate medical school and hospital in difficult economic times, which is what the chairmen reasoned should have been his focus in his new position.

---

[36] The Campus Club can be a depressing place. The fourth-floor lounge-library in those days was where, by midday, you may have found some of the senior liberal arts faculty asleep in leather lounge chairs, oblivious to the outside world. Usually there was a newspaper (*Pravda?*) lying alongside their chair, having slipped from their hand to the floor as they dozed off. I often imagined that there was an attendant who made the rounds from time to time to make sure all the professors were still breathing or to see if they fogged a mirror. By evening, quite often, the lounge air, like similar other faculty lounges, was so thick with mastermind utopian redistributionist solutions to the world's problems, it could have been cut with a knife.

Figure 22. A leper with his bell

When the attack on the medical school first began, the academic health sciences were approximately one third of the 1.7-billion-dollar university budget. As it turned out, Hasselmo and his administration, as well as those who followed him, became the consummate looters of the medical school's private practices. In the opinion of the clinicians, the university administration believed we all had lime green and white blood running in our veins. Hasselmo and his administrative team disregarded President Morrill's Regents' Rules of Practice, proving by his actions that property rights have never been a concern of liberals or progressives or communists or whatever they call themselves these days.

The chairmen left the University Campus Club meeting knowing full well the final battle had begun. We had just experienced the term from the recent spelling bee—*guetapens* (Fr. for ambush). I turned to a colleague on the way out—I think it was Joe Buckley in anesthesia—and opined, "As they said in World War II when Germany invaded Poland, the balloons just went up."

The administration's attack on private practice at the medical school more than likely also had the concurrence of the liberal governor at the time, the dearly departed Rudy Perpich, may he R.I.P. In addition, it could not have moved ahead without the concurrence of the Board of Regents. The university regents, although technically "democratically" elected by the legislature, were for the most part "political" appointees. The 1972 general election in Minnesota also exacerbated this problem at the university, as it turned legislative control over to the Liberal caucus, from the Conservative caucus—this explains a lot. The aforementioned sequence of events helps to confirm my thesis that liberals or "libtards" always leave a trail of ruin in their wake.

Based on his actions and word-of-mouth pronouncements before and after the aforementioned meeting, Hasselmo had, in the opinion of many of us, several goals regarding the medical school. He meant to severely restrict the power of the strong chairmen and thereafter seize control over patient-care fees. We also thought, based on leaks from our friends in central administration, that Hasselmo intended to restructure the medical school by diminishing the importance of individual physicians and increasing control over them by reducing them to civil servants (as per Fleming's prediction). As to the current state of affairs for the clinical departments at the university post Hasselmo, read Henry Buchwald's classic article "A Clash of Culture—Personal Autonomy Versus Corporate Bondage" listed in the suggested reading at the end of the book, in which Buchwald stated, "Physicians went from autonomy into corporate bondage." Buchwald's article is a fitting prequel to this book.

Hasselmo's vitae explains why he supported such policies. Born in socialist Sweden, he received his education and worked in the pestholes of leftism (the modern American academy) never having had, as far as the medical faculty or the people who vetted him could determine, any private-sector experience. In Minnesota the lack of affinity for the private sector of any undertaking is not necessarily a negative, especially among progressives. Also, his vitae showed no previous connection to the medical field. In my opinion, Hasselmo's values and the policies he advocated were perfectly compatible with his experiences and inferred ideology. By the way, at one point in his career, he was awarded the Order of the North Star; there were many of us who thought Order of the Red Star would have been more appropriate.

Over time, Hasselmo's actions showed the chairmen that he clearly looked at medical school clinicians as having a honeypot of money into which he, like *Winnie the Pooh*, could stick his nose. In fact, before Hasselmo, the money controlled by the clinical department was one of the few large pools of resources within the university that were not controlled by central administration. As the clinical departments became weaker financially, resulting from the deteriorating reimbursement structure, Hasselmo and the medical school dean-led scavengers closed in, and the half-century-old dream of the moochers and looters to seize control of the medical school practice monies became reality. (Often my mind went back to the only question that mattered to my recruiters at Varco's house before I came to the university, which was, "What do you think about private practice?") The havoc that followed in the medical school after the administration seized the medical practice funds made the wisdom of my recruiters even more evident to me.

This aforementioned process to collectivize the practices was a no-holds-barred fight, which witnessed wholesale spurious attacks on many of the chairmen that were conducted according to the Alinsky playbook.[37] The administration honored liars and perniciously promoted mediocre people who helped tear the clinical departments apart. Administrators ran many prominent clinicians out of the

---

[37] These radicals were clearly following Saul Alinsky, who advocated, "Isolate and demonize your enemies and seize the moral high ground by the ferocity of your attack."

school because the looters knew the strong chairmen would resist them after having spent a lifetime building something that they would have fought to preserve. In the end, bureaucracy replaced private practice with "group" practice, which has taken on a life of its own and now controls the practice money and, thus, indirectly, the very lives and economic freedom of the physicians. Needless to say, bureaucracies like this have a human cost associated with them that far exceeds any benefit they bring to the table.

It is my prediction that life will come full circle and the medical school will soon be demanding big taxpayer subsidies just to continue to exist in a state that has a projected $6 billion deficit in the next biennium. That is, unless they find other sources of funding. The tragedy is that those responsible for diminishing the medical school will, for the most part, have passed on into the sea of entropy that surrounds us without ever having been held accountable for what they did. If no one was imprisoned or lost his or her job over 9/11, then it follows no one will ever be held to account over what happened at the university.

Needless to say, the clinical enterprise at the University of Minnesota School of Medicine and Hospitals has slipped, at least in terms of rank order in American medicine. In 1969 the hospital ranked eleventh-best in the United States, which is no longer true, and the medical school was highly ranked against its peers. In the last *U.S. News & World Report* (2011) rankings, the medical school ranked thirty-fourth in the country. I know Dick Varco and Lyle French and Owen Wangensteen would be most unhappy with that slide. That the medical school still survives is, in part, the result of funds provided at one point by the money confiscated from the shareholders of the tobacco companies, which, incidentally, are still to this day selling legal products like cigarettes and related items. Between what happened to the medical school and the "mobacracy" that glorified the stealing of the shareholders of tobacco companies' monies both within Minnesota and elsewhere, therein rest some of the most sordid and immoral chapters in modern Minnesota and United States history.

JOHN NAJARIAN AS THE METAPHOR

What deserves separate comment relative to the aforementioned events is how the university, under its chief administrative officer and its attorneys, the federal government, and other assorted bureaucracies were willing to criminalize minor administrative missteps by some of the renowned medical faulty, especially Professor John Najarian. The administration did this as a means of pursuing its agenda, the central purpose of which was to gain complete control over the medical faculty, including their private practices and their money. What the university and federal government attempted to do to him is described in detail by Professor Najarian in his 2009 book entitled *The Miracle of Transplantation*, listed in the suggested reading at the end of this history, which outlines exactly what he experienced at the hands of rapacious bureaucrats. I was surprised and disappointed how benign John was in describing what was done to him, but maybe the long fight and trial wrung the fight out of him.

The background on the Najarian story is as follows. For several years, Najarian's department produced an antirejection drug called ALG (antilymphocyte globulin), which was used all over the world to prevent organ rejections in transplant patients. (Najarian developed ALG in California before the medical school appointed him as chief of general surgery, succeeding Owen Wangensteen. So he brought the ALG program with him to Minnesota.) ALG was the best drug of its kind at the time. Consequently, many if not most transplant physicians made ALG their drug of choice for preventing organ rejection, so it saved countless lives. That fact is not in dispute.

The department of surgery and the administration of the medical school were providing the drug to other transplant centers at a cost sufficient to reimburse the U of M department for the "costs of producing ALG." In fact, the university built an elaborate new facility to produce ALG just before the storm clouds appeared. This arrangement went on for many years with the concurrence of both the US government and the university central administration without any suggestion of impropriety being raised. As Federal Judge Richard Kyle stated after the Najarian trial, both the university and the US government treated the program with benign neglect for years. Of course, a lot of money came into the surgery department that funded not only the ALG program but also, as it turned out, various projects for the dean; the dean often turned to John when he needed extra money to recruit new faculty or for other projects. One of the university's regents, a physician by the way, actually raised the question before things went bad as to why the department of surgery was not charging more for the ALG. (That question is in the transcript of the regents' meetings for anyone who is interested in looking it up.)

However at some point for reasons still unknown to most of us, but possibly spurred on by a pharmaceutical company with a competing drug it wanted to market, the FDA and the government through the United States Attorney's office went after Najarian for, among other charges, "selling" a drug that had never been approved for sale to humans by the FDA. (By the way, the FDA has never approved aspirin for use in or sale to humans either.) The instigation of the attack on Najarian remains shrouded in mystery because bureaucrats are often "men behind masks." For example, as I was writing this book, Congress and the American people still do not know who was behind the gun-running fiasco referred to as the *Fast and Furious scandal*. One of a bureaucrat's greatest talents is covering his or her tracks in the face of trouble. The prosecution of John Najarian relied on the same type of tactics used by many of the federal prosecutors in the news lately, such as Patrick Fitzgerald, the federal prosecutor that had to trump up additional charges just to give credibility to his activities, especially in the case of "Scooter" Libby.

As the process related to Najarian unfolded, we all saw government and university bureaucrats run amok. At one point, the FBI raided the department and seized all the department's records and computers, and at the same time, broke into the homes of some of the department's administrators looking for incriminating evidence. The late James Coggins, Najarian's chief administrator back then, told this author that the FBI burst into his home without warning and without a search warrant and ransacked it, and in the process, knocked his wife to the floor; the Feds also yanked Jim naked from the shower, and he slipped and fell, injuring himself. This sounds unbelievable in the United States of America, doesn't it? Well, it certainly happened, and worse. And to put the finishing touch on this episode, Jim died shortly thereafter of some type of cardiac event that more than likely was caused by the stress he had endured.

In other words, one of the university's clinical superstars and world-famous surgeon was somehow all of a sudden an evil man who in so many words deserved to be in prison to mingle with child predators, rapists, drug lords, and murderers. The university, in what will never be known as its "finest hour," also turned on Najarian and company. The buzz was that the US government threatened the university, claiming that unless the U cooperated in the case against Najarian, the school would lose all of its federal funding and grants. Most of us think that threat was a bluff that would never have been tolerated by Minnesota's congressional delegation, but we recognized that congressmen have their own well-known backbone problems on occasion. We can only speculate about what the Feds would have done.

The cave-in to government tyranny by the university administration, its attorneys, and the university regents reminded me of that statement by Teddy Roosevelt to the effect, "I have seen better backbones carved out of bananas." The university's performance, as it turned out, could thus be summarized in the opinion of many Minnesotans as a profile in fecklessness. Even Governor Arne Carlson severely criticized the university's performance in the Najarian affair.

As a result of all the government's investigations, the US Attorney indicted Najarian on a variety of charges ranging from embezzlement to tax evasion. It appeared to us outsiders that as prosecutors sank farther and farther into a quagmire of their own making, they realized that the original reason they gave for starting the attack on the ALG program did not hold water. As it turned out, Federal Judge Richard Kyle threw out many of the charges against John even before the trial began. Kyle also issued strong public admonishments from the bench to the US Attorneys for having brought many of the specious charges in the first place. The court, of course, acquitted Najarian of the remaining charges in a trial that was swift and to the point.

The following is Judge Kyle's ending statement from the transcript of the case:

> This has been a long, rough case. I am sure the defendant is relieved with it, but I don't read the verdict as saying that everything that went on with the ALG program was done properly ... but the jury has rendered its verdict and that verdict is, as indicated, not guilty. I have some question as to why we are here at all, quite frankly. Not because there weren't things that were wrong with the program, but it was a program that was looked at by the FDA for 15 to 20 years with what I guess I could describe as benign neglect ... converting all of this to a criminal proceeding of the magnitude that we saw here, it seems to me has gone or did go beyond the bounds of common sense. We had a program here in Minnesota which, for

all its problems and shortcomings was a good program, literally saved thousands of lives. It should have been run better and it wasn't, but I have serious doubts as to whether that type of program should have been subjected to a criminal proceeding of this kind (United States v. Najarian, Transcript of February 21, 1996).

Eventually, other antirejection drugs became available, and the aforementioned events have faded into history. The university stripped Najarian of both his professorship and his chairmanship ("First the verdict and then the trial"—from Alice), but recently, enough private money was raised to endow a university chair in clinical transplantation in John Najarian's name. Who says that there is no economy operating in the universe that guarantees the triumph of good over evil?

As the public became aware of all the facts, many Minnesotans concluded the US Attorney and staff had been into "resume padding" in hopes of subsequently seeking political office, having triumphed in a high-profile trial. One of the attorneys for the government had been in his previous iteration a hard-left Paul Wellstone political operative. This suggests he probably thought that bringing down a "rich doctor" would be his ticket to higher office. But he and his cronies misread the Minnesota public, many of whom supported or were at a minimum sympathetic to Najarian despite their political leanings. Minnesotans never forgave the individuals involved for what they tried to do to John.

One of the government prosecutors did run for public office in a primary election. But I was told several citizens followed him on the campaign trail, and when he began to speak on the stump, they shouted out from the audience, "What about what you did to Dr. Najarian?" Eventually that individual allowed, apparently in a moment of public candor, "I wish I had never heard of Doctor Najarian." Some wag said that a gaffe in politics is when a politician accidentally tells the truth. In any event, the Najarian pursuer's campaign for that, and other, reasons failed and he did not get the nomination he sought.

I offer here a proposal for a new law to prevent prosecutorial abuses: make it illegal for any federal prosecutor to seek public office until at least five years after he or she ceases being a federal prosecutor. That law would at least discourage future prosecutorial abuses driven by a political calculus and resume padding.

Prosecutorial abuse or judicial activism is not that infrequent in our country. We have witnessed several decades in which the hard left, who can't get their policies implemented in fair elections, turned to the court to make policy by legislating from the bench.

What happened to Professor Najarian is an ominous development, and similar events are happening with increasing frequency. Bureaucrats of various stripes, but mostly of the left, are not only willing, but eager, to use the criminal justice system or a governmental regulatory body like the EPA in particular to not only cover up their own malfeasance, but when necessary, to criminalize differences in policy or interpretation of administrative procedures by making an innocent party into a criminal. This is exactly what they tried to do to Professor Najarian.

A sidebar to the Najarian affair was the role played by arguably the worst daily major newspaper in the United States—the local *Minneapolis Star-Tribune,* another fish wrap. The paper failed to support either Najarian or the university medical community in any respect. Some believe the paper actually colluded with the university's central administration to help them and the government in their case against Najarian as well as other medical faculty. The paper's slanted reporting inflamed and sensationalized the situation much more than was necessary. It is rumored that when President Hasselmo called Najarian to "fire" him as department chairman, a zealous *Star-Tribune* reporter sat in Hasselmo's office, and the reporter could be heard in the background yelling, "Fire him! Fire him!" as Hasselmo and Najarian talked.

It even has been rumored, but never proven, that one of the *Star-Tribune*'s leading reporters was tied into the forces that started the assault on the ALG program and that he had a financial incentive for doing so. Now that would be a real story. Many Minnesotans believe the *Star-Tribune*, now operating under bankruptcy protection, has been one of the most pernicious influences in the state for years, with its implacable and reactionary mindless liberalism. Remember what Mark Twain said: "If you don't read the newspaper, you are uninformed; if you do read the newspaper, you are misinformed."

The Locusts Prevailed, and the University Inherited the Whirlwind

"No one has seemed in the least aware that everything
which is paid for must be paid for out of production,
for there is no other source of payment."[38]
—Albert Jay Nock

In the opinion of most of the chairmen of my era, there were a lot of hardball makers versus takers in play in the university during the whole time the locusts were eating what we had created and what we were producing. To say this whole unseemly mess put a stain on the University of Minnesota by the way they mismanaged the crisis is an understatement for the ages. One thing for sure, by their actions, the university destroyed, or greatly diminished, more than one hundred

---

[38] Nock, A. J. (1943) *The Memoirs of a Superfluous Man.* Lanham, MD: University Press of America.

years of surgical history, and the department of surgery may never fully recover, at least for several generations.

During this time when the bureaucratic locusts ate, and in the aftermath when the medical faculty reaped the whirlwind, the multiple destructive political and prosecutorial forces simultaneously delivered a terrible blow to the medical school and the physicians, the effect of which persists to this day. One result of the financial and programmatic calamity that befell the school of medicine is that the university hospital had to be sold to a private hospital corporation (Fairview), so at least the hospital is now run better and is more patient-friendly than it was previously when it was staffed by civil servants. Fairview's purchase of the hospital was an example of the private sector bailing out the public sector. Certainly sustaining these institutions involves the private sector because of the amount of money involved and because governments everywhere are approaching insolvency. Americans must be informed as to how important these academic medical centers are in determining the type and quality of health care awaiting them on the day they need surgery—or any advanced medical procedure.

Looking back, I think how difficult it was in the beginning, but in 1969 I operated within a framework that allowed our hardworking and creative staff to overcome the problems that were outlined in this book. In a word, we lived in nirvana by comparison with the problems facing medicine, and particularly academic medicine, in 2014. In that sense, I believe any young academic chairmen today assume their responsibilities at a time when much of their economic freedom has been taken away and they will be practicing in an environment in which there will be less incentive to work or excel. There is no question they and their faculty will be increasingly dependent on government largess to survive.

It is no wonder I do not envy any new academic chairmen, but I hope they will also find a way to overcome. Any of their achievements will be far greater than anything the chairmen of my era ever did, considering the challenges they are facing. To quote my grandfather once again, "All achievement is relative to where you start." All of us owe the academicians of today and the future so very much for trying.

A real bright spot in this story has been the high quality of the recent appointee Badrinath Konety as chairman and professor of urology at the University of Minnesota. Professor Konety is an able administrator and has a reputation as an excellent clinician. Konety came to this country originally to work with a former Minnesota trainee, Perinchery Narayan, in his laboratory in California. Then he had his urology residency with Tom Hakala in Pittsburgh, and later he spent time with Dick Williams at Iowa. So from the time he touched down in America, he has had plenty of Minnesota influence preparing him for his position at Minnesota.

Epilogue

This history was, of course, autobiographical in nature, so there are a lot of I's and me's in the text. This is uncomfortable for the author because, simply put, whatever small achievements there were during the time chronicled, none would have come about except for the "comets" like Paul Lange, Ralph Clayman, Richard Williams, Tom Hakala, Bill DeWolf, Arthur Smith, Ami Sidi, Pratap Reddy, Keith Kaye, and Clyde Blackard, among others. In addition to the faculty and those who chose an academic pathway, we were blessed by excellent residents. To these names I add the individuals in the laboratory: Art Elliot, Bob Vasella, and David Bronson and their associates, and our medical editor, Judy Bronson.

Figure 23. Twenty-fifth anniversary of Fraley chairmanship

In addition, we had a superb secretarial staff, headed up by the one and only Marlene Lindquist, who was a combination of mother confessor and mother hen, not only for me, but for the residents, and even many of our patients. Hiring Marlene was one of my best moves during the entire run.

And finally, over the years, we had many superb residents who added luster to the program and who became invaluable to their chosen field. These residents may have labored in the shadows, but their contributions to the program were mighty, and despite the fact they never became famous, I have reason to believe they are providing a high level of patient care, which is, in fact, the most important result that any training program can achieve.

We also had help along the way from many university faculty colleagues. Among the best of them were B. J. Kennedy and his entire staff, John Najarian, Richard Varco, Seymour "Sy" Levitt, Roby Thompson, Kurt Amplatz, Mike Paparella, Konnie Prem, Bill Thompson, Al Michaels, Bob Vernier, Jack Delaney, Henry Buchwald, and last but certainly not least, Neal Gault, who served as dean during the best of times, before the locusts ate.

It is important that the "first ladies" of the residents, and especially the spouses of those who went the academic pathway, be recognized. As William Shakespeare once said, "The general's wife is the general's general." First, not a single one of our group experienced divorce while they were in Minnesota, and only one divorce occurred among our group after they left. The way these individuals conducted their personal lives is not only a tribute to the solid humanity and character of the husbands, but also to the character of the wives. Those very young women were as committed to what their husbands were doing as were their spouses. Their marriages were truly professional partnerships. Among other sacrifices, these wives tolerated having less time with their husbands and less material rewards than they would have had if their husbands had gone directly into private practice. As Coach Lou Holtz said, "One word characterizes greatness: sacrifice."

Figure 24. The Comettes, the generals' generals
L to R: **Beverly Williams, Jeanne Fraley, Lucy Lange,**
Jan DeWolf, Carol Clayman, and Kay Smith
With thanks to Manoj Monga, MD

The late Clyde Blackard is one person not mentioned sufficiently in this history. Clyde made a tremendous contribution to our training program. Clyde, who in the beginning served as head of our clinical service at the Veterans Administration Hospital, was a good administrator and a superb clinician. Also, Clyde served as a loyal helpmate and a stabilizing influence on both residents and junior staff. Clyde was one of the most decent individuals I have ever known, and now that he is gone, I miss him terribly. There is no more important function in writing this history than to pay tribute to Clyde's memory and, therefore, to give him due credit for his immense contributions to the university urologic surgery training program. In the beginning, he pitched in after the VA and university residencies were combined and made that transition almost seamless. I realized he was in a position to make my life difficult when I had so many other problems to deal with, but he did not do that, despite the fact that combining of the VA and university training programs was imposed on him. Clyde, ever the good soldier, chose a better way by being cooperative and remaining positive. In brief, Clyde helped make the VA clinical service and laboratories important additions to our residency program, and as a bonus for me, we became good friends. Clyde had a natural shyness and reserve that prevented some people from knowing him well, but beneath Clyde's apparent diffidence, he was a person with broad interests and extensive knowledge, ranging from opera to the history of the War Between the States. My memories of Clyde and his humanity continue to enrich my life to this day. I am not certain Clyde knew the full extent of the high regard in which he was held by everyone who knew him, and especially me, but if he did not, that was a failing by all of us that must be corrected someday.

Figure 25. Clyde Blackard, MD
With thanks to Louise Blackard and family

My Fond Conclusion

To end this history on a very high note, one of the things that has pleased me the most has been the way that the bonds of friendship and a sense of having been in a special place during a special time with very special people has helped hold many of the former faculty and residents close personally through time. It is not unusual that when men and women work in such close proximity with lives at stake and under great stress, they bond very intensely. In World War II when wounded soldiers were taken to the rear, many of them would, as soon as they were able, tear off their dressing and even jump through windows in an attempt to return to the front and their comrades.

The continuing fellowship of the Minnesota people reminds me of the following passage from Saint Crispin's Day speech in Shakespeare's *Henry V*:

> Be in their flowing cups freshly remembered.
> This story shall the good man teach his son;
> And Crispin Crispin shall ne'er go by,
> From this day to the ending of the world,
> But we in it shall be remembered—
> We few, we happy few, we band of brothers.

The End

SUGGESTED READING

King of Hearts: The True Story of the Maverick Who Pioneered Open Heart Surgery. G. Wayne Miller, Times Books and Random House, New York, 2000.

The Social Transformation of American Medicine: The rise of a sovereign profession and the making of a vast industry. Paul Starr. Basic Books, New York, 1982.

The Meaning of Money: Ayn Rand. The Ayn Rand Institute, Online, 1988. www.aynrand.org

The Rise of Surgery: From Empiric Craft to Scientific Discipline. O. H. Wangensteen and Sarah D. Wangensteen. University of Minnesota Press, 1979

The Memoirs of a Superfluous Man: Albert Jay Nock, Harper & Brothers, New York, 1943. Anyone who reads this book and can prove it to me will, if they so desire, be inducted into the Nockian Society, and will from that day forward be known as a "Nockian." The Nockian Society has no meetings, no dues, no officers, no publications, no bylaws, and no constitution. The only requirement for membership is that you love and value freedom. You can become a Nockian only by recommendation of another Nockian, and the author is a proud member. So call me if you want in. I alone will judge whether you are worthy. This is a rare book, but copies are available at Amazon.com The book is required reading for all who desire to become a Nockian. Become a Nockian, and your life will be transformed forever.

United States Debt Clock: For a dose of financial reality about our national debt in real time, go to http://www.usdebtclock.org/.

Conflicting Visions: Walter E. Williams. Two visions of human nature: restrictive and unrestrictive, and why the left believes it is their role to perfect human nature. http://econfaculty.gmu.edu/wew/articles/fee/oct99.pdf

The Politics of Bad Faith: The Radical Assault on America's Future. David Horowitz. Free Press, 1998. How the left engages in the politics of personal destruction.

The Road to Serfdom: Friedrich A. Hayek. University of Chicago Press, 2007. This is a classic on the nature of collectivism and its destructive effect on society. Reagan and Churchill both list this as a favorite read, and they often referred to this seminal work in their writing and speeches.

Presidential Address: *A Clash of Culture—Personal Autonomy Versus Corporate Bondage.* Henry Buchwald, MD, PhD: *Surgery,* 1998; OCT; 124(4):595–603. This is a terribly prescient analysis of what is happening to physicians in general and surgeons in particular. The article is clever, erudite, and creatively written. Professor Buchwald's analysis of how bureaucrats operate is spot-on.

The Miracle of Transplantation: The Unique Odyssey of a Pioneer Transplant Surgeon. John Najarian, MD. Phoenix Books. Los Angeles, CA. 2009

Never Enough: America's Limitless Welfare State: William Vogeli. Encounter Books, 2010. A discussion of the course and meaning of America's limitless welfare state. A must read for all Americans.

Health Reform: The End of the American Revolution? Lee Kurisko, MD. Alethos Press LLC St. Paul, MN. 2011. Lee Kurisko immigrated to the United States from Canada in 2001. He is a Canadian-trained radiologist, who also worked in primary and emergency room care in Canada. His book is a chilling indictment of the Canadian health-care system. Just as importantly, he analyzes the impact of ObamaCare on Americans.

Through The Portals of Pigs and Manure: The Story of the Minnesota Influence on American Surgery. Arnold S. Leonard, MD, PhD. Cancer Research Fund, Minneapolis, 2012

Appendix 1:
IN MEMORIAM: MARLENE LINDQUIST, RIP

Such a sad, sad day when we learned of Marlene's passing. She was so much a part of our entire family's life for twenty-five years, almost from the time I arrived in Minnesota until I retired. And even after we parted, she called me on my birthday every year just to remember.

I found Marlene because the university had hired for me an incompetent young secretary with a wandering eye before I arrived. I fired the young vixen in short order after asking all over the medical center as to who was the very best secretary in the whole complex. Marlene's name came up in the first three inquiries, and that was enough for me. I met her in the Mayo coffee shop and told her she was going to work for me, and I made her an offer she could not refuse, so to speak. She was old school with a sense of propriety, so even though I wanted her to come to work the next day, she insisted on giving two weeks' notice. Hiring her was one of the very best decisions I made during the twenty-five-year run. At times I think she agreed that coming to work in urologic surgery was a good move for her.

Marlene was better than competent and the best and fastest typist on earth. Those were the days of IBM typewriters with ribbons and ink-stained fingers on the operator. She was able to bang out numerous long grants and papers for publication flawlessly on that primitive equipment, with time to spare for her Avon business, which she ran from her desk. I asked repeatedly for a cut on the Avon but never saw a dime.

Marlene was in a sense the human guardrails for the whole department. I would give her an order or write a letter when I was mad as hell or frustrated or both, and she often refused to carry out the orders or mail a hot letter—in my best interest. I got so angry with her when she thwarted my intentions I fired her so many times *I lost count*. Every time she started to clean out her desk, I of course relented and helped her to reload her desk because I could not imagine life there without her. She also knew I was as monogamous as a swan. Often when she fell ill, I would send her flowers with a note to get back to work or be fired. And hiring her back required a raise as an inducement for her to stay. So firing her became very expensive for me! Besides, she had a filing system akin in complexity and illogic to a pirate's treasure map so that only she could find things within it. I finally came to understand that filing system was her job security. Marlene had an uncanny sense to recognize the one or two delusive individuals who passed through the department over the years. Toward the end when working at the university was like crawling through the steaming, hissing ruins of Chernobyl to get to work, she looked up at me one day with the saddest eyes and said, "I think the bad guys are winning."

Marlene was both father confessor for me and mother hen for the residents and the patients. I notified many of the great residents we trained about her passing, and they all got right back to me stating how sad they were at her death and how important she was to the department. The following adjectives were often repeated in their comments about her: caring, kind, loyal, competent, an important part of the department, and so on and so on.

Marlene was a good and faithful colleague with a great capacity for loyalty and caring. But loyalty starts at the top and goes out to others who work for you before it comes back to the boss. New members of the department soon realized that being critical of Marlene was taking them down a path from which there might be no return. Her passing, along with those of other friends and associates, leaves a little dark, empty room in my heart. I will miss not knowing she is here.

There is an ancient aphorism on the wall as you exit the Holocaust Museum in Israel that states: *"You are alive as long as you are remembered."* Marlene will be remembered as long as we all are alive.

Our thoughts are with her entire family.

APPENDIX 2:
THE CASE FOR A NOBEL PRIZE OR LASKER AWARD—JULY 17, 2012: THE INVENTION OF ENDOUROLOGY BY MEMBERS OF THE UNIVERSITY OF MINNESOTA'S DEPARTMENT OF UROLOGIC SURGERY—THE GROWTH OF MUSTARD SEEDS

"He set another parable before them, saying, 'The
Kingdom of Heaven is like a grain of mustard seed,
which a man took, and sowed in his field; which indeed
is smaller than all seeds. But when it is grown, it is
greater than the herbs, and becomes a tree, so that
the birds of the air come and lodge in its branches.'"
—Matthew 13:31–32, *World English Bible*

"Few discoveries are more irritating than those
which expose the pedigree of ideas."
—Lord Acton

The rumored orthodoxy of the medicine Nobel Prize among
the medical cognoscenti is that that prize is awarded mainly for
seminal contributions to the biological sciences and not just for

"treatments." An example would be the prize awarded to Watson, Crick, and Wilkins for illuminating the structure of DNA or the award to Enders, Weller, and Robbins for discovering how to cultivate the polio virus in vitro, which made the polio vaccine possible. Many other prizes have been awarded with less relevance to clinical medicine. However, careful review of previous prize awards, including the award to the Harvard surgeon Joseph Murray for organ transplantation and the work of Charles Huggins cited herein, suggests that significant, innovative new treatments are also considered by the wise and sophisticated Nobel Prize committees for the physiology or medicine award, popular misconceptions notwithstanding. The Lasker Award, in contrast to the Nobel medicine prize, has a track record of recognizing clinical advances, to whit a Lasker was awarded to the cardiac surgeons at the University of Minnesota in 1955. The same surgeons should have been awarded a Nobel Prize.

There have been two Nobel Prizes awarded to urologists. The first was given to Werner Forssmann (1956) and the second to Charles Huggins (1966).

Huggins won his prize for showing that altering the hormone environment of a cancer could diminish a cancer's rate of growth through hormone receptor signals. Huggins's work eventually led to the use in urology and medical oncology of estrogens or the surgical procedure orchiectomy (removal of testis—the main source of testosterone in men) to treat advanced cancer of the prostate, and his work also led to the hormone treatment of cancer of the breast by altering that cancer's hormonal milieu. So in the case of Huggins, his Nobel was closely related to new treatment for patients. The later development of Tamoxifin was based on the same concepts—that is, blocking hormone signals. Huggins shared his prize with Peyton Rous of the Rockefeller Institute, who discovered a sarcoma virus in fowl.

Forssmann illustrated that he could gain access to his right heart by passing a cannula (or catheter) retrograde through the antecubital vein (near the elbow) into his right atrium. After he passed the device into his heart, Forssmann walked to radiology, where an X-ray (chest radiograph) showed the catheter in his right atrium. Forssmann was an urologist when the prize was given to him, but he passed the catheter into the heart while he was a resident in surgery. The cardiologists soon extended the application of Forssmann's work, and the medical specialty of interventional cardiology was born. Forssmann shared his prize with Dickinson Richards and Andre Cournand. Urology is the only surgical specialty to have been awarded two Nobel Prizes in medicine.

It is historical irony that the work in Minnesota that may merit a Nobel Prize or Lasker Award was not unlike Forssmann's contribution in principle, insofar as the Minnesotans devised new, less-invasive treatments for a variety of diseases of the urinary tract, rather than the heart using the percutaneous or less-invasive approach to the kidney, ureter, and bladder. This work evolved into a new subspecialty within urology, now designated by the appellation endourology.

The invention of endourology began in the mid-seventies in the department of urologic surgery at the University of Minnesota, and that work changed the paradigm of urology. Prior to 1979, however, a few relevant mustard seeds were being sewn, as for example, when in 1912, Hugh Hampton Young at Hopkins passed a pediatric cystoscope percutaneously into a massively hydronephrotic kidney—a mustard seed. In 1955 the late Willard Godwin at UCLA published a report that demonstrated access to the kidney was possible percutaneously using radiological guidance and without open surgery—another mustard seed. In 1976, Fernström and Johansson even performed a percutaneous nephrostomy (PCN) specifically to remove a kidney stone—one more mustard seed. But none of this work was exploited until the late 1970s, when nephrostomies were still done open with an incision and, in addition, kidney stones also continued to be treated by open surgery. So this work and that by others were the pedigrees of what came later—namely, endourology.

The above beginnings of using minimally invasive surgical techniques (MISTs) in urology was little noted in our department until Paul Lange called some publications on percutaneous nephrostomy, including Godwin's paper, to my attention and proposed that nephrostomies at Minnesota should be done thereafter percutaneously, in almost all cases without open surgery and with the collaboration of our radiological colleagues, who would help guide us to access to the urinary tract. This was truly an inflection point in urology in this country. That first step to apply broadly a less-invasive approach to the urinary tract was not unlike a big bang in the universe of urology, and the treatments of urological diseases by MISTs have continued to expand in number and complexity since that time. Many new innovations in medicine are met with scorn or derision and progress is thus thwarted, but not in Minnesota. The Minnesota environment had a long tradition of encouraging innovation in medicine that began with the heart surgeons who carried out the first open-heart surgery in the world. This Minnesota work in heart surgery, as mentioned previously, was rewarded with a Lasker Award in 1955. It should have received a Nobel Prize.

The other two early movers in this field in Minnesota besides Paul Lange were Arthur Smith and Ralph Clayman, who working cooperatively and with radiologists, especially Bob Miller at the VA Hospital, were primarily responsible for developing the new field of endourology. These outstanding young men at the time cross-fertilized ideas with each other and rapidly expanded the scope of what they were doing. It was the beginning of open surgeons' thinking about employing less-invasive approaches to surgery, which would result in reducing patient morbidity and costs.

Minnesota's work in urologic surgery also stimulated the growth of MISTs in other surgical fields. The application of minimally invasive techniques across the surgical disciplines led to significant decreases in both costs and morbidity for patients with a wide universe of diseases not only in urology but also in other surgical fields.

As activities using MISTs continued to expand, it was important to create an all-encompassing term that would describe and codify this new field as a subspecialty within urology. It was important that this new field be forever recognized as a branch or subset of urology and not just one more activity of, for example, interventional radiology. The first iteration of the term devised by me to define the new field was endo-urology, which evolved into endourology, and the unhyphenated term stuck and is a new word for *Dorland's Medical Dictionary*. The word *endourology* first appeared in an abstract in the *Journal of Urology* in which we defined the new field and its potential for urological patients. Thus, not only did the Minnesotans invent a new field; Minnesota university urology also invented the *word* by which it will forever be named. Today almost all major scientific meetings in urology have a major part of the program devoted to endourology, so the appellation for the field has been accepted universally. In fact, several new freestanding meetings and publications are now entirely devoted to the field; some of them are enumerated below.

As the work expanded, the Minnesotans' first treatments were evolved primarily to treat kidney, ureteral, and bladder stones. New instruments and technologies were developed or improved to remove or shatter urinary stones in situ. Stones were broken by the endourologists into small enough fragments within the urinary tract so that usually the fragments could pass out of the body with minimal difficulty, or if they did not pass, the fragments were removable with forcepslike devices. When the lithotripter came along, the skills of the endourologist were often required to definitively rid the patient of the stone fragments irrespective of how they were created. As endourology pushed forward, treatments for other diseases or disorders ranging from congenital obstructions to certain other lesions such as iatrogenically damaged ureters were evolved. I recently attended a lecture by Ralph Clayman during which Ralph demonstrated new treatments for small polar kidney cancers using endourological techniques, showing just how far the field has expanded.

Even though Ralph had already done the first laparoscopic nephrectomy using minimally invasive techniques, it was only possible to enlarge the field of endourology by developing new instruments, catheters, and other devices that could be placed inside the urinary tract as means for effecting treatments for one condition or another. Several companies and the Minnesota radiologists, especially Kurt Amplatz, Bob Miller, and Willie Castaneda, all cooperated with our urologists to further progress in the field.

The training and techniques that were developed by the Minnesota endourologists facilitated the rapid expansion of the use of both the lithotripter and robotic-assisted surgery. The ideal individual to apply robots and the lithotripter as adjuncts to surgery was the well-trained endourologist. The application of all three methodologies has facilitated the advance of applying MISTs in urologic surgery.

Finally, Minnesota played a seminal role in teaching the craft of endourology to thousands of urologists around the world because the work in Minnesota also gave birth to many instructional hands-on courses, scientific papers, and textbooks far too numerous to count that have served to keep practicing urologists current in the field wherever urology is practiced. The work in Minnesota led to the founding of the *Journal of Endourology*; the annual World Congress of Endourology (now in its thirtieth year to be held in Istanbul), which draws upwards of 1,500 urologists from over sixty countries; and the founding in 1984 of the Endourology Society. The Minnesotans were instrumental in founding the endourology periodicals and societies, and they also served on the editorial boards of most of the new journals. These facts alone demonstrate the profound extent to which endourology has bent the arc of progress of the specialty of one of medicine's oldest disciplines—urology.

In summary, the development of the new field of endourology merits consideration for either a Lasker Award or a Nobel Prize in physiology or medicine. The work has decreased morbidity and mortality as well as treatment costs for some of the most common urological diseases in countless numbers of patients. In addition, what happened in Minnesota stimulated the advancement of minimally invasive surgery across many other surgical fields. And further, the concepts and techniques evolved in Minnesota continue to be applied in patients worldwide. The field of endourology has historical roots dating back to the Egyptians, who began "cutting for bladder stones," which was one of the first operations of any kind done in man. The mustard seeds planted more recently by Hugh Young, Willard Godwin, and others finally grew and matured under the husbandry of our group in Minnesota. That Minnesota work deserves recognition because it is a proud history that was made possible at least in part by the atmosphere and academic and professional freedom at the university at a time that encouraged innovation and creativity. The relationship between freedom and achievement is best demonstrated by the fact that since 1900, seventy-two Nobel Prizes in medicine have been awarded to Americans.

Elwin E. Fraley, MD
Former Professor and Chairman
Department of Urologic Surgery
University of Minnesota School of Medicine

About the Author

Some teachers and professors are builders of themselves, their achievements and their reputations. A few, very honored others, are "Builders of People", builders of the young men and women they teach, often at the expense of their own fame and glory. Dr Fraley illuminates the latter.

Elwin Fraley's family was of modest means, but with the support of others in the community, he graduated from Exeter, Princeton University cum laude and Harvard Medical School. He then trained in Urology at Massachusetts General Hospital under Dr. Wyland Leadbetter, after which he left Boston for two plus years as a senior investigator at the National Cancer Institute. During this time he developed one of the first human tumor and serum banks in the world.

At the age of 32, never previously having had any experience in a large academic surgical department, Dr Fraley was offered, and took on the most challenging position of Professor and Chairman of the Division of Urology at the University of Minnesota. During his tenure he not only developed this into a world class department but in addition trained, stimulated and encouraged numerous young urological surgeons, who went on, in their own right to become luminaries in the field.

The intense esprit and collaboration he initiated with his trainees, staff and other departments, led to the development of the world-changing, minimally invasive surgery field of Endourology – a term in fact coined by Dr Fraley. This has revolutionized the field and seen the world adopt all sorts of minimal invasive techniques, laparoscopic and robotic surgery. In addition he developed a serum bank and urologic tumor bank which propelled the use of PSA for prostate cancer care and numerous other innovative surgical procedures.